Philosoph.
and the Priority of Questions in
Religions

Expanding Philosophy of Religion

Series Editors:
J. Aaron Simmons, Furman University, USA
Kevin Schilbrack, Appalachian State University, USA

A series dedicated to a global, diverse, cross-cultural, and comparative philosophy of religion, Expanding Philosophy of Religion encourages underrepresented voices and perspectives and looks beyond its traditional concerns rooted in classical theism, propositional belief, and privileged identities.

Philosophical Hermeneutics and the Priority of Questions in Religions

Bringing the Discourse of Gods and Buddhas Down to Earth

Nathan Eric Dickman

BLOOMSBURY ACADEMIC
LONDON • NEW YORK • OXFORD • NEW DELHI • SYDNEY

BLOOMSBURY ACADEMIC
Bloomsbury Publishing Plc
50 Bedford Square, London, WC1B 3DP, UK
1385 Broadway, New York, NY 10018, USA
29 Earlsfort Terrace, Dublin 2, Ireland

BLOOMSBURY, BLOOMSBURY ACADEMIC and the Diana logo are trademarks
of Bloomsbury Publishing Plc

First published in Great Britain 2022

Cover design by Louise Dugdale
Cover image © ICHIRO/Getty Images

A catalogue record for this book is available from the British Library.

A catalog record for this book is available from the Library of Congress.

ISBN: HB: 978-1-3502-0215-3
         PB: 978-1-3502-0214-6
       ePDF: 978-1-3502-0216-0
      eBook: 978-1-3502-0217-7

Series: Expanding Philosophy of Religion

Typeset by Integra Software Services Pvt. Ltd.
Printed and bound in Great Britain

To find out more about our authors and books visit www.bloomsbury.com
and sign up for our newsletters.

Contents

Preface   vi

Acknowledgments   ix

Introduction: Questions in Deific Discourse   1

Part 1 Elements of a Hermeneutic for Interpreting Questions in Religious
Narratives

1   Questioning Has Hermeneutic Priority   19

2   Religious Narrative Is Literature   35

3   What Is at Risk with Questions in Deific Discourse?   59

Part 2 The Exegetical Hermeneutic Circle: Questions in the Direct
Discourse of Deific Figures

4   *HaShem* Asks, "Where Are You?"   85

5   Ancestor Ma Asks, "Why Are You Seeking Outside?"   101

6   Jesus Asks, "Who Do You Say I Am?"   117

Part 3 The Existential Hermeneutic Circle: Questions Posed by the Deific
Voice of the Text to Readers

7   A Divine Voice Asks, "Where Do You Stand?"   137

8   A *Dharma* Heir Asks, "Why Conceive of Fulfillment as Outside
     Yourself?"   151

9   An Evangelist Asks, "What Do You Have to Say for Yourself?"   165

Conclusion: Human Responses to Questions Asked by Deific Figures   175

Bibliography   183
Author Bio   201
Index   202

Preface

This book is a response to the fact that sacred texts and traditions often depict supreme beings or figures of ultimate religious authority—such as Gods or Buddhas—as asking questions. Moreover, readers and oral audiences experience these texts themselves as questioning them and calling on them to respond. I find it shocking to see Gods and Buddhas asking questions in religious narratives because I always assumed they had all the answers. It is also remarkable that religious practitioners experience texts as asking them questions. People who turn to their religions for answers do not seem to make a sufficiently big deal of this. While I explain my approach, argument, method, and book outline in the Introduction, I want to provide a few words about the purpose and origins of this project in the preface.

My aim throughout is to isolate questions in "deific discourse" to illuminate their ambiguity, to put readers in a position of abeyance where they must decide for themselves their own answer to the question of why Gods or Buddhas are depicted as asking questions and why people experience sacred texts as asking them questions. Are any of the questions that Gods and Buddhas (or sacred texts) ask genuine? If Gods and Buddhas or sacred texts *never* ask genuine questions, can they really be models for endeavors like interdependent interpersonal relationships—or, on a broader scale, deliberative democratic society? Between the extremes of theocracies, such as the Taliban or secular absolutism like the hijab ban in France, is there a paradigm where religious motives might have a place in the ideal of democratic egalitarian discourse? Despite the purported separation of Church and State in the United States, we know—with extremist examples such as the "Moral Majority" and "The Family"—that there are numerous ways that religions influence governance (see Sharlet 2008, and Gibney et al. 2019). In "Religion as a conversation-stopper," the American Pragmatist Richard Rorty argues that religions should never influence democratic governance and that we ought to hold people suspect who defer to special revelation within their religions in political debate (Rorty 1999). The appeal to "higher" authorities is a recognizable method of argument. Employees turn to managers or human resource officers to mitigate disputes. Even Covid-19 vaccine resistors often say, "My doctor said" such and such about either the virus or vaccine, which they take to legitimate their resistance. People in the United States can appeal legal decisions all the way up to the Supreme Court. Higher "supernatural" authorities, for Rorty and others, exceed the conventional democratic agreements of what constitutes appropriate authority and expertise. One crucial aspect of this criticism is the nature of religious or ultimate authority: Does it consist solely of revealed answers or can supernatural beings also *ask* genuine questions as well as answer them? Thus, an indirect but significant implication of this study concerns religious influence in politics. I will discuss this briefly in both the Introduction and the Conclusion.

The first time I wondered about this topic was as a whim. There was a call for papers for the annual graduate Jakobsen conference at The University of Iowa in 2006, and I sketched a quick abstract, flippantly asking whether the god of the Tanak could ask a genuine question, titled "Can 'God' Ask a Genuine Question? The Virtues of Dialogue and the Personhood of God." Not only was the abstract accepted for presentation but the final paper won first place in the Humanities division. This took me by surprise because I only showed up to the award announcement for the snacks. I was prodding my fellow grad students to leave early with me to go to the local watering hole when the organizers announced my name for winning first place. I walked up to receive my award to laughter because everyone could see the surprise on my face. From that moment on I figured I could work on this topic. The basic argument was as follows: Genuine questions are a key virtue of dialogue, and dialogue is a crucial element of what it is to be a person, so whether a god asks genuine questions is definitive for that god's personhood. Taking this God as a case study, I looked at several questions in the Tanak. For example, this God asks Job lots of questions—but all those questions are patently rhetorical.

As a scholar of comparative philosophy of religions, however, I'm not satisfied merely to examine this God's direct discourse—though at the same time, I recognize this alone is worthy of one's scholarly lifetime. Moreover, in light of training in hermeneutic phenomenology, I'm interested in religious literature and interpretation, not metaphysical issues concerning the (non) existence of some omnibeing of institutionalized philosophy of religion. For example, some might find it fascinating to ask how an omniscient, or all-knowing, entity can have a genuine question. Such a topic concerns the nature of some actually existent omnibeing. My topic, alternatively, looks at the questions attributed to deific voices or figures of ultimate authority in religious literature—whether Gods and Buddhas within the texts or the voice of the texts themselves. Is dialogue a definite feature of the world of the text where HaShem, Buddhas, and Jesus ask questions, this world unfolded by reading communities? These worlds function as regulative ideals by which devotees orient their lives. What would Jesus do? Would Jesus ask a genuine question? If not, why would someone who seeks to be Christ-like do so—

especially in the context of democratic processes? Does Gautama Buddha ask questions? Does the Messenger?

Much of the groundwork research was undertaken for my doctoral dissertation (see Dickman 2009). However, after many years of thinking through and revisiting this material, I have revamped my approach and its significance, as well as consulted a growing scholarly conversation on related topics. My hope is that this book will help all of us become more self-conscious and deliberate in our use of genuine questions in our relationships and in our social or political projects.

Acknowledgments

I want to thank a number of mentors, colleagues, friends, and current and former students for their conversations and support throughout my reflections and research on this topic. You all have my gratitude for humoring my explorations through all these topics and providing critical yet constructive feedback on my writing: David Klemm, Jay Holstein, Ralph Keen, Morten Schlütter, David Stern, Ben Landsee, Adrienne Ho, Brian Kanouse, Christine Darr, Christoffer Lammer-Heindel, the late Matthew Wilhite, Denise Kettering, Sarah Dees, Ezra Plank, Joshua Allen, Benjamin Landsee, Kendall Marchman, Joy Spann, Bethann Bowman, Roxana Chicas, Taylor Davis, Alyssa Lowery, Mason Mitcham, Nicole Drake, DJ Bohannon, Anderson Moss, Andie Weaver, Thomas Johnson, Alejandro Lemus-Gomez, Khalid Johnson, Courtney Huskins, Emily Todd, Elizah Huff, Joseph DeFrank, Xavier Jacobs, Astheris Miller, Kate Greene, Kristen Brown, and Jacob Perry. I also want to thank my many Institute of Continuing Learning retiree students in Young Harris, GA, for our lively discussions in my course on these topics over the summer of 2015. I also appreciate the extensive feedback from the series editors, J. Aaron Simmons and Kevin Schilbrack, as well as anonymous reviewers.

Throughout the book, some sections are updated revisions of research that previously appeared in the following:

Dickman, Nathan Eric. 2009a. *Dialogue and Divinity: A Hermeneutics of the Interrogative Mood in Religious Language*. Dissertation. The University of Iowa.

Dickman, Nathan Eric. 2014. "Between Gadamer and Ricoeur: Preserving Dialogue in the Hermeneutical Arc for the Sake of a God that Speaks and Listens." *Sophia* 53(4): 553–73.

Dickman, Nathan Eric. 2016. "The Questions of Jesus and Mazu: Human or Beyond?" *Literature and Theology*. 30(3): 343–58.

Dickman, Nathan Eric. 2018a. "Hermeneutic Priority and Phenomenological Indeterminacy of Questioning." In *The Significance of Indeterminacy: Perspectives from Asian and Continental Philosophy*, edited by Robert H. Scott and Gregory S. Moss. New York: Routledge.

Dickman, Nathan Eric. 2018b. "Call or Question: A Rehabilitation of Conscience as Dialogical." *Sophia*. 57(2): 275–94.

Dickman, Nathan Eric. 2020a. "Master Questions, Student Questions, and Genuine Questions: A Performative Analysis of Questions in Chan Encounter Dialogues." *Religions* 11(2): 72. https://doi.org/10.3390/rel11020072.

Dickman, Nathan Eric. 2021a. *Using Questions to Think: How to Develop Skills in Critical Understanding and Reasoning.* New York: Bloomsbury.

Dickman, Nathan Eric. 2021b. "The Hermeneutic Priority of Which Question? A Speech Act Clarification of Interlocutionary Acts." *Informal Logic* 41(3): 485–508.

Dickman, Nathan Eric. 2022. "Anapotheotics: A Hermeneutic Approach to Religions as Symbolic Languages." In *What Paths – What Summits: A Multi-Entry Approach to Philosophy of Religion,* edited by Timothy Knepper and Gereon Kopf. New York: Bloomsbury.

Introduction: Questions in Deific Discourse

In the Gospel attributed to Mark, Jesus asks, "Who do you say that I am?" In the Chan (Zen) discourse records about him, the classical master Mazu asks, "Why do you seek outside?" In the first book of the Torah, HaShem asks, "Where are you?" Religious narratives depict Buddhas, Gods, prophets, oracles, demons, Bodhisattvas, gurus, and more as asking questions. Moreover, many readers experience these questions as addressed not merely to other characters within the narratives but to the readers themselves. Why? What are readers or listeners to make of these depictions? How do religious texts call on readers to answer such questions for themselves?

Aren't Gods and Buddhas Supposed to Have the Answers, Not Questions?

Before we get too far, I want to make it clear that I am speaking about what we will call "deific voices." I use this to set off not only the voices of Gods and Buddhas from institutional religious leaders like imams or rabbis or priests but also the voices of texts that speak to people spiritually from other texts or stories. I use "deific" in the sense that these voices are treated as "god-like." This may strike some readers as odd since Buddhas are not Gods. Indeed, Buddhist traditions are often stereotyped in Western societies as being "atheistic" (Faure 2009, 59). Yet on close inspections of cultures in which different Buddhist traditions have influence, there are indeed many Gods (or *devas*)—some carried over from the ancient Indian pantheon, such as Indra and Brahma, and others are indigenous deities from regional cultures, such as Guanyin in China. More importantly for my purposes, however, Buddhas (such as Shakyamuni or Amitabha) and Bodhisattvas (such as Avalokiteshvara) take on roles superior to Gods (Faure 2009, 63). As Gautama Buddha teaches, "Even the gods envy those who are awakened" (Müller 2013, §181). That is, just because someone is a god, that does not mean they have realized *nirvana* and awakened—which translates the Sanskrit term *bodhi*, from which the title "Buddha" is derived.

For further conceptual clarity, we can relate my notion of "deific voices" to the philosopher of religions Kevin Schilbrack's notion of "superempirical" beings (see Schilbrack 2014, 152). This term gathers under one notion Gods, spirits, and nonpersonal powers that are: (a) not empirical, and (b) not the product of empirical things. Even if we disagree about which ones exist, if any do, we can agree that many people in religious communities define their religion as consisting of at least one or more of such beings. For example, in Mahayana Buddhist traditions, such as Zen, the *Dharmakaya* or "Truth body" of Gautama Buddha is such an entity. We can also include figures such as Brahman in Advaita Vedanta, the Christ in Christian traditions, the Dao in Daoist traditions, and more. There is also the God in Jewish religious traditions, whom we will respectfully refer to as *HaShem* ("the Name") throughout this book in place of this God's personal name. This God's personal name is represented by the Tetragrammaton, rendered in English as Yahweh or YHWH. I mention it here just once to emphasize that the word "god" is not a name but a title, and that despite people using the title "god" as a name, it is crucial to remember that this God has a personal name. I address this further in Chapter 4. The term "superempirical" excludes things like nations or sports teams because these are or are produced by empirical things. Superempirical things do not have to be treated as objects of ultimate concern or be more fundamentally real than other things. A specific God or power might be superempirical yet might not be the center of a person's life.

I want my phrase "deific voices" to capture *superempirical beings who speak*, but also to capture those *texts that religious communities take as speaking to them* when they are read. This is different from the status of specific books as objects of devotion, such as the Lotus Sutra in Nichiren Buddhism. For example, the founder Nichiren believed that chanting praise to the book itself was the only truly effective Buddhist practice in the face of what he perceived to be worldly decline (Lopez 2016). As I will explain, it is not about the cult of the book but about understanding what a text *asks* of readers. My point here for introduction is simply to emphasize that not only are Gods and Buddhas depicted as asking questions in religious narratives, readers often experience texts themselves as asking questions of readers. Hence my need to isolate these sorts of voices as "deific," as god-like voices speaking to readers in the depth of their being. This is what I hope strikes many readers as surprising, given how many people (religious or not) assume Gods or Buddhas are all-knowing and all-powerful or that sacred texts provide all the answers. When we look at questions in the direct discourse of literary figures or experience being asked questions by the texts themselves, these seem to stand in tension with what people think metaphysically about superempirical beings as all-knowing or the books as holding all relevant answers. If you already know something, then you probably will not have any sincere questions about it.

These deific voices stand apart from institutional religious leaders, such as imams, priests, rabbis, nuns, monks, and preachers, or even inspired human figures in religious narratives such as minor prophets or other visionaries. Institutionally backed religious authorities are like other secular institutional roles, such as clinicians, doctors, teachers, officers, presidents, and judges. That is, although they might be ordained by a religious community to convey spiritual messages, they also are responsible for administration of the institution, from collecting money to mobilizing enough members of the community for collective action—such as getting enough kids from youth group to join together to rake leaves in cemetery. Of course, people filling these roles might ask many questions, from the mundane ("How much is the electric bill?") to the profound ("Can our object of devotion redeem all humanity?"). Yet when we look at many religious leaders in these institutional roles, we see that they often present themselves as the ones with *the* answer(s). Consider, for example, pilgrims trekking to Plum Village to ask questions of and listen to the teachings of the Zen master Thich Nhat Hanh. Although Thich (the Vietnamese Buddhist surname) might ask many questions, they are often designed rhetorically for him to provide advice and wisdom to patrons (see Thich 2011, 15).

I am confident if you pay attention to politicians that you have heard many of them say the phrase, "The question is…" to introduce a point or proposal they want to make. That is, they pose a question as a prompt to provide the answer themselves. Just like this tactic among politicians, so also do most preachers use many questions as devices to prompt the messages they provide to their communities. Do Gods and Buddhas just use questions this way, as a prompt for the substantive message? I want us to be truly clear that the focus of this book is on questions asked by voices of ultimate religious authority, not questions asked by institutional leaders. While these institutional leaders might have some authority—and might even have a lot of it—whatever authority they have is construed as sanctioned by superempirical beings or texts within which they are depicted. All of these are voices of ultimate religious authority.

Perhaps readers of religious narratives are so used to seeing these figures ask questions that it is not surprising or shocking to read them asking questions. Perhaps some readers are thinking: "Just look at the sacred texts! They ask questions all the time. So why be surprised?" I want to provide some motivation here. First, consider religious leaders and institutions in many societies today. We can see among religious institutional administrators a preponderance of what we can call "religious certainty." Embodied religious identity is characterized often by certainty and insularity, where community members resist exposure to and connection with people of other religious or nonreligious communities (Wuthnow 2005). The leaders are authoritarian in their certainty and community members monitor and police one another to prevent anyone from having doubts (see Hunsberger et al. 2002; and Altmeyer and Hunsberger 1992). That is, doubt is construed as antithetical to belief. This is true for many forms of fundamentalisms in different religious traditions across the globe.

Moreover, many members of religious communities turn to their traditions for *answers* to their questions. We can distinguish some broad patterns here. The early Buddhist teachings attempt to "answer" or address people's experience of suffering. Modern European philosophers such as David Hume and Karl Marx agree that people turn to religions to address their suffering. Religions provide answers to laments such as, "Why do I suffer? Why is our community disenfranchised?" As the philosophical provocateur Friedrich Nietzsche points out, many religious priests answer this question with, "You yourself are to blame" due to sin, karma, ignorance of the divine, or what have you (see Nietzsche 2008, 106). Another cliché here, however empirically false it turns out to be, is "There are no atheists in foxholes." Perhaps religions do not help people make rational sense of their experience or completely end their suffering, but they do seem to help people cope with their experience of suffering. Yet especially with regard to oppressed peoples, through colonization and white supremacy, some religions provide inspiration for resistance to brutal and violent power (see, for example, X 1992). In this way, people turn to religions to answer their questions, to be empowered with existential courage in the face of institutionalized social and political oppression or natural disasters.

There are also ways that privileged people turn to religions for answers, perhaps in ways that placate their complicity with systems of exploitation of others. In fact, some institutional leaders recognize this pattern and attempt to address clichés such as "It's a mystery, and we just need to accept it" or "It's all part of God's plan" or "Jesus is the answer (or, alternatively, the Bible has all the answers)" and more (see Olson 2007). According to the evangelical theologian Roger Olson, these clichés wither under the onslaught of secularism, and so Christians of this variety need to develop better "answers" (Olson 2007, 20). A problem is that it is not clear what the questions even are that Christians are supposed to answer, or whether Christians are really even asking those questions to themselves. In a way, they are not answers but satisfaction—often a smug satisfaction. Or the questions are focused on individual needs, such as whom one should marry or what career one should choose. This is not local to Christian traditions. Writings for teenagers in

Conservative Jewish communities address "tough questions Jews ask," such as "What happens to us when we die?" (Feinstein 2005, 105). It is as if religions are supposed to work like a Magic 8-Ball. These questions and clichés end up placating people who use them to accept and even perpetuate institutionalized status quos.

Second, there is a tension between what many people believe about supernatural beings—such as the belief that a God or Bodhisattva is omniscient—while simultaneously reading in sacred literature the characters supposedly representing these beings asking many questions. In fact, omniscience is a standard topic in institutionalized philosophy of religion textbooks and courses (see, for example, Pojman 2003, 231–50). It is a fascinating topic. If there is a creator God that is all-knowing, and this includes knowing all your future actions, can you really be free to choose your actions? This God would seem to know what you are going to do from the beginning of created time, and so if you were to choose other than that action, that would make this God wrong about what the God knew. Of course, in this institutionalized framework for thinking about an omniscient God, one might say that a God that gets things wrong isn't a God worth believing in. The same is said about Gautama Buddha's night of enlightenment, that the Buddha learned everyone's past, present, and future karma. Can the Buddha's knowledge be wrong? If it can be wrong, then it was not really knowledge. If what we are going to do is known already, are we ever really free? To get back to questions, though, can an all-knowing God (or Buddha) ask genuine questions?

Is questioning a power or weakness? Is it something we are only capable of due to our finitude? Is there any kind of question that is a power? It seems that most questions emerge out of need or deficit, such as the need for an answer so that one may accomplish something else. I need my keys to drive to work, but do not know where they are, and so I ask, "Where are my keys?" Imagine someone responding with, "Huh. That's a good question—what does it really mean for keys to be in a place?" When we ask a question out of need, we are only satisfied with *the* answer; we do not find dwelling in shared wonder at the question satisfying. There also seem to be some questions that we ask not out of need but out of a surplus of wonder. Consider the following question: Are "good books," good reads (see Wiggins and McTighe 2001)? Or the following: What is a "close" friend (see Aristotle 1999)? These sorts of questions invite dwelling together, where we can consider and evaluate multiple responses.

Given these two major types of questions, deficit-driven ones and surplus-driven ones, we can reflect on two issues relative to deific voices. First, do they ask deficit-driven questions? This would suggest that they have limited knowledge and can come to know even more. It seems to depend on whether Gods and Buddhas, etc. have epistemic needs. When HaShem asks HaSatan, "Where did you just come from?" in the Book of Job (1:7), does this God really not know where Satan has been? Yet later in the same book (Job 38:4), HaShem asks Job, "Where were you when I laid the earth's foundation?" Does HaShem expect a genuine response? Gautama Buddha asks, "Is there in this world any man so restrained by shame that he does not provoke reproof, as a noble horse the whip?" (Müller 2013, §143). Isn't this merely a rhetorical question to set up his point that, "Like a noble horse when touched by the whip, be ye strenuous and eager, and by faith, by virtue, by energy, by meditation, by discernment of the law you will overcome this great pain, perfect in knowledge and in behaviour, and never forgetful" (Müller 2013, §144)? When Jesus asks in the Gospel of Mark (5:30), "Who touched my clothes?" does he have a gap in his knowledge? In the Gospel of Matthew (11:16), Jesus asks, "To what shall I compare this generation?" Isn't this just a set up for his critique of the community?

In light of these sorts of questions, some might wonder whether an entity without knowledge of all the facts can truly be considered a voice with ultimate religious authority. What is interesting here is that most people assume that figures of ultimate religious authority have no epistemic needs—they are, in some way or other, all-knowing. If this is so, then it is incoherent to claim that these figures can or do ask deficit-driven questions. Inasmuch as a question like "Where are my car keys?" emerges from a deficit, a lack of knowledge of the facts about the keys, then someone who asks it sincerely lacks at least this one bit of knowledge. Therefore, this being could not be said to be all-knowing.

On the other hand, do they ask surplus-driven questions? This would suggest that they can have their horizons broadened through understanding another person's perspective. Can Gods and Buddhas, etc. dwell with others to consider pluralities of responses? What is interesting here is a wonder about expansion of horizons. Whatever one's epistemic status, it seems that through dialogue we can have our horizons expanded. Even someone who knows all the facts about something still might learn something new through dialogue with another person. Gautama Buddha asks, for example, "How is there laughter, how is there joy, as this world is always burning? Do you not seek a light, ye who are surrounded by darkness?" (Müller 2013, §146). Could this start a conversation with potential followers? Jesus asks in the Gospel of Luke (10:26), "What is written in the law? What do you read there?" He is asking how another person interprets the law, and this could lead to a conversation about applications of it. The book of Jonah ends with HaShem asking Jonah a question (4:11): "And should I not be concerned about Nineveh, that great city, in which there are more than a hundred and twenty thousand persons who do not know their right hand from their left, and also many animals?" Does HaShem invite a response from Jonah?

While we might not gain knowledge of new facts through dialogue, we might have our perspective on those facts or our interpretation of the significance of those facts changed. Our perspectives, indeed, all perspectives, are limited. For a perspective to be what it is, there must be limits; otherwise, it is not a perspective or point of view. A perspective opens from a specific standpoint out toward a horizon of significance. Facts available within such a purview are imbued with significance and relevance relative to that trajectory. Yet, only through recognition of an alternative perspective can we recognize our own *as a perspective*. This is to recognize the limits of our own perspective. Do deific voices speak from a perspective? Do they have perspectives at all? Do they somehow transcend perspectives? It seems that only if they have perspectives, like us, can we consider them participants in the humane universe of discourse where our horizons expand through dialogue. Without a perspective, such speakers are incoherent to us. I am especially interested in whether Gods and Buddhas, as well as sacred texts that speak to readers, ask these surplus sorts of questions. Are not Gods and Buddhas supposed to have the answers? Are not sacred texts the sources of answers, not questions? What could they gain from dwelling with others, from fusing horizons with others?

These are not quite the questions I *really* want to address, though. When they are put abstractly like that, they focus our attention on the actual existence (or nonexistence) of superempirical beings. I want our attention focused in a different direction. What do depictions of these figures as asking questions, or our experience of being asked questions by sacred texts, mean about us, about the human condition? What is it to be asked questions by deific voices? My argument is that *if* there are exceptional cases where these voices speak *with* us in dialogue, rather than *at* us in deific dictates, we have a clue pointing toward an existential ontology where we are enabled to be responsive. That is, genuine surplus-driven questions in deific voices indicate that although religious sources might dictate absolute pronouncements that subordinate human beings to their commands, these sources also— and perhaps more importantly—unfold in living dialogue with us. It is not merely that HaShem, Mazu, and Jesus speak *at* their listeners but that— more importantly—they seem in some cases to speak *with* them. It is not merely that the sacred texts themselves speak *at* their audiences but *with* them. If so, their dialogue partners are endowed with a deep and abiding form of responsibility (literally, the ability to respond) grounded in being heard and received by the ultimate, as ones capable of response to even an overwhelming authority. Such questions bring Gods and Buddhas "down to earth," in that they belong within our humane universe of discourse.

This possibility of being asked genuine questions by deific voices depends on our hermeneutic, however. So an essential step in developing my argument includes the rigorous determination of the hermeneutic priority of questioning. Questioning takes priority. In this way, we change the very grounds by which people usually appeal to "higher authorities." As I noted in the Preface, when people get into a disagreement, they often try to settle it by appeal to an authority, such as taking cases all the way to the US Supreme Court. Or, in the case of some religious attempts at explanations, people might say this or that event (like a death in the family) is part of "God's plan" or a result of past karma. In the hermeneutics of sacred texts, such as biblical hermeneutics, "history" or historical criticism is often lauded as having priority in any interpretations worth their salt. Perhaps you have heard politicians say, "History will be the judge of my presidency." That is, just like "god," "karma," or "science," history is also often used as the criterion by which we weed out some interpretations rather than others. Yet we know that just like religion and science, history can also be put to political or socioeconomic purposes. As the historian of ancient Mediterranean religions Elaine Pagels explains, the historical characterization of Jesus' resurrection, for instance, has a political function because it legitimates power and authority (Pagels 1989, 6). It serves to validate the succession of bishops, defining their authority. This parallels the Zen transmission lineage, which purportedly stretches back all the way to the historical (Gautama) Buddha (McRae 2003). I am not going to argue that we remove history altogether, but in developing the hermeneutic priority of questioning, I show where historical criticism is relevant to but not the whole of interpretation. I argue that there are four relevantly distinct layers of questioning that must be coordinated in interpretation. Two layers concern what is "in" the text, and two layers concern how the text "speaks" to readers. I develop my book aligned with this necessary division of labor: explaining the hermeneutic priority of questioning (Part I), examining what is "in" the texts (Part II), and examining how the texts "speak" to readers (Part III).

It should be helpful to provide the broad framework I'm working within, particularly in terms of defining religions and philosophizing about religions. Religious traditions are sets of beliefs, practices, and institutions that orient individuals and communities toward ultimate fulfilment, and which provide fundamental interpretations of experience or narratives within which events make sense (see Taves 2011; Geertz 1993; and Tillich 2001). Because I focus on character development within sacred stories, I emphasize, in particular, the linguistic aspect of religious traditions, their discourses—whether written or spoken—and the symbols and myths that make up key notions within those discourses. This is not to grant discourse some hierarchical privilege over embodied practice or lived experience. Inasmuch as religious discourse ties intrinsically to embodied practice and lived experience, religious discourse is what we can call a "first order" discourse or object language (Dickman 2017). Philosophy is a "second order" discourse or metalanguage, where we conceptualize and interpret first order discourses or object languages. In philosophizing, we use conceptual analysis, dialectical reasoning, postcolonial critique, deconstruction, and more to make explicit what is often implicit in images, symbols, and myths.

A further feature of my framework responds to a general theory of the relation between philosophy and religion in recent phenomenology and some twentieth-century liberal Christian theology. As the philosophers of religion J. Aaron Simmons and Bruce Benson explain, whereas earlier phenomenologists such as Edmund Husserl and Jean-Paul Sartre seemed to avoid positively engaging religion in their writings, late twentieth-century phenomenologists engage it in a way that correlates phenomenology as questions and religion as symbolic archives for formulating answers to those questions (Simmons and Benson 2013, 84; 99; cf. Janicaud 2000). While new phenomenologists such as Emmanuel Levinas, Jean-Luc Marion, and others refuse to allow institutionalized religious authorities to count as "evidence," they do think that religious narratives and institutions can be drawn on as symbolic archives for interpretation into "answers" (Simmons and Benson 2013, 134). The problem new phenomenologists (and others) have with institutionalized religions is that they seem to start with already settled answers (Simmons and Benson 2013, 94). Phenomenology raises questions, however, and religions provide resources for possible answers to those questions (Simmons and Benson 2013, 94). The phenomenologist Jean-Louis Chretien explains his motive for turning to religion is that "philosophy poses questions to which it cannot respond in an ultimate fashion" (cited in Simmons and Benson 2013, 107). The hermeneutic phenomenologist Paul Ricoeur emphasizes that phenomenology of religions must investigate the ambiguity of the notion of "response," where people can respond to a question but also can respond to a call (Ricoeur 2000, 128). This exploration of phenomenology as posing questions and religions as resources for answers relates to the twentieth-century philosophical theologian Paul Tillich's "method of correlation." In Tillich's method of correlation, religious symbols are coordinated as resources for answers to philosophical questions (see Tillich 1951, 8). As Tillich writes, "It tries to correlate the questions implied in the situation with the answers implied in the message" (Tillich 1951, 8).

That is, questions are located solely on one side of the method and do not—at least on the face of it—have a role in religious symbols and myth.

In this broad framework, then, religions—particularly the symbolic and mythic resources—answer existential questions. This is not to say that people who do not participate in standard or institutionalized religions do not have resources to address existential questions. It is that existential questions are a fitting way in which to interpret inherited symbols. Or, put in another way, as soon as someone makes use of something—such as money, or a national flag, or a mountain—to address their existential questioning, they turn these things into symbolic resources for addressing their questions. In this way, the object becomes a "god" for them (see Tillich 2001, 2). These fundamental questions do not need to be posed in terms of a specific religious system but require some broad philosophical paradigm for conceptual clarity to pose the questions. One question might be: "How do we lead a flourishing and fulfilling life in light of death?" Different religious traditions approach this question with their own strategies communicated through their symbolic notions, such as heaven, nirvana, immortality, moksha, and more. *If this broad correlation between questions on the side of phenomenology and resources for answers on the side of religions is so, then we should expect to find no questions in deific voices.* However, there are numerous questions in their direct discourse as well as experienced by readers! Are these questions merely further symbolic resources in need of philosophical or phenomenological translation into answers to human existential questions? Or are the questions asked by such figures an exception to this general correlation in phenomenology? My argument, again, is that this exceptional experience of questions in deific voices reveals a shared horizon, bringing Gods and Buddhas down to earth.

Many religious practitioners turn to speak with ancestors and recently deceased relatives at gravesites and other memorial shrines (see Corcione 2018). Other religious practitioners turn to divine figures with prayers. The twentieth-century Jewish philosopher Martin Buber, for example, describes human relationships with the divine as a dialogue (see Buber 1996). What does it mean to speak *with* such beings? Is it a monologue, where living practitioners speak *at* these beings? Or is it, like Buber asserts, a dialogue? What constitutes differences between monologues and dialogues? For this project, shared questions distinguish dialogues from monologues. Do these figures to whom we petition and devote ourselves ask us questions? An additional element is the nature of these figures. Are they persons (see Tillich 1955)? Is dialogue, particularly dialogue through genuine questions, a crucial criterion for the distinction between persons and nonpersons?

My emphasis on genuine questions and working through global-critical philosophy of religions, where I investigate multiple religious traditions, suggests ways that people can be more hospitable to religious and nonreligious others (see Dickman 2020c). If religions are—or have—resources for answers to life's questions, then when two representatives of alternative religions attempt dialogue with one another, it might end up being a collision of monologues and not a dialogue. Who could have a question in a context where you already have all the answers? Imagine a Christian and a Buddhist: "Have you accepted Jesus as your lord and savior?" "Well, have you realized nirvana?" It is like oil and water. The representatives merely speak *past* one another, not *with* one another. What is the purpose of interreligious dialogue? Is it merely to learn information about other religions? If this is all, the information can be acquired through other means besides dialogue. We can, for example, look up the information in an encyclopedia. Dialogue seems to have an entirely distinct purpose from mere acquisition of information. In dialogue, we reach an understanding with others and we fuse horizons of meaning. What results occur when representatives of different religions fuse horizons? Is it the creation of a new super-religion—in this case "Buddhianity"?

My project is indirectly relevant for ongoing scholarly conversations and research concerning tensions between religious belonging and participation in ideal deliberative democracy (see Stout 2004). I will return to this briefly in the conclusion in a discussion about shared questioning and antifascism. Consider this illustration. Can you imagine Donald J. Trump, Kim Jong-un, or any number of authoritarian leaders asking a genuine question? However, some fascists or authoritarians use questions to police and interrogate their subjects and victims. They use questions as a tactic to create a feeling of guilt in their victims—even when the victims know they are innocent. When someone asks a question where they are not in the position to expect an honest answer, it is like there is a setup where the person admits to doing something nefarious even if they refuse to answer. Their silence makes them seem suspicious. As Zizek explains, it is as if authoritarians say, "It is *we* who will ask the questions around here!" (see Žižek 1989, 182). The scholar of linguistics Roberta Piazza explains the pragmatics of similar sorts of questions, where they are conducive to getting the person questioned to admit to something even if the person questioned does not want to answer the question (Piazza 2002, 511–13). Do deific voices model authoritarianism with their questions, or do they model the sorts of shared questioning necessary for deliberative democracy? Moreover, what is the place of religion in US democratic discussions? Inasmuch as many institutional religious leaders express certainty and insularity, and even interject this certainty and insularity into politics, then the leaders stand in tension with what might appear to be genuine epistemic humility on the part of superempirical beings asking genuine questions in sacred narratives. Despite wearing a bracelet that says "WWJD?," perhaps these leaders do not really live up to being Christ-like? Would emulating deific voices include the question, "Would Jesus [God, the Buddha, the Prophet, etc.] ask a genuine question?" Questions are crucial for truth-seeking and justice-seeking in pluralistic societies (see Patel 2012, 75–7).

Many people know, for example, the evangelical Christian movement called "The Family" or the fellowship has undermined US governing processes through their complicity with Russian interference in the election of Donald J. Trump as president in 2016 (see Sharlet 2008, and Gibney et al. 2019). Their answer is that their God can work perfect plans through imperfect people, based on a peculiar reading of the story of David. They use this as an analogy for their total embrace of Trump—where the more problematic he is, the more their God's grace abounds. This is not unique to Christianity. We can recognize religious strides for dominance in many eras and cultures, such as the Taliban's drive for total theocracy or the persecution of Muslims by Buddhists in Myanmar. Of course, not all Christians support evangelical devotion to Trump, not all Muslims agree with the Taliban's conservative patriarchal version of Islam, and not all Buddhists accept ethnic cleansings in Myanmar. Nevertheless, such extremisms persist and claim to be motivated by their religion. How is democracy possible in light of extremist devotion?

The primary relevance for this book, though, is to philosophical hermeneutics—particularly theory about how to interpret religious texts. How can and should readers interpret questions in the direct discourse of superempirical beings, and what significance does the experience of questions posed by the texts themselves have for readers? My book attempts to develop the art of interpreting divine questions in explicit detail. Let us turn to provide an overview of how I go about it.

Overview of the Book

In the first part of the book, we will develop a hermeneutic framework for approaching questions in deific discourse. Chapter 1 isolates a unique kind of question that we will call "genuine questions." Such questions have hermeneutic priority in that interlocutors need to ask them to be able to be in dialogue with others. These questions suspend the synthesis of subjects and predicates. Consider the question "Where are my car keys?" The subject "car keys" radiates predicative possibilities. They might be "in your book bag," or "locked in the house," etc. Most importantly, the questions need to be *shared* in order to reach an understanding with others. Readers, for example, must ask the question to which a text responds to be able to understand what a text says. Sharing questions allow us to fuse horizons with others or have our horizons expanded.

Chapter 2 develops how religious texts need to be approached as literature so that we can appropriately isolate questions in deific discourse—whether or not superempirical beings exist outside of the text or in reality. This is crucial for comparative study of religions. We cannot assume that one religious narrative or book represents reality more accurately than other religious narratives or books. Before religious texts are direct historical records or mere myth, they are compositions. As such, they are composed artfully; they are works of art. There are two main structural levels on which to analyze literature—the level of story and the level of discourse. Stories not only have content such as characters, atmospheres, and conflict, stories also are told by someone to someone else. So, our work on questions in deific discourse concerns both levels—questions as acts of speech performed by characters within the stories and questions as discourse engaged by reader and text in the process or dialogue of interpretation. What reading or hearing religious stories unfold is what we will call "the world of the text," like an imaginative pop-up book emerging through interpreting and weaving together lines of text. Is dialogue an essential element in the story-world of the text? Or is genuine questioning solely something for the level of discourse between reader and text? These two levels determine how I organize Parts II (story) and III (discourse) when I turn to look for exceptional cases where deific voices ask genuine questions.

Chapter 3 examines what is at stake for reading questions in religious texts. I employ a refined schema from literacy pedagogy, an approach to teaching students how to interpret texts by addressing four questions concerning "lines" in a book. The first set of questions address what is "on the lines," the basic complete thoughts explicitly expressed in discourse, whether written, spoken, or signed. What did the big bad wolf do? He huffed and puffed. The second set of questions address what is "between the lines," what is suggested but not explicitly stated. For example, a reader can infer a character has a particular trait or virtue based on a number of actions explicitly attributed to the character. These two sets of questions enable an interpreter to construct or unfold the story-world in detail, the story dimension of literature (Part II). The dimension of discourse or narration (Part III) also has two further sets of questions. The third set of questions addresses what is "behind the lines," what went into the production of the text—from historical context to a writer's intention. For example, historical context provides constraints on what a text could have meant at its inception. The founding fathers of the United States, for instance, could not possibly have meant AK-47s when they established the right to bear arms. A fourth set of questions address what is "beyond the lines," what a text can mean to an interpreting audience. What will contemporary readers do with the text when they have understood it? We will see questions in deific voices both on the level of story and on the level of discourse. These questions stand in need of demythologization, an existential interpretation of them (Bultmann 1989). What do deific genuine questions mean for our fundamental affections and dispositions? If religions are archives of symbols, if they are resources for developing "answers" to life's deepest questions, then what does a deific question do for us (see Simmons and Benson 2013)? What do questions posed by deific voices indicate about our being in the world? These topics are addressed in my Conclusion.

Part II of the book focuses on three case studies of questions posed by deific voices on the level of story—the God depicted in Jewish scriptures, the classical Chan (Zen) master Mazu in his recorded sayings literature, and Jesus as he is depicted in canonized Christian Gospels. In principle, my method is transferable to depictions of deific figures in other texts and traditions. I just happen to be most familiar with these three. Yet there are nonarbitrary reasons to believe that these three are particularly illuminating for our hermeneutic inquiries. For those familiar with Zen Buddhism, we know that—especially in the Rinzai sect—the master-student dynamic is wrought with questions and interrogations. *Koan* practice emerged from earlier "transmission of the lamp" literature of the Tang and Song dynasties, particularly in the genre called "encounter dialogues" or brief vignettes portraying a master interacting with one or more students. It is a hot medium, requiring readers imaginatively to fill in missing details surrounding the snapshot (see McRae 2003). Elite literati of the Tang and Song dynasties voraciously consumed these writings of "recorded sayings." How do questions operate in these encounters? In Christian-influenced popular culture, many people ask, "What would Jesus do?" Jesus is depicted as having a propensity *not* to ask sincere questions but regularly confronts others with rhetorical questions. Would Gospel authors construct an image of Jesus asking genuine questions or would that be counter to their interests in promoting Jesus as a messiah? The Jewish God is among the most enigmatic figures in world literature. It seems that, as I will show, this figure's first spoken interaction with primordial human beings begins with a question, that this figure is the first in the Torah to ask a question. Perhaps this is significant?

Chapter 4 focuses on the God's questions in the Tanak, primarily in *Bereshit* or Genesis. This God is a figure who speaks, and—at least in this regard—is anthropomorphic. Anthropomorphism presents a God that is radically distinct from the abstract omnibeing of institutionalized theistic philosophy of religion. While an omnibeing might be omniscient, and thus ask no genuine questions, this God is depicted asking numerous questions. Many of this God's questions are rhetorical or interrogating. Are there any that might be genuine questions, aimed at shared asking and broadening horizons? This would prove to be exceptional. We will consider some prime examples but look most closely at this God's first question to the primordial human beings: "Where are you?"

Chapter 5 turns to Mazu, the eighth-century progenitor of the most irreverent versions of Zen. We will examine the constructed quality of Dharma transmission records or genealogies, with an aim at clarifying the literary rather than historical character of encounter dialogues. The recorded sayings of Mazu provide not only some of his sermons but a surplus of brief encounters with students where—in many cases—he provokes students with questions. While the majority of his questions examine students' quality of insight, there seems to be places where his questions could just as well be genuine. If so, this would prove to be exceptional. We will look, in particular, at his question to his Dharma heir named Hui Hai, where he asks, "Why are you seeking outside?"

In Chapter 6, we will look at Jesus' questions, primarily those in the canonized Gospels. Because Gospel portraits conflict in many ways, we know that the Gospel portraits—like the transmission records—are constructions in accord with the interests of the writers and their communities. Thus, we are not looking at whether Jesus historically asked a genuine question but ways Gospel writers depict Jesus. Do they construct him as the kind of person to ask genuine questions? The majority of Jesus' questions, as we noted above, are patently rhetorical—such as when he asks, "To what shall I compare this age?" If any of his questions are genuine ones, this would prove to be exceptional. We will look, in particular, at his famous question to Peter, where he asks, "Who do you say that I am?"

Part III returns to the three case studies, but on a reflexive level by looking at narration, where a dialogue occurs between reader and text. The topic shifts from whether characters internal to a composed story can ask genuine questions to whether readers can experience being asked a genuine question by the text itself. Demythologization answers the demand that religious texts be interpreted not literally but existentially (Bultmann 1989). The issue here is less whether characters ask a genuine question but more whether readers are empowered through religious symbols, specifically the religious symbol of a genuine question posed by a deific voice. To interpret a text is not merely to find the question(s) to which the text answers but also to respond to questions the text asks you as a reader. Chapter 7 returns to the Torah, but this time looks at the reader's interaction with the voice of the text. What were the historical conditions that gave rise to the production of the text? Who is the voice of the text, and what does it ask of the reader when the God is depicted asking human beings where they are? Chapter 8 returns to Mazu's recorded sayings but this time positions the reader as the student of the master-text. What were the historical conditions that gave rise to the production of the text? Who is this voice confronting the reader, and what does this voice ask of readers who pick up the text in pursuit of insight? Chapter 9 returns to the Gospels, but this time looks at the reader's reception of the fundamental question of Jesus' identity. What were the historical conditions under which these texts were produced? Who is it that asks this of a reader, and what can this tell us existentially about the reader's accountability?

I conclude with a meditation on human responses to divine questions, an inversion of Tillich's method of correlation where—for him—religious symbols provide deific answers to human questions (Tillich 1951). For us, it is about human responses—indeed, human response-ability—in the face of questions posed to us by deific voices. As we will see, my book contributes to a religious humanist program through an ontology accounting for how one's own voice is being heard by and within being itself. Religious humanism navigates between two extremes: hypertheism of evangelical or fundamentalist literalism, on the one hand, and overhumanization of neoliberal and naturalist capitalism, on the other (Klemm and Schweiker 2008). Moreover, my book also contributes to antifascism and antiauthoritarianism by promoting questioning together and taking responsibility for our answers in contrast to subordination to authoritarian answers from above.

Part One

Elements of a Hermeneutic for Interpreting Questions in Religious Narratives

Chapter 1: Questioning Has Hermeneutic Priority   19

Genuine Questions Are Not Interrogations   21

Genuine Questions Suspend Copulation of Subjects and Predicates   24

Shared Questions Facilitate Fusion of Horizons   26

Implications of the Hermeneutic Priority of Questions for Interpreting Religious Literature   32

Chapter 2: Religious Narrative Is Literature   35

Literature Has Two Dimensions: Story and Discourse   40

A World Opens within the Text for Imaginative Dwelling   48

Religious Fiction Precedes the Categories of Myth and History   51

Chapter 3: What Is at Risk with Questions in Deific Discourse?   59

Questions on the Level of Story: On and Between the Lines   65

Questions on the Level of Discourse: Behind and Beyond the Lines   68

Questions Asked by Deific Voices Stand in Need of Demythologization   77

Before examining and interpreting specific questions attributed to deific figures and sacred texts themselves, I want to use Part I to provide a general theory and method for interpreting questions in religious literature. I will first define what questions are and explain their role in reaching an understanding with others. Second, I will delimit our domain of inquiry to religious narrative, particularly in its literary rather than historical or mythical character. Third,

I will pinpoint four ways questions function in the process of interpretation of texts as well as conclude with a call for demythologization of questions in religious narrative. This framework will help us get our bearing for engaging divine questions in a critical and comparative way without ranking some religions as "truer" than others. As a reminder, questions in the discourse of deific voices should strike us as surprising, if not downright disturbing. People seem, on the whole, to turn to such figures for answers, not more questions. Inasmuch as this is so, why are they depicted asking questions at all, and as asking so many questions at that?

Before proceeding, I want to point out that Part I is a paradigm for text interpretation informed by literacy pedagogy, literary criticism, and phenomenology (see Iser 1972). This matters because, on the one hand, phenomenological hermeneutics and literary criticism often neglect engagement with empirically researched literacy acquisition strategies used in reading instruction. It is one thing to theorize the nature of understanding; it is another thing entirely to work with children in the process of learning to read. Put simply, asking and answering questions with regard to sentences of a text is a crucial element of reading success. We know, however, that there are different kinds of questions. One kind of question might be checking a reader's retention of basic information disseminated via the text, and another kind of question might be asking for a reader to contrast her own perspective on a topic with that unfolding via the text. Literacy is demonstrated by answering such questions.

This also matters because, on the other hand, studies of religious texts are often bound either to advancement of their home traditions or involve historical contextualization and criticism to inoculate us from ideological eisegesis (see Porter and Stovell 2012). That is, the faithful often study their texts dogmatically; others distance themselves from dogmatism by placing texts in historical contexts. For many self-identifying faithful religious people, their texts directly and transparently describe reality. For others, many of whom also consider themselves religious, the texts prove to be historically inaccurate in content but nevertheless potentially informative about the interests of the writer, original audience, and broader culture of the era. By using literary criticism in general, and phenomenologies of reader-response theory in particular, we can resist both extremes—rejecting the narratives because they prove to be historically inaccurate and dogmatically seeing the narratives as transparent descriptions of some transcendent reality. We can use a suspension of disbelief, or what I will call a "hermeneutic reduction," to bracket out the normal attitude of demanding that religious narrative be either true or false in some directly descriptive sense.

Let us turn to isolate the hermeneutic priority of questions.

Questioning Has Hermeneutic Priority

This chapter will explain what it means to say that questions have hermeneutic priority and explain why this is the case. My argument in this chapter is twofold. I argue that understanding is specific to discourse, to sentences in particular. And I argue that understanding sentences requires actually asking the questions to which those sentences answer. Just to provide some preliminary clarification of terms, we need to start with defining hermeneutics. For our purposes, I want us to consider "hermeneutics" in a broad sense of the science and art of interpretation of written texts. While we can extend interpretation to phenomena that are not written texts, this extension is by way of an analogy where we model something that is not a written text *as if it was* a written text. So, while some people might assert that "dance" or "video games" are texts, reading these well or interpreting these is an extension of our ability to read and interpret written texts. In fact, I am constraining "texts" to written ones to be helpful, but we should also keep in mind how this excludes spoken discourse and signed discourse. As I will elaborate later in Chapter 2, there are a number of unique oddities about written discourse in contrast to spoken and signed discourse, such as the fixation of discourse in writing and the liberation from restraints of face-to-face dialogue. Let us agree for now to focus primarily on interpretation of written texts, knowing that our discoveries can be extended by analogy to things other than written texts. Moreover, hermeneutics stands in contrast to rhetoric(s). Hermeneutics focuses on *reception and understanding of discourse*, whereas rhetoric focuses on *production and making of discourse*. Although much of our work here might help us say something new, our aim is first to understand something that has already been said.

To interpret a text, at the very least, is to identify its topic and the major predicate or complete thought concerning that topic. This complete thought holds other elements of the written work together into an integrated whole. Like a thesis statement of an argumentative essay or the major plot for the protagonist in a story, this main subject matter and predication about it establish an integrated hierarchy of topics and complete thoughts where minor conflicts or minor premises serve the purpose of supporting the main point (see Ricoeur 1974). This should help us see why we can get into interpretive disagreements with other readers. They may find the main topic to be different from what we believe is the main topic. Or, we might agree on the main topic, but they might see one complete thought as the primary thesis, while we see a different complete thought as the primary thesis. Of course, through discussions about our competition of interpretations, we may come to realize we overlooked obvious details and realize that their interpretation is better because it, for example, integrates details that our interpretation forced to be anomalous. However, we could also come to see that both interpretations have sufficient support to leave us in interpretive abeyance between both (or more) options.

Nevertheless, however many conflicting interpretations there might be for a given written text, all of them need to answer two questions: What is the main topic? What is being said about that topic? It is precisely in this way that questions have hermeneutic priority. Without asking and addressing those questions, we have not yet interpreted a text. This comprehensive plot or thesis statement shapes the rest of our interpretation however thorough or superficial it may be. The same priority of questioning occurs per part composing the whole. Each chapter of a book has a main topic and predicate concerning that topic. Each paragraph does as well, and so does each sentence. I am confident many of us have had the experience of "reading" a page of a book or an essay or article, and—upon getting to the end—asking ourselves, "What did I just read?" That is, we know we looked at the words, and we even know what (most of) the words mean, but yet when we try to isolate what holds all the words together, we come up short. Looking at a page like this is not to read or understand the page. What is required to understand the sentences is asking the questions to which they answer as well as asking the question to which the text as a whole responds.

A fundamental axiom of philosophical hermeneutics is: to understand a question is to ask it, but to understand a complete thought is to understand it as an answer to a question (see Gadamer 2013). Without asking the question to which a complete thought responds—whether in the form of a plot, or in the form of a thesis statement, or in the form of a minor premise supporting the thesis, etc.—the complete thought is lost on us. It is like looking at a page of written sentences, even being able to sound them out phonetically, yet not understanding what the sentences are saying. That is, while we can see or hear a sentence, we can only understand a complete thought. A sentence only makes sense when we understand the complete thought it materially embodies. *It takes actually asking the question a sentence answers to transform that sentence merely seen into a complete thought understood* (Dickman 2021). We should be able to tell that this axiom of questioning's hermeneutic priority applies on the micro and macro levels of texts. If we do not have at least an implicit sense of a question to which a specific sentence responds, it will not be understood, whether that sentence is a minor point in a footnote or the major point defended by the entire work.

We should be feeling at least slightly reflexive if not quite uncomfortable right now. If questioning's priority is, in fact, true, does that mean we are asking the questions to which these specific sentences written on this very page are answering? When I pay attention to my own reading of these sentences or even my own writing of these sentences, I do not experience or perceive myself explicitly asking questions for each discrete sentence. We will return to this problem in much greater detail in Chapter 3. There we will break down questions in the reading process into discrete classes, but for now allow me to point out that what we call literacy or fluency—derived from the same Latin root as the word "fluid"—is where we can process answers to questions unfurling at lightening speeds. Yet we also know that our anticipations of questions can be premature, where we believed a sentence would answer one question but as we collect a greater quantity of complete thoughts, we realize that a sentence actually answered an entirely different question. What studies of children learning to read help us comprehend is that the process of becoming literate involves slowing down by breaking down the reading and interpretive process into its discrete steps or classes of questioning. As I said, we will return to this later on, but for now I want to isolate the complex phenomenon of questioning itself to clarify a number of features of questioning that are particularly relevant for our main topic: Can deific voices ask a genuine question?

Genuine Questions Are Not Interrogations

Studies of law enforcement distinguish between police interviews and police interrogations (see Hartwig et al. 2005, and Kassin et al. 2007). Interviews use questions merely to gather information. Interrogations use questions with the aim to get a suspect to make a confession. These correspond to two general question types in the logical analysis of questions, what we can call the "make me know" type of question and the "tell me truly" type of question (see Harrah 1982). On the one hand, people ask questions when they do not have a piece of knowledge, where they ask another person to supply them with that knowledge. It is a request to make me come to know that thing. On the other hand, such as with interrogations or—perhaps less insidiously—with questions that teachers ask of students, people use the questions not to acquire requested information but to test whether the answerer knows the information. That is, we use these questions to get reassurance that the other person knows the information we want or need them to know. Nevertheless, both of these types are reducible to what, in the logical analysis of questions, have come to be called "epistemic imperatives."

Epistemic imperatives are typical interrogative statements. From the perspective of epistemic imperatives, a question is just a command that the questioner come to know something or other. To clarify with an example: the question "What is your name?" amounts to the same thing functionally as the command "Tell me your name." In every case of typical interrogatives, they seem reducible to an imperative. Without this structure, we would not be able to construct logical analyses of questions. Logic and reasoning, in general, have come to be operations on declarative sentences or propositions. Thus, before we can do a logic of questions, we need to transpose questions into sets of propositions. To return to our example, the more precise transposition of "What's your name?" is "Select one from the following options: My name is Muhammad. My name is Ruth. My name is [etc.]." The options for answering consist of all possible names one might have, in a complete thought. Notice that this more precise transposition clarifies the two elements: the "select one… " is the imperative element; and the set of knowable propositions is the epistemic element—what the questioner should come to know. What we realize through this analysis is that questions, at least paradigmatic ones used in the logical analysis of questions, presuppose sets of propositions. The question word in wh-questions like our example (who, what, where, etc.) functions like an algebraic variable for which we need to solve. However, let's take a simpler question: "Is it snowing?" This epistemic imperative needs to be transposed as: "Select one: it is snowing; it is not snowing." This is a grammatically closed question, with only two options. With wh-questions, alternatively, the questions are grammatically open ones. That is, grammatically closed and grammatically open questions have to do with the presupposed set of propositions which are the possible answers. Does the set have two (or three) options? Then it is closed. Does the set have potentially infinite options? Then it is open.

I want to take a moment to challenge such reductionist tendencies in conceiving of questions, which I have done elsewhere in more detail (see Dickman 2018; and Dickman 2021). I believe we need a notion of questioning that cannot be reduced to commands to protect questioning from critics dismissing it as a mere authoritarian power move (see Comay 1991, Žižek 1989, and Wang 2006). It is not accidental that critics perceive questions as cloaked devices for control of others since, as I just mentioned, questions are reducible to commands in the logical analysis of questions. Even if we turn to pragmatics and speech act theory, this reduction seems unavoidable. For example, of the five primary illocutionary acts we can perform with language, questions belong in the "directive" genus (see Searle 1969, and Bell 1975). The verb "to ask" is unique among other command verbs. Most command verbs, including "ask," can work grammatically in the sentence: "I command [demand, urge, ask, etc.] you to go." However, only "ask" works in the following: "I ask [command, demand, urge, etc.?] you when you last saw your parental guardians." As the speech act theorist Martin Bell explains, asking a question "is a special kind of commanding, distinguished in that to ask a question is to command specifically a linguistic act" (Bell 1975, 206). The issue, even in pragmatics, is not whether a question is a command but the unique kind of force of asking as compared to other forms of command. A further dimension of its uniqueness is that asking commands a linguistic act, namely, an articulated answer. Whether from a logical analysis or from a pragmatic analysis, questions seem reducible to commands; interrogative sentences seem reducible to imperative ones. These are sincere questions, where we need an answer or even "the" answer. However sincere this sort of question might be, though, I want to distinguish sincere questions from what I prefer to call "genuine questions" (see Dickman 2018; and Dickman 2021).

I want to isolate one kind of questioning that circumvents such reduction to commands for linguistic response, and thus is inoculated from criticisms of questioning as intrinsically authoritarian at large. Recall that our focus on deific voices concerns the nature of ultimate religious authority and our tendencies to appeal to higher authorities. In some cases of question asking, we do not seek either a confession or a definitive answer. In these cases, we seek shared asking of the question so that we might dwell together in conversation and thought, exploring possibilities for answering the question together. The Ancient Greek philosopher Aristotle uses this possibility of sharing thoughts as definitive for the essence of complete friendship (see Aristotle 1999). Consider the question: "What year is it?" Of course, depending on the circumstances and orientations of the conversation partners, this might simply be a command for specific articulate information. Yet it is not impossible to imagine one friend asking this, and another friend responding with, "Yeah, what year is it, really?" Such a conversation might unfold into exploration of varying conventions of era-dating systems, metaphysics of time, and more. We know it is only 2021 CE relative to one era-dating system, one complicit with Euro-Christian global hegemony. But there are other era-dating systems found in other religious traditions, such as the Islamic and Jewish calendars. Such a shared asking of the question opens up the possibility for exploration and critique of colonialist conventions. Part of what grounds questioning's hermeneutic priority is precisely this possibility for *shared asking of a question that allows for a dialogue* rather than a compulsive conclusion with "the" answer. It suspends rather than demands the answer. I want to clarify further how these questions suspend answers, and then elaborate further on what shared asking of questions accomplishes.

Genuine Questions Suspend Copulation of Subjects and Predicates

We know that all complete thoughts consist of a subject, a predicate, and the copula synthesizing the two together. A complete thought, though, is greater than just the sum of its parts. A complete thought is not merely a pile of signs (see Ricoeur 1976). Something new emerges, a new dimension of experience emerges, through the synthesis of signs into sentences. Indeed, the copula just is this new being or entity, what we usually call a "meaning." I do not intend to use this word as a synonym for lexical definitions in dictionaries, or for mental intentions, or for objects indicated by labels or signs like a referent. While the word "meaning" does get used in these ways, for this book I want us to restrict it primarily to complete thoughts. Recall our hermeneutic axiom about questions having priority: understanding a complete thought requires understanding it as an answer to a question. Otherwise, we are just looking at a pile of signs. To put it differently, it takes asking the question to transform a sentence perceived into a complete thought or meaning understood (see Dickman 2021). Keeping in mind that answers to questions are complete thoughts with subjects and predicates will help us pinpoint just what makes genuine questions relevantly distinct from typical interrogative sentences.

Let us look at another example. Imagine someone saying, "We are facing Mecca." This sentence—to transform into a complete thought understood rather than merely a sentence seen—answers a question such as, "What direction are we facing right now?" If we are only familiar with cardinal and egocentric directions like south and backward, a sentence using Qibla compass coordinates might be so unfamiliar that the complete thought the sentence embodies might be lost on us. Without the question, the sentence would strike us as coming out of nowhere and would not make sense. While performance artists might want to "make a statement" outside any context, our hermeneutic paradigm for understanding meanings or complete thoughts requires at least a question for context to make sense of a statement. The question about what direction we face seems to be seeking "the" answer. If we break down the answer, we note there is a subject (our orientation) and a predicate (facing Mecca). Notice that the opposite or negation of the example sentence is "We are not facing Mecca." I highlight this because we might be inclined to conceive of questions as the opposite of declarative statements. This assertion with a negation in it is not a question, though.

That is, questions are not the opposite of or negations of assertions. This is the case even for epistemic imperatives. What if the question is not merely seeking "the" answer as in an imperative but opening a conversation about contestations over regimes of orientations (see Ahmed 2005)? That is, we might be "facing forward," or "facing north," besides "facing Mecca." It is not obvious that an Islamic model for orienting us in space and time is more fitting than our cardinal model or egocentric model. Whether seeking "the" answer or opening out toward a reflective conversation, questions suspend assertions, holding multiple combinations of subjects and predicates together and apart in the domain of possible answers. That is, the propositions presupposed or forming the content of a question (like the set of "My name is Muhammad, Ruth, etc.") are not actual complete thoughts but subjects and predicates *held in suspense.*

Part of what the logical analysis leaves out is *this abeyance and fluctuation* of subjects and predicates, like *a tensive ontology* where things both are and are not (see Ricoeur 1975). Questions suspend the copulation of subjects and predicates, not presuppose sets of already synthesized complete thoughts. This is what allows the set to consist of *possible*, not actual, answers. Without this moment of suspense, we cannot transition from a question to an answer. From a phenomenological perspective, the suspense happens when we become conscious of a subject matter in its mode of questionability (see Schumann and Smith 1987). In our example concerning our orientation, the subject radiates predicative possibilities—"facing Mecca," "facing forward," "facing north," etc.—where all of them are held in suspense. These different frameworks for orienting ourselves, these different possible predicates, are live options but we are not settled yet. In fact, we might not feel any particular urgency in settling things, and instead enjoy exploring each possibility held in suspense or exploring the very conditions under which these rather than others are the live possibilities. In this way, we should relocate such questions away from the directive or command genus of speech acts to another genus, perhaps even inventing another genus that we can call "suspensives" (see Dickman, 2021b). These sorts of exploratory questions that disclose the questionability of things are not declarations or assertions, they are not commands or commissives, and they are not merely self-expressions. These five types of discourse are considered exhaustive in speech act theory. However, speech act analysis of questions breaks down here because *such questions are less an act of speech and instead more an event of listening.* Just as listeners literally make utterances as they listen, with such hearing-tokens as "mmhmm" and "yes," so also do listeners embody their listening by asking questions (see Bublitz 1988). In listening, we suspend judgments—which is not the same as saying we have *no* judgments. Like the suspension of disbelief we employ in our enjoyment of fiction allows us to make judgments within the fictional universe, this suspension of judgments allows us to make judgments within the field of questionability.

A further aspect of suspense here can be brought out by distinguishing what we can call "deficit-driven questions" and "surplus-driven questions." Some questions, as we have pointed out, seek "the" answer. Such questions are asked out of need or lack, perhaps even under conditions of perceived or real urgency. These are deficit-driven questions. We experience an absence and need it filled, such as, "It's time to go. Where are my car keys?" Such a question is a tool or means to an end, a tool that can be replaced by other means—for example, just scanning the room for the keys. That is, there is nothing essential to asking the question to finding the keys. Surplus-driven questions, alternatively, are genuine questions. These are not rooted in need or lack. Instead, they emerge out of a desire of one who "lacks nothing," a desire oriented by what Levinas calls, echoing Plato, "the order of the Good" (Levinas 1969, 102). Our surplus, our flourishing, is expressed in our sheer enjoyment of questioning. That is, we can ask questions for the joy of them, tarrying with what questions open to us, where we do not feel deprived of "the" answer. It is naïve to subordinate questions to answers, as if the purpose of all real questions is just to get answers. Some questions elicit questions. And some questions elicit shared asking of the questions. That is, the point of some questions is less to get an answer and more to get another person to ask the questions with us. By sharing a question together, we connect with others. We can clarify this connection with more precision through the model of fusing or broadening horizons of understanding.

Shared Questions Facilitate Fusion of Horizons

While I hope we can all appreciate how questions help transform sentences observed into complete thoughts understood, how do we come to understand what another person says? I want to elaborate more thoroughly here on how shared questioning facilitates reaching an understanding with others. To get at this, it is helpful to return to our axiom for philosophical hermeneutics: to understand a question is to ask it, but to understand a complete thought or meaning is to understand it as an answer to a question. The first clause indicates that sincere or genuine questioning is not really an action but a passion. It is something that happens to us or occurs to us more than it is something we can deliberately control. We get caught up by a question, inspired to ask it. What is even more, there is not really a potential attitude of questioning. As the hermeneutic philosopher Hans-Georg Gadamer points out, there is no "tentative or potential attitude of questioning… Even when a person says such and such question might arise, this is already a real questioning that simply masks itself, out of either caution or politeness" (Gadamer 2013, 383). While we might decide it is against our interests to utter a question aloud depending on the circumstances, we cannot decide whether or not a specific question occurs to us. I am not trying to claim we do not have moments where we do not understand questions. For example, if someone asks me a question in a language in which I do not have fluency, I will not understand the question. Moreover, even if someone asks me a question in my native tongue, I might not understand it if there are conjunctions with which I lack familiarity. The point is solely that understanding a question is simultaneously to be asking it. The asking *is* the understanding. While sentences are potential complete thoughts seen and complete are sentences understood, interrogative sentences are questions seen but questions asked are interrogative sentences understood.

The passivity or nonintentional character of questioning is crucial for explaining how we can reach an understanding with others about a subject matter. When I understand another's question whether written or spoken or signed, *I also ask that question with the other person*. That is, their question becomes my question, too. In other words, rather than it being your question or my question, it is *our* question. We share responsibility for the questioning, even if we end up not liking the answers or other consequences of our questioning. In fact, we share this responsibility despite the fact that we did not deliberately decide to ask the questions. The shared questioning puts us in *a synergistic relationship of mutual responsibility*, one that subordinates neither party to the domination and power of the other person. It is shared questioning that allows our account of genuine questions to circumvent critiques of questions as power or dominance moves.

What is more, through this shared questioning I am positioned to consider their responses to the question as possible answers. Without this shared questioning, what they say would be lost on me, what they say would not make any sense. This happens in reading written texts or listening in dialogue or comprehending through sign language. That is, I can understand what someone is saying because I have a sense of the questions to which they respond. This happens in face-to-face dialogue, but also happens— indeed must happen—in the reading process, where only in asking the questions addressed can I grasp and not merely see what is written. I want to emphasize that while I cannot merely consider asking their question— because to consider it is to be asking it—I can consider their answers without necessarily appropriating their answers as my own answers. That is, only through sharing their questions do I come to grasp what they say *as* an answer, as a complete thought that can be understood. I can comprehend why they might propose this or that complete thought as an answer, but that does not entail that I take their answer as "the" answer for myself. An extra step of existential appropriation of their meaning is required of me to achieve this—whether it is taking their answer as one of my own or making their answer "the" answer for myself. As we have already explained, questioning exposes the questionability of subject matters, holding subjects and predicates in suspense, where subjects radiate predicative possibilities without any one of the possibilities being selected or determined yet as "the" answer. Just because shared questioning allows me to *consider* what they mean, that does not entail that I too mean what they mean, that I agree with what they mean.

Upon sharing questions with another, I am positioned to appropriate existentially what they mean by agreeing with what they say in response to the question(s). Reaching agreement seems to be the aim of a dialogue where we fuse and broaden our horizons of understanding. A fusion of horizons is realized concretely, according to Gadamer, when dialogue partners reach some form of agreement concerning a subject. I take "subject" here in a particular way: the subject of a complete thought. A fusion of horizons is realized when we find shared predicates fitting for that subject. A question is not a judgment because a question is not a synthesis of subject and predicate. And yet, a question is not the negation of that one synthesis or any other synthesis. The peculiar nature of questioning is, as Gadamer writes, "that it stands closer to a statement than any of the other linguistic phenomena, and yet it allows no logic in the sense of a logic of [complete thoughts]" (Gadamer 2007, 102). It is by virtue of the shared question that I can start to try out these predicative possibilities for a specific subject, and when I find a predication that works, it expands my horizon and enriches my world. Moreover, through the partnership of questioning, the questions specify a horizon within which the transferal of meaning is made possible. In this way, hearing what another person has to say, accommodating them in discursive space, as well as suspending resolution with regard to that which they speak about precedes all abstract making of a "statement." Consider the question, "What direction are we facing?" Through dialogue, we can consider predicative possibilities, and reach agreement. If we reach agreement concerning those pertinent predicates, then we also can be said to "fuse horizons." How so?

Our historical situatedness, or what some critical feminist philosophers such as Pamela Sue Anderson identify as our standpoint, opens us to horizons of possible meanings (see Anderson 1998). Because human beings are always in a situation, our understanding is always unfinished and incomplete. We have new experiences that change our understanding of something we thought we already grasped. Many people read a book for the second time and get something else out of it that we did not from the first reading of it. Hence, the need for the application of the concept "horizon" here. We need a superior breadth of vision in trying to reach an understanding and fuse horizons. As Gadamer writes, "To acquire a horizon means that one learns to look beyond what is close at hand—not in order to look away from it but to see it better, within a larger whole and in truer proportion" (Gadamer 2013, 316). Horizons include all that can be seen from this point of view. Yet the notion of fusion of horizons seems to imply that there are two separate horizons, mine and yours, which fuse when we reach agreement (see Gadamer 2013, 314). It seems as if there are distinct individual subjects with points of view opened to distinct horizons. This would entail, however, that there are "closed" horizons. This is incompatible with the relativity of horizons (see Warnke 2016). Horizons move as people move, preserving an opening with us. *There is no such thing as a "closed" horizon.* When we reach an understanding, we are not empathizing with another person where we try to enter into their situation and horizon. We are not merely trying to feel what another person feels. *We can empathize without understanding; we can understand without empathizing.* So, when we think about it, people do not try to understand others precisely, but instead people try to understand what others have to say in response to living questions generated by historical situations. In this way, we are all part of one great horizon. By reaching an understanding and fusing horizons, we "rise to a higher universality," a greater breadth of perspective in which it is possible to share meanings with one another or to consider things from multiple points of view (Gadamer 2013, 314). The term "universality" is not some metaphysical truth that stands eternally. Instead, hermeneutic universality indicates those complete thoughts and their questionings that can be shared by ever-greater swaths of humanity.

Fusing horizons transforms us because we open ourselves to new possibilities of meaning not only for consideration but also for appropriation and ownership. *Responsible understanding involves coming to speak otherwise than I have ever spoken before because, when I grasp answers to questions, I make gains in greater linguistic fluency.* Insofar as speaking differently reflects being different, to what extent might one also become otherwise in responsible service to others when we are in dialogue with them? One can become completely other than who one has been if one is loyal to responsible understanding. But are we not then faced with a hard choice: either loyalty to understanding or commitment to my current identity? Reaching an understanding involves a transformation of ourselves (Beatty 1999, 295).

When we understand what one another says about something, we cannot help but be transformed into a communion in which we are no longer be the exact same person (Gadamer 2013, 371). Understanding that expands our horizons, putting our very selves at risk. Regarding our perspective as revisable entails regarding our very selves as revisable. As philosopher Joseph Beatty writes, "To listen to another with openness is, then, to open the self to the possibility of taking seriously meanings of the sort that can transform it. Such openness requires, therefore, not merely the willingness to rework and rethink experience and its ingredient opinions but the willingness to rework character" (Beatty 1999, 295). Every time we listen, in other words, our very selfhood is at stake. We cannot maintain a closure where we have already made a decision, come what may. When people use the cliché "stick to your guns" to encourage another person to maintain their position despite opposition, this sort of thinking inhibits listening and growing in character. To share questions is to be open to the possibility that we will need to change our mind.

The event of fusing horizons is transformative because in it "you" and "I" become "us." We can explain this by examining what happens when we become concentrated in playing a game. A game moves and has its essence beyond the particular intentions or deliberate consciousness of each of the players. Games draw us in and simultaneously fill us with their dynamic spirit, like "team spirit." This spirit surpasses all of us as isolated individuals. Consider the "wave" in stadiums. Games mediate and moderate each individual's intent by transforming us into parts of a greater whole. And just as with games, so also with being-at-one on a subject and reaching an understanding. As Gadamer writes,

> A [dialogue] does not simply carry one person's opinion through against another's in argument, or even simply add one opinion to another. Genuine [dialogue] transforms the viewpoint of both. A [dialogue] that is truly successful is such that one cannot fall back into the disagreement that touched it off. The commonality between the partners is so very strong that the point is no longer the fact that I think this and you think that, but rather it involves the shared interpretation of the world which makes moral and social solidarity possible.
>
> (Gadamer 2007, 96)

In games, players align their actions with movements appropriate for the game. Consider see-saw or teeter-totter. A good match consists of the uninhibited performance of the to-and-fro balance worked out by the two participants. This movement is irreducible to some further end or purpose.

Participants in games are overcome by the playfulness of the movement and animated by it. A game only fulfills its purpose when the participants, so to speak, "lose" themselves to the movement. As Gadamer writes, "It is at this point that the concept of the game becomes important, for absorption into the game is an ecstatic self-forgetting that is experienced not as a loss of self-possession, but as the free buoyancy of an elevation above oneself" (Gadamer 1977, 55). In games, we are liberated for *re-creation*. We literally re-create ourselves in games. The form that the re-creation takes constrains the field of possible action, but is experienced not as restrictive. It is liberating. Without the game situating players thusly, they would not be freed to play. Without the rules of driving, we would not be free to get anywhere! The constraints governing the field of the game are the condition of the possibility of the playful variety of activity. *Furthermore, the goal of re-creation is fulfilled not in winning or solving the puzzle of the game but with simply exhibiting the dynamic form of the game.* The mode of being of such a game is not winning or losing but is "self-presentation." What the game means for the participants does not depend on finishing or winning the game. Rather, players "spend" themselves out on the task of the game and "play" themselves out in it. In this way, the game takes a stand in and through the participants. This excursion into games shows us the way in which "who we are" is at stake in play, and even more in listening to what another person has to say.

Shared questioning that leads to a fusion of horizons is not just a conjunction of individual intentions. Consider pushing a car with another person. It is not that "I" am pushing the car and "you" are pushing the car. My so doing and your so doing are a part of "our" pushing the car. If "I" discover that "you" were faking it, then not only was I wrong about what you were doing but I was also wrong about what I was doing (see Searle 1992). Dialogues are collective activities, and the intentional contents of a participant's self-understanding and intention, even though it may differ from the content of other participants' I-intentions, conjoin in some way to a common we-intention. Through shared questionings we can come to consider others' responses as meanings to understand and own. Shared questioning is not the sum of the individual actions having the same intentions, such as when individual and solitary hikers all take shelter from a storm in the same bunker. The understanding achieved in dialogue is more than the sum of its parts. Understanding and dialogue are something we accomplish with others, not by ourselves. This is especially true about genuine questions as they are distinct from sincere questions, where sharing a question precedes any need for "the" answer.

One final element crucial for explaining how shared questions facilitate fusion of horizons is, as we have already mentioned, *we do not understand others but understand what others say.* Questions, because they have hermeneutic priority, make it possible for sentences to appear as complete thoughts or meanings for understanding (see Ricoeur 1975, 97). As Gadamer writes, "Being that can be understood is language" (Gadamer 2013, 490). Not merely sentences perceived but sentences understood as complete thoughts are language. Moreover, only sentences have the potential to be understood as meanings. This might feel like I am atrophying our understanding because in our natural attitude we feel we ought to understand everything, not "merely" language. We express despair and disappointment when we do not understand some things. The anthropologist Talal Asad writes the following toward our experience of death and horror about suicide bombings: "Breaking into this paranoid [frenzy] may be the sudden realization that in any death there is nothing to understand—that there's no role for the meaning-making subject. The thought that makes chance deaths more horrible is that they cannot be redeemed by a comforting story" (Asad 2007/2008, 129). If only sentential answers to asked questions can be understood, then this despair is not a problem of our understanding properly speaking but *a problem of our inflated expectations for understanding* where we try to smear it across all things. When someone asks, "What is the meaning of life?" As response we can make given this framework is that "life" has no meaning because "life" is not a complete thought that can be understood. We cannot understand such things because they are not sentences or complete thoughts that answer to questions. We participate in events, undergo experiences, meet others, make something of ourselves, and all these generate in us a desire to speak up or make us poetically productive. We understand discourse—no more, no less.

Implications of the Hermeneutic Priority of Questions for Interpreting Religious Literature

Before turning to specify what we mean by religious literature, I want to delineate our findings here about the hermeneutic priority of questions as well as draw out what we should look for as we progress through the rest of this book. There are two primary features of the hermeneutic priority of questioning. On the one hand, questions make possible the transformation of sentences seen into complete thoughts understood. Just because we see or hear sentences does not entail we understand the sentences. It takes asking the questions to which sentences answer to render them into meanings to be understood. On the other hand, genuine questions also transform isolated individuals into a community, through the event of shared questioning.

When someone else asks a question, we ask it with them if we understand it. Their question, then, becomes our question. We need to keep these two features in mind when we inquire whether or not a God or Buddha (or texts themselves) can ask a genuine question. Can they share questions with others and have their horizons expanded?

When we apply this to our engagement with deific voices, we need to keep clear two levels of application. First, pinpointing whether a God can ask a genuine question involves focusing exclusively on the constitution of the figure within religious literature. Even though we notice numerous interrogative sentences attributed to Buddhas, Prophets, Gods, and more in religious literature, that does not entail any of those questions are sincere or genuine. In the case of sincere questions, those that aim at acquisition of "the" answer or specific information, it would require that the religious figure does not already have knowledge of all the facts. Do prophets, Gods, or others ever need information and use questions to get it? In the case of genuine questions, those that aim at shared asking and dwelling with others, it would require that the religious figure can be existentially transformed via such an encounter with another. Do Buddhas, Gods, or others ever risk their identity and become transformed through a fusion of horizons with another? While these questions emphasize how deific figures are constructed in narrative, additional questions apply to deific voices on the level of discourse or the reader's engagement with a text.

Second, then, pinpointing whether or not a God can ask a genuine question depends on how readers interpret religious texts. Questions have hermeneutic priority not merely between characters in a narrative but, perhaps even more importantly, between reader and text. For a reader to interpret sentences they read requires that the reader positions oneself to ask the questions to which the sentences answer. The writer, composer, or redactor constructs both an ideal narrative voice and an ideal reader. This voice internal to the text asks and addresses questions; they do not merely make statements in semantic or hermeneutic outer-space. Thus, the reader needs to share those questions with the narrative voice to be able to transform the sentences seen into complete thoughts understood. This is merely to understand the narrative. However, presumably—inasmuch as religious narratives seek to engage and transform readers' lives in the here and now— the text asks questions of readers, questions that do not shape the content of narratives but questions that engage readers existentially, as in, "What do you, reader, have to say for yourself in light of this narrative?" Can religious texts engage readers with genuine questions? Can readers engage religious texts with their own genuine questions?

In this chapter, I have argued for restricting understanding to complete thoughts or meanings, and that complete thoughts are really only understood in relation to actually asking the questions to which those sentences answer. Let us turn to pinpoint features of narrative within religious texts, where texts are concatenations of sentences.

Religious Narrative Is Literature

My argument in this chapter is twofold. First, I argue that religious texts are not merely representational. Second, I argue that religious narratives are best conceived of in terms of "fiction," using this as a term to navigate between historical accuracy and mere myth. One main difficulty with engaging religious texts, especially in advanced capitalist Eurocentric societies, is how religious texts are treated within a positivistic framework (see Smith 2017; and Kotsko 2018). Positivism, as I mean it here, is a view about how language works, stemming from Wittgenstein's early philosophy, where sentences are only meaningful if they accurately represent or correspond to facts in the world. A global transformation occurred near the sixteenth century due to the collision of the scientific revolution, the Protestant Reformation, the modernist retrieval of classical humanism, the rise of the modern nation state and colonialism, and the Industrial Revolution (see Dupre 1993). In the centuries since, a positivist framing of religious texts has taken two extremes.

On the one hand, we have witnessed a viral spread of religious literalism, where communities now take their religious texts to depict accurately physical and metaphysical realities. Unlike their ancient and medieval counterparts, modern religious fundamentalists reject poetic, allegorical, and anagogical readings of sacred texts (cf. Aquinas 1993). Perhaps you have heard some say, "Seven days is seven days." However, contemporary readers know—whether they admit this to themselves or not—that, for example, there is no three-tiered hierarchy to the human drama on earth positioned between a heaven and a hell as it often appears in Christian works (see Bultmann 1989). Contemporary readers know that the Buddha could not really go "down" to one of the hells to teach the Dharma to those enclosed there by their karma. Let me put this differently. Despite our conventions of talking, we know there is no such thing as a "beautiful sunset," but only beautiful earth-spins. When we point "upward," we know that it is really pointing "outward," since there really cannot be an up or down on a round object. Many premodern peoples understood their position in the cosmos differently, where the Earth was the meaningful center, where human actions seemingly had cosmic significance. Today we know that there probably is no center to the universe at all. The point is that contemporary literalism requires a comfort with cognitive dissonance or bad faith, where their religious worldview conflicts with the worldview they embody every time they, say, get on an airplane. Moreover, literalists purport to be true to original religious communities. For example, despite Orthodox Judaism's claim to be consistent with precedent Jewish traditions, the distinctively Orthodox movement as we know it today emerged in reaction to the establishment of Reform Judaism in the 1800s. Like Orthodox Judaism (not all of whom are literalists), literalists in general work under an aura of a claim to represent authentic tradition tracing back to their religious foundings (see Bell 2009). It is, however, sheer anachronism, misrecognizing the rhetorical strategy happening in the present to bolster present authority and authoritarianism. It could make for a fascinating study to examine how literalism functions in our advanced capitalist global economy. Who profits from it, and why does its branding sell so well? We will leave this for a different project.

On the other hand, we have witnessed a sensationalized anti-religious atheism that rejects all or most religious texts because, from this perspective, religious texts are inaccurate in their attempts to depict physical and metaphysical realities. Because religious texts are obviously false from this perspective, believers are also seen as delusional (see Dawkins 2008). Even more, in light of the way religious texts get used politically, these texts are seen as particularly dangerous in stirring up and mobilizing peoples against alternative ways of living or thinking. Militant atheists construe religious texts in comparably literalist terms, and in this way contribute to literalism's dominance in the religious marketplace. They seem only able to thrive off one another, such as when we see sensationalized debates between representatives of the two sides, like the Ken Ham and Bill Nye "debate" in 2014. Both of these extremes share a common positivistic assumption: religious language attempts to represent accurately facts about reality. Even moderates on this continuum presuppose positivism when they promote some middle ground, where although religious texts may be inaccurate in exact details, they are correct overall, such as when some progressive-leaning Christians discuss the first creation narrative in Genesis as, say, a day being billions of years for the God. They preserve their religious text as accurate to reality, just loosely rather than technically speaking. Thus, even moderates remain committed to believing that the function of religious language is to represent reality.

Such a framework for reading religious texts leads to questions like the following. Did Jesus' resurrection really happen historically and physically? Did Bodhidharma really sit in meditation until his legs withered? Did the first human beings have bellybuttons or the trees in Eden have rings? In a way, these questions might strike us as entirely natural. And they are... for people living in the modern world. Our natural attitude for "big" questions like these is one of seeking to know what is and what is not real, and a positivist framework enables this perspective. Either Bodhidharma lost his legs or he did not. Either the first human beings had bellybuttons or they did not. Either Jesus rose from the dead or he did not. The first place we can see serious scholarship on such questions is in the mid-1700s through the 1800s. For example, in *Ompholos: An Attempt to Untie the Geological Knot* (1857), the naturalist Philip Henry Gosse investigated the possibility of Adam's navel. Yet we know how to suspend our natural attitude that seems to compel us to ask such deficit-driven questions. Every time we enjoy a novel or movie or cartoon, we suspend our disbelief. We stop asking questions about whether what is depicted is "real." We stop asking questions about whether what is depicted is factual and historical. This is not the same as assuming the content is false. By suspending our natural attitude, the question of a story's factual truth or falsity is rendered impotent or unimportant *in comparison to what a story means.*

In technical terms, the suspension of disbelief is the first step of phenomenological method: the phenomenological reduction. The father of contemporary phenomenology Edmund Husserl describes this step as an *epoche* or bracketing out of our natural, positivistic, and naïve attitude (see Welton 1999). Our capacity to bracket this out opens us up to experience phenomena more meaningfully. Instead of some positivist concern about whether a story is factual, we can see what significance and power the story has in its own right. We can attune ourselves to understand what is being said rather than what it purports to refer to. Given phenomenology's influence on hermeneutics, I want to call this step in our engagement with religious literature the "hermeneutic reduction." This interpretive *epoche* puts us in a state of nonengagement with the "real" world, with regard to action and perception (see Ricoeur 1979). It puts meaning in a neutralized, rather than a positivistic, atmosphere. The world we can experience thanks to the hermeneutic reduction is not the mere empirical or positivist environment but a totality of relevance and meaning (see Taylor 1989). Before religious texts can be positivist descriptions of some reality, they are works of art and compositions. Before we can positivistically determine whether a text is accurate, we need to understand what it is saying. Thus, using the hermeneutic reduction, religious texts should be approached first as literature. Our efforts to understand the texts should precede asking whether a text is factually true or false. As the Hebrew and comparative literature scholar Robert Alter puts this,

> Subsequent religious tradition has by and large encouraged us to take [a religious text] seriously rather than to enjoy it, but the paradoxical truth

of the matter may well be that by learning to enjoy [religious] stories more fully as stories, we shall also come to see more clearly what they mean to tell us about God, man, and the perilously momentous realm of history.

(Alter 1981, 235)

What makes some literature distinctively religious, though? What distinguishes nonreligious literature and religious literature? For one, religious literature contributes to the constitution of the identity of a community in ways nonreligious literature does not. Communities see in religious literature an all-encompassing metastory, one that is open-ended and ongoing (see Ricoeur 1995). Individuals within such communities are empowered to see their own actions as part of this ongoing story. Religious literature provides communities with an orientation, one that projects a total world horizon that informs "intentions by which actions are projected into that world" (Crites 1971, 298; see also Ahmed 2006). Moreover, religious literature is traditional, authoritative, and liturgical (see Ricoeur 1995). What makes it traditional is that its content is told a certain way, which grounds its continuing to be told in that way. What makes it authoritative is that its content is separated off as canonical from the so-called "heretical." What makes it liturgical is that religious literature achieves its fullness of meaning when recited and performed in devotional contexts. Through these features, religious literature explodes the distinction between the imaginary and the real world. It gives adherents' lives ultimate orientation and intelligibility. Adherents understand themselves in light of religious literature, such as the characters developed in religious narratives. What would Jesus do? What would Bodhidharma do?

This should not neglect, however, aesthetic pleasure taken in producing and interpreting literature, as if religious literature can only have moral or didactic purposes and can never have playful or even irreverent purposes (see Alter 1981, 18–21). As Alter writes, "Implicit in such a contention is a rather limiting notion of what a 'religious' narrative is or of how the insight of art might relate to religious vision" (Alter 1981, 18). Packaging religious texts "as literature," such as textbooks or courses on "The Bible as Literature," superficially compartmentalizes sacred texts away from other world literature. It is not like other literary courses do this—imagine a course titled "Hemingway as Literature." Alter notes this is needlessly concessionary to religious literalists and condescending toward literature. He writes, "I would prefer to insist on a complete interfusion of literary art with theological, moral, or historiosophical vision, the fullest perception of the latter dependent on the fullest grasp of the former" (Alter 1981, 20). Some practices with religious texts preserve an aesthetic dimension of engagement, such as Quranic recitation contests, Torah scroll calligraphy, Buddhist mantra meditation, and more. This is not literary aesthetics, though. Such a separation from "mere literature" tends to serve institutional interests of religious businesses (see Bell 2009). Consider Nietzsche's condemnation of institutional Christianity's destruction of, say, the library of Alexandria and its ruining "taste in *artibus et litteris*" (Nietzsche 2008, 107). This criticism, he writes,

> refers to the basic text of Christian literature, its model, its "book of books." Even during the era of Greco-Roman splendor, which was also a splendor of books, in the face of an ancient world of writings that had not yet succumbed to decay and ruin, at a time when you could still read a few books we would nowadays give half of whole literatures to possess, the simplicity and vanity of Christian agitators—we call them Church Fathers—dared to decree: "we have our own classical literature, we don't need that of the Greeks." And so saying, they proudly pointed to books of legends, letters of the apostles and apologetic little tracts, rather similar to the way the English "Salvation Army" today fights Shakespeare and other "heathens" with similar literature.
>
> (Nietzsche 2008, 107–8)

In naming their bible "*The Bible*," Christians characterized their collection of materials not just as "the book," which translates the Late Latin term "biblia." Rather, it is not just "*The* Book" for them but "*The* The Book," purportedly the only thing worth reading or "the greatest story ever told." How has institutionalized use of religious texts undermined our capacity to enjoy them as "good reads"? Instead of reading, many people treat religious texts like a Magic 8-Ball oracle, shaking them up to get a random and contextless line that purportedly speaks to us about some divine or karmic purpose for their lives in broad outline or in a specific moment. My wager—with Alter (1981), the hermeneutic philosopher Paul Ricoeur (1974), the philosopher of Buddhism Peter Hershock (2009), the Jewish New Testament scholar Amy-Jill Levine (2015), and others—is that it is possible to read religious texts literarily, not literally.

Because I am focused on questions asked by deific voices, we need to focus our attention in particular on religious narratives. It is within narratives that characters perform actions like asking questions, and where narrational voices engage readers. We need to keep in mind, however, that such narratives are always nested in other modes of discourse (see Ricoeur 1995). Genealogies, laws, and poetry accompany the narratives in *Bereshit* or

Genesis. Sermons and genealogies accompany the episodic narratives known as "encounter dialogues" in the *Mazu yulu*. Letters and sermons accompany the canonized Gospel narratives. The point here is that a range of material is distributed between "the two poles of storytelling and praise" (Ricoeur 1995, 245). Nonnarrative discourse accompanying religious narratives prompts communities toward explicit philosophical, theological, or Buddhalogical discourse. Nonnarrative discourse inaugurates the process of transferring adherents from recitation of stories to a full grasp of the significance and meaning of the stories. Ricoeur refers to religious narratives as "embryonic theological thinking" (Ricoeur 1995, 248). Using the hermeneutic reduction to isolate religious narrative ought to help us resist premature theological and Buddhalogical conclusions. Although some of what we cover might help us to produce new doctrinal discourse, that is properly the domain of rhetoric or poetics more broadly. Centered in hermeneutics, we need to stay focused on the reception and understanding of discourse.

Literature Has Two Dimensions: Story and Discourse

I want to take up some crucial distinctions made within the structuralist approach to narrative. This brief detour will help inoculate us from naively psychologizing deific voices as if they represent real historical individuals with real motives, traits, and more. Our temptation in asking about HaShem's questions or Mazu's questions, or the authors' questions, is to construe them as if they are real people doing things like intending to question in certain ways. *Our detour into some elementary theory will help us persevere in our hermeneutic reduction, rather than following a shortcut through religious narrative to some (metaphysical) reality it supposedly represents.* Before we can say that "Jesus asked genuine questions" as a claim about a historical person, we need to interpret narrative compositions, where we are talking primarily about "Jesus" as a literary construction. These narratological distinctions will help us provide both a thick description of content of narratives where religious figures ask questions as well as a thick description of narrative discourse where content is given from text to reader.

There are differences between a story told and the telling of a story, between what Levinas calls the "said" and the "saying" (see Levinas 1998, 150). Narrative structuralists distinguish these two fundamental coordinates of narrative as *the level of story* and the *level of discourse* (see Todorov 1969, Barthes 1975, and Chatman 1978). These two dimensions of story and discourse form a hinge between the internal configuration of a literary work (story) and the external re-figuration of a reader's life where a text "speaks" to them (discourse) (see Ricoeur 1986, 127). On the one hand, the story configures parts into a whole. On the other hand, the discourse engages a reader's self-understanding, and—if successful—transforms the reader. Interpreting narratives involves readers taking hold of that hinge between a work's configuration as a story and the potential re-figuration of their life on the level of discourse, where readers' horizons are broadened through understanding themselves in light of the story.

These two aspects of narrative help us clarify a standard hermeneutic distinction between what we can call the "exegetical" hermeneutic circle (Part II) and the "existential" hermeneutic circle (Part III). In the exegetical hermeneutic circle, relations between parts and whole of a story guide it, where parts inform the meaning of a whole and the whole informs the meaning of a part (see Schleiermacher 1977). For example, the parts of a complete thought—a subject and a predicate—compose that thought, but the whole thought affects the definitions of the subject and predicate. Just so with narratives, where a character (a part) informs the meaning of a plot while the plot informs the meaning of a character. In the existential hermeneutic circle, reader's expectations and anticipations of meaning are revised in light of what a text says—its discourse (see Gadamer 2013, 278–310). These anticipations lead readers to put parts and wholes together in different ways, yet they also transform readers as an understanding of a story is achieved.

The main elements on the level of story to which I want us to give discrete attention are plot, event, action, and character. The fundamental feature that distinguishes narratives from other genres is "plot." Emplotment brings parts of a story together into a broader whole. Plot is not a static structure but an integrative process, synthesizing disparate elements such as discrete events and actions into more than merely a serial succession of sentences (see Ricoeur 1986, 122). Plots unify widely divergent parts into stories— from agents of actions and patients undergoing those actions to accidental and expected confrontations, from characters in relations of conflict or cooperation to means for achieving goals and results from enacting those means, and more (Ricoeur 1986, 122). We have inherited a number of genres for the composition of plots, which are sedimented models whereby we can distinguish, say, short stories from myths or comedies from dramas. Yet this sedimentation cannot be exhaustive because the models help make innovation possible, where they guide further experimentation (see Ricoeur 1986; see also Alter 1981, 57). Afrofuturism, for example, brings together elements of science fiction and African diasporic genres. Thus, these inherited models govern, but do not completely determine, narrative innovations. We can only recognize innovations against the backdrop of settled genres. As Alter writes,

> The process of literary creation, as criticism has clearly recognized from the Russian Formalists onward, is an unceasing dialectic between necessity to use established forms in order to be able to communicate coherently and the necessity to break and remake those forms because they are arbitrary restrictions and because what is merely repeated automatically no longer conveys a message.
>
> (Alter 1981, 74)

When we set out to provide descriptions of religious narratives, it is important to keep emplotment in mind. Descriptions should not merely gravitate toward isolating specific elements like an act of questioning but also gravitate toward integration of those elements into a broader plot.

Events and actions are basic units of narrative. "Event" and "plot" mutually define one another (see Ricoeur 1979a). There is no event in a story without a broader significance; there is no plot without events conjoined by it. As Ricoeur writes, "A story is made out of events to the extent that the plot makes events into a story" (Ricoeur 1979a, 24). Outside the context of relevance in a story, events are mere occurrences, like accidents, thwarting expectations and anticipations sedimented by the way things have gone before. An occurrence is transformed into a narrative event through a "retrograde necessity" ascribed to it via emplotment (see Ricoeur 1992, 142). Actions are distinct from events because whereas events merely happen, an action is "what makes things happen" (Ricoeur 1992, 61). Moreover, actions have an internal and necessary logical relation to "motives." They are mutually implicated. We cannot speak of an action without simultaneously discussing the motive to which it belongs (Ricoeur 1992, 63). To mention a motive, however, is to mention the agent (Ricoeur 1992, 95). Actions are either "mine" or "yours," "his" or "hers" or "theirs." That is, actions are in someone's power. Events, alternatively, merely are caused and bear only a contingent connection to their causes. We need to keep in mind here that by "motive," we are isolating a narrative element, a semantic category, not some psychological cause referring us to an actual person.

Questions in the direct discourse of deific figures are actions they perform, and thus connect to a motive revelatory of their character. Characters are themselves subordinate plots to the main narrative plot (see Ricoeur 1992, 143). In the construction of characters, readers determine their "traits" or abiding and relatively stable qualities of their personalities (see Humphreys 2001, 14). A trait is more general than a habit because it arises from the interconnection of habits. As film and literary critic Seymour Chatman writes, "If a character is constantly washing his hands, mopping already clean floors, picking motes of dust off his furniture, the audience is obliged to read out [an implicit] trait like 'compulsive'" (Chatman 1978, 122). Traits persist over the entirety of the story, or at least significant episodes of it. Moreover, traits are relatively independent of one another. That is, contradictory traits might exist in a single character. A character's traits integrate into a somewhat coherent whole enduring over time within the narrative, but this whole can be modified by growth or decay. The whole typically is given a proper personal name or some other designation. That is, characters stand out from a backdrop of mere cast members in a narrative due to these sematic relations of name, character, traits, motives, actions, physical descriptions, and more (see Alter 1981, 116–31).

Most important for our purposes is that characters keep track of information they receive in order to construct facts within the narrative as well as traits of other characters (see Todorov 1990, 46). In this way, characters often form a bridge between the "what" or content of a story and the "how" or discourse of a story's being told. Characters often mediate stories as much as they are parts of stories (see Ricoeur 1985, 37). A character might be an object of description at one point but also provide a point of view within the story through her own direct discourse. Since characters have a point of view, they can be asked for it. An omniscient narrator might see the entire narrative labyrinth in intricate detail, Alter explains, yet characters at least have a grasp on broken threads of it as they seek their own way (Alter 1981, 197). Deific figures in religious narratives are characters within stories, and questions are often among their various actions. Do they share omniscience with the omniscient narrator? Do they have grasps on broken threads as they seek their own way? What can questions in their direct discourse tell us about their character traits? Just as their expressions of anger or disappointment can clue us into how we ought to construct their character, so also can their questions. Do figures of ultimate authority ask questions of other characters, prompting these others to mediate the story not only to readers but also to the divinities themselves? This capacity for characters to mediate stories helps us transition from the level of story to the level of discourse because, *among the characters who form elements of a story is the narrator*, the main voice giving the story over to an audience, a figure who may or may not be identical to a character within the story.

On the level of discourse, readers engage with modes of authorial intervention, elements of point of view, and variations of representation. As the poststructuralist theorist Roland Barthes writes, "This ultimate, self-designating, form of narrative (i.e., the [level of discourse]) transcends both its contents and its properly narrative forms (functions and actions)" (Barthes 1975, 264). A narrative work is not merely an integration of story elements, but *a discourse given by a voice to readers to receive it and thereby change their acting* (see Ricoeur 1984, 53). The presence of both the narrative voice and the reader is detectable within the narrative itself. When a narrator says "I" in self-reference or "you" in a direct address to the reading audience are obvious traces. Moreover, anytime a narrator rehearses facts within the story that the narrator already perfectly knows, there occurs, writes Barthes, "a sign of the reading act, for there would not be much sense in the narrator's giving himself information…" (Barthes 1975, 260). The main elements on the level of discourse to which I want us to give discrete attention are implied reader and actual reader, as well as writer, implied author, and narrator.

The implied audience of written texts is, ultimately, anyone who can read. Yet a more particular role for a more specific reader is prestructured in a text (see Ricoeur 1988, 171). Consider, for example, Nietzsche's disparagement of his contemporary readers, and his calls to his readers "of the future" or the readers whom he calls "my own" (Ricoeur 1980, 176). That is, traces within the text lift out ideal or implied readers from the anonymity of reading publics at large. The implied reader guides all actual readings. In actual readings of a text, the actual reader transforms the role of an implied reader (Ricoeur 1988, 171). An actual reader gives us leverage to make our notion of a "text" more precise. A text is not an abstract structure in itself, where reading is extrinsic to it. *Artifacts that can be put on a shelf are mere books, not texts. A text is a semantic field opened by an actual reader's hermeneutic reduction.* Without an actual reader, there is no text but merely a book (see Dickman 2014).

Such transformation helps us explain why the same reader can get different things out of the "same" book upon reading it at different times over one's life. One way to explain this phenomenon is that actual readers undergo changes between readings, where the meaning of a book changes because "I" have changed. The Reformed philosophical theologian Nicholas Wolterstorff, for example, says readers are rewarded by new insights when they return to books because "each of us at a particular stage in our lives is cognitively privileged with respect to certain facets of reality and cognitively underprivileged with respect to others" (Wolterstorff 1995, 185). Historically changing circumstances affect our "cognitive privilege" or consciousness, where we project anticipations of a book's meaning and revise those anticipations in light of what the text says (see Gadamer 2013, 279–81).

Another way to approach this, though, is through the model of interpretation as a dialogue, a dialogue between an actual reader and the voice of a text. To interpret and understand a text involves asking the questions to which it responds, even if those questions are not written explicitly in the text (see Ricoeur 1988, 174). That is, texts presuppose questions, and—at times—those questions are explicit in the text itself. To interpret is to ask the question to which the text answers (see Gadamer 2013, 378). As Gadamer writes, "We understand the sense of a text only by acquiring the horizon of the question—a horizon that, as such, necessarily includes other possible answers" (Gadamer 2013, 378). However, it is not merely that texts respond to implicit or explicitly stated questions that readers must share so that what a text means can be transferred to readers for understanding. Even more significant for our purposes is that *texts themselves pose questions to readers*. That a text is interpreted means, according to Gadamer, "that it puts a question to the interpreter… Interpretation always involves a relation to the question that is asked of the interpreter" (Gadamer 2013, 378).

Ricoeur claims that the properly hermeneutical question is: "What does the text say to me and what do I say to the text?" (Ricoeur 1988, 175). Active readers "talk back" to the texts they read. Obviously, they are *not* talking back to the writers, especially in those cases where the writers are already dead. Who is it then that poses questions to readers? And, insofar as questions are a mode of listening, who is it that listens to what readers have to say (see Dickman 2018)? *The text says something different because, in asking questions of a reader, it listens to what the reader has to say in response and thus changes what it says in kind*. That is, just as we often say that "texts speak," we should also say that, through questions, "texts listen" (see Dickman 2014). This speaker/listener cannot be the writer of a book, considering convenient classical examples of ancient writers who are long dead. Yet even with those classic texts, they say different things to a reader upon different readings of them. The fact is that writing explodes the conditions of face-to-face dialogue. Writer and reader in the event of reading do not correspond to speaker and listener in the event of dialogue. The reader is absent from the act of writing, and the writer is absent from the act of reading. In asking questions of readers, *texts themselves display listening*. Upon having heard readers' responses, texts then can say something different to readers on their next reading of the text. That is, we get different things out of the "same" book because our dialogues with texts are ongoing rather than complete upon one reading (see Dickman 2014). When a text purports to be *the* transmission of the Buddha's Dharma, or when a text purports to be *the* word of a God, these interpretive dialogues take on a horizon of ultimate significance.

In light of this, it is helpful to make a few clarifications about the level of narration or discourse. We need to keep distinct the writer, the author, and the narrator. Barthes writes, "The one *who speaks* (in the narrative) is not the one *who writes* (in real life) and the one *who writes* is not the one *who is*" (Barthes 1975, 261). Just like we need to resist the temptation to circumvent a textual character to get at some real or historical person existing behind the book, we need to resist the temptation to circumvent the textual narrator and author to get at some real or historical writer existent behind the book. Just as "character" is a semantic, not psychological, category, so also are "narrator" and "author." We need to preserve our hermeneutic reduction even on the level of narrative discourse. Narrators and authors are essentially, as Barthes puts it, "paper beings" (Barthes 1975, 261). An illustration might be helpful here. Consider Mark Twain's *Adventures of Huckleberry Finn*. Samuel Clemmons is the writer, a historically existent person. The author, however, is Clemmons's performative character, Twain—someone readers only get to know through texts and performances that display his character traits. The narrator, however, is Twain's main protagonist, Huck himself. When engaged in the dialogical process of interpretation in reading, is the reader engaged with Clemmons, Twain, or Finn? We could provide similar layers for, say, the ancient Greek philosopher Plato's *Republic*, or the sixth patriarch of Zen Buddhism Huineng's *Platform Sutra*, or the Christian existentialist Søren Kierkegaard's *Either/Or*. When the voice of a text poses questions to a reader, it is either the narrator or the author, not the writer. For our purposes, the reason it is crucial to isolate this narrative voice is that—just as characters within the story might ask questions to others—this voice asks questions of readers.

Someone questions, someone asks questions of the reader, from the text itself. This voice, Ricoeur writes, "is an instance of the text" (Ricoeur 1995, 191; see also Foucault 1998). *This questioner, this speaker, is not behind the book but in front of the text*. The author or narrator gives us a way to locate Ricoeur's notion of "semantic autonomy" of texts with more precision. This helps us enhance why we need to separate the exegetical hermeneutic circle (Part II) and the existential hermeneutic circle (Part III) in our studies of religious texts. What does it mean to say that a text is semantically autonomous? Texts that continue to speak to further generations of readers exceed the imaginative capacities of writers, where their texts spread beyond just their original audience. That is, no writer can anticipate or intend in any controlled way just what their texts might come to mean for people. As Gadamer writes,

> If by the meaning of a text we understand the [writer's intention], that is, the "actual" horizon of understanding of the original Christian writers, then we do the New Testament authors a false honor. Their honor should lie precisely in the fact that they proclaim something that surpasses their own horizon of understanding—even if they are named John or Paul.
>
> (Gadamer 1977, 210)

Interpreting does not involve the mere recovery of a writer's psychology or a writer's intention. It is not about just repeating or merely empathizing with what the writer intends but about understanding what the text says. In this way, a text as a composition, what is said in a text, separates from a writer's intention. The text's semantic autonomy means that it is not a mere function of writer intentions (see Ricoeur 1976, 30). It is independent of those. At the same time, however, the text is also independent or autonomous from readerly whims, where readers take complete control to make a text say whatever the readers want. There is a speaker, a "thou," who is an element of the text. As philosophical theologian David Klemm explains, "In this vein…, texts can manifest a subjectivity quite separate from that of their [writers] and thereby assume a voice of their own" (Klemm 2008, 62; see also Scharlemann 1993). This subjectivity deserves the same respect we should show to people face to face. When we ask whether Gods and Buddhas can ask genuine questions, we are not merely talking about characters internal to the story but also asking about these deific voices of the texts. Can the authorial voice ask readers a genuine question?

There is one further crucial element of the voice of the text I want to emphasize. Because writing and reading explode conditions of face-to-face dialogue, readers must make the text speak (Gadamer 2013, 382). That is, only through the reader are written marks transformed into complete thoughts that readers can understand—and this happens, as we saw above, when readers ask the questions to which sentences of the text answer. *Readers have to resuscitate textual agency to bring what a text says to speech.* To force another to speak in face-to-face dialogue, however, can be just as dehumanizing as robbing another of her voice. This voice of the text, though, only emerges in actual events of reading. Through interpretation in reading, the text becomes *like* speech. Of course, a book does not literally speak, does not utter conventional noises. Of course, books do not literally listen, receiving and understanding what another person says. Instead, the same general features of reading aloud apply to silent reading to oneself (see Gadamer 1989, 47). When we read aloud, like recitation, we do so for an audience. That is, we read *to* and *for* someone else. To do so well, we need to bring the resonance of the words and sentences into harmony with the sense of what is said (see Gadamer 1989, 47). This is just what guardians do when they sound out the voices of characters in children's bedtime stories, such as voices for the wolf and the three little pigs in different registers. When students are called on in class to read a passage of an assigned text, the teacher *can tell by their sound and rhythm of reading* whether students understand what is said. In this way, readers graft their reading voice to the composition or "code" given to them by the text (see Barthes 1975, 265; and Ricoeur 1986, 130–1). When we see Quranic recitation competitions, this is precisely a goal in the quality of contestants' performances (Sells 2007). How do we perform deific voices? Silent reading is an advancement, where we internalize this dialogue and cacophony of grafted voices, where we "read to ourselves." A text provides a score by which the reader orchestrates a dialogue between two distinct interlocutors or subjectivities: *the reader as the one reading and the reader as the one read to.* There is, then, the reader grafted to the voice of the text who says something, and the reader as the receiver to whom this something is said.

Let us turn to look at what we can call "the world of the text," the crucial feature of semantic autonomy in our approach to religious narrative as literature rather than as mere history or mere myth.

A World Opens within the Text for Imaginative Dwelling

The author, or narrator, to whom the reader gives voice in interpretation emerges before or in front of the text. This is not the writer behind the book. Questions about whether Bodhidharma really lost his legs are trying to get behind the book. Questions about what a God wants of a reader are trying to get behind the book. Questions about a writer's psychology or intention go behind the book. The semantic field—including narrators, characters, plot, and more—in front of the text unfolds thanks to readers' hermeneutic reduction. Without readers, no world unfolds before the text. That is, a text is not some abstract structure in itself where reading is extrinsic to it. A text is not an artifact. A book is an artifact, something we can put on and take off a shelf. In a classroom, all the students have physically different books. They all read the same text, though. The text is that which readers engage in dialogue, in the process of interpretation involving questions and answers. *Through this process, readers unfold the world of the text. It opens up like a pop-up book or a blossoming flower.* Instead of cardboard cutouts unfolding into three-dimensional shapes or petals uncovering stamens and carpels for pollination, the reader unfolds an imaginative world through understanding and interpolating complete thoughts.

We might be tempted to model imagination on sensation, that images are residual remainders of sensory experiences from which we compose fantastical figures, like combining a horse with a horn to make a unicorn. This approach to imagination and understanding as deriving from sensation is hegemonic for how we theorize them, and we should be able to see how this fits with the positivist conception of language. Either our image of a unicorn "corresponds" to an actual one and so is true, or it does not correspond and so is false. To persevere in our hermeneutic reduction, though, we need to develop a semantic approach to imagination and understanding. As Ricoeur points out, the reverberation of poetic images comes "not from things seen, but from things said" (Ricoeur 1979, 130). Semantic images do not merely reproduce reality like a photocopy. They are, instead, productive (see Ricoeur 1979, 123). They produce a virtual world in which readers might dwell imaginatively. To form an image or imaginary universe through reading is not to hold a picture before our "mind's eye" but to weave sentences together under the aegis of a main plot or thesis statement. Do you "see" what I mean? Our ocular-centric metaphor for thinking occludes its semantic, not sensory, character. The world of the text is a semantic structure rather than an ocular hallucination, where disparate complete thoughts are combined into relevantly meaningful wholes. In creative writing circles, this is called "world-building."

Written texts and reading liberate us from the immediacy of environments. It is thanks to writing and reading that we live in meaningful worlds rather than merely persist in environments. Environments just are the conditions on which living organisms depend. All organisms are dependent on and embedded within environments. Language, particularly written language, grants us freedom from environments by allowing for a peculiar orientation or stance toward them (see Gadamer 2013, 460–2; and Ahmed 2005). We know, for example, that our sun does not set, that our environment is such that the planet spins while the sun remains relatively stationary. However, this does not keep us from having significant moments with others, where we enjoy sunsets together. That is, a world of significance emerges despite its tensions with what we know about our environments. Artworks, especially literature, open such worlds of possible experience, experience of interconnected webs of significance (see Heidegger 1971, 47–58). Poetic works of art bring forth things to radiate their significance, revealing to us "what is" (Heidegger 1971, 51). It is not about accurate or correct representation but the *presentation* of a kind of truth we would not recognize without such works. Literature unfolds these virtual worlds, these interconnected webs of significance. Ricoeur brings this together nicely in stating,

> For me, the world is the ensemble of [significances] opened up by every kind of text, descriptive or poetic, that I have read, understood, and loved. And to understand a text is to interpolate among the predicates of our situation all the significations that make a [world] out of our [environment]... Only writing... in freeing itself, not only from its author and from its originary audience, but from the narrowness of the [face-to-face] dialogical situation, reveals this destination of discourse as projecting a world.
>
> (Ricoeur 1976, 37)

When we successfully interpolate predicates from religious narratives onto our experiences, we transform our environment into a meaningful world of ultimate significance.

Comprehension of the world of text and its plot happens only through reader engagement in dialogue with the text. There is no such virtual world apart from its construction in particular readers' imaginations. This world of significance, though, projects or unfolds in front of the text, constituted beyond any writers' intentions and anticipations. Grasping a narrative is not merely to grasp a description of the world of the text, though. A plot integrates elements within the narrative world and establishes a hierarchal relation among the parts that straddles the narrative sequence (see Barthes 1975, 243). This hierarchal relation of significance is what *opens a new dimension accompanying the sequential dimension*. As we know from recent proliferations of fanfiction as well as prequels and sequels, gaps between a narrative plot and the horizons of the world of the text allow for further exploration and development of alternative plots. Consider the *Star Wars* universe or the *Marvel Comics* universe.

The world of the text, as a virtual world, differs from the environments in which we live. In opening a horizon of possible imaginative experience, this virtual world belongs both to the experiential horizon of the work imaginatively and to readers' action concretely. Readers enter the world through the dialogical process of interpretation, guided by the voice of the text. The world is not something we see, though. It is a meaning we understand. As Barthes writes, "The passion that may consume us upon reading a novel is not that of a 'vision;' (in fact, strictly speaking, we 'see' nothing). It is the passion to discover meaning, it is a striving toward a higher order of relation" (Barthes 1975, 271). Our hermeneutic reduction affects an *epoche* or bracketing of reality, suspending readers' attention to it, and placing readers in a state of nonengagement as to actual action and perception. It suspends reality by neutralizing it as meanings. As Ricoeur writes,

> In this state of non-engagement [with reality] we try new ideas, new values, new ways of being-in-the-world… But this positive function of [literature], of which the epoche is the negative condition, is only understood when the fecundity of the imagination is clearly linked to that of language, as exemplified by the metaphorical process… We grasp this truth: we first see some things to the extent that we first hear them.
> (Ricoeur 1986, 134)

Reading, and opening the world of the text for exploration, is not a mode of perception or sensation, although in our reading, we sometimes "see" and "hear" as well as "smell" and "touch." Reading is about grasping meanings, a consciousness informed by words, not sensations of things. Literature is like a moral and existential laboratory. And, when it works well, such experimentation can change readers' lives. Consider, for example, activists who have been inspired by moral messages from the *Harry Potter* series in the Harry Potter Alliance organization. A world of the text opens in front of it for possible appropriation by readers, an appropriation or making it their own where their horizons fuse with the horizon of the world of the text. By changing readers' lives, literature changes the "real" world.

When looking at deific voices, we need to examine what features are and are not necessary elements of the world of the text. For example, is dialogue a necessary feature of the mythic world where primordial earthlings interact with the God in Genesis? Perhaps it is not. Perhaps what we witness in fanatical fundamentalisms is reader appropriation of narrative worlds without dialogue, appropriation of a divine authoritarianism. In striving to appropriate the meanings of Gods as regulative ideals in our own lives, such as when people attempt to emulate the Buddha or the Christ, perhaps dialogue is not a necessary practice for them. Alternatively, if genuine questioning is an essential element of the world of the text, particularly with deific voices, then perhaps we can show fanatical fundamentalists misinterpret their sacred texts. Before moving to the next chapter to provide step-by-step principles for asking questions in the process of reading and interpretation, let us make one last clarification about religious narrative.

Religious Fiction Precedes the Categories of Myth and History

Religious literature, as it unfolds under the hermeneutic reduction, stands apart from the spectrum spanning from *mere* myth to accurate history. It is not helpful to describe religious narrative as somehow standing between these extremes, as if it were superior to one or the other by incorporating aspects of both. As we started this chapter criticizing the positivistic model of Post-Copernican literalism, we conclude this chapter by returning to it. To take religious narrative as literally true or false because it is accurate or inaccurate to objective facts presupposes that religious language is essentially representative, as if it is supposed to correspond to facts. As our detour through elements of narratology has helped us specify, religious narrative—as narrative—is not reproductive but *productive*. Religious narratives produce worlds of significance in which readers might dwell imaginatively as moral and existential laboratories, where readers are empowered to appropriate meanings they understand there as their own, applying those meanings within and to their own lives. We can know, for example, that we are not merely facing north but are facing toward Mecca. The significance of our orientation is disclosed by the world of the text(s) definitive within Islamic traditions. If religious narrative is neither accurate history nor mere myth, what can we make of it? Note that I am saying religious language is not historical, and this is because religious language is *not* positivistic or representational. I am not saying it is false, though.

I would like, with intellectual predecessors such as the philosophical theologian Rudolph Bultmann and Tillich, simply to call religious narrative "mythic." We live in an era, however, where "myth" is often associated with the opposite of truth, such as pop shows premised on "myth-busting." This is despite the popular success and influence of comparative mythicist Joseph Campbell on the power of myths and his impact on the *Star Wars* universe. Campbell and *Star Wars* show that the word "myth" is ambiguous in contemporary society. On one side, myth means false. On the other side, an empowerment is donated to listeners through myths. In speaking on this in relation to the Hebrew Bible, Alter writes,

> The prevailing emphasis of the narratives... does move away from mythology. What is crucial for the literary understanding of the Bible is that this impulse to shape a different kind of narrative in prose had powerfully constructive consequences in the new medium that the ancient Hebrew writers fashioned for their monotheistic purposes. Prose narration, affording writers a remarkable range and flexibility in the means of presentation, could be utilized to liberate... personages from the fixed choreography of timeless events and thus could transform storytelling from ritual rehearsed to the delineation of the wayward paths of human freedom, the quirks and contradictions of men and women seen as moral agents and complex centers of motive and feeling.
>
> (Alter 1981, 28)

Nevertheless, we can isolate a critical notion of "myth" that is not reducible to a simple positivistic rejection of it or an assumption about "myth" as archaic ritual performance. Demythologization is Bultmann's term for the process of interpreting myths, the existential interpretation of myths that primes readers to receive their donative and transformative power (see Bultmann 1989). As Tillich builds on this, we should say that religious narrative is "no less" than myth, not "mere" myth, because only myth and symbols can give the ultimate dimensions of our experience the honor due to them (see Tillich 2001, 60).

Through myths, we tap into and are empowered by the deepest resources of our being in the world.

Let us clarify a few features of myth in this sense of the term. As the anthropologist Clifford Geertz puts it, myths act "to establish powerful… moods and motivations in people by formulating conceptions of a general order of existence and clothing these conceptions with such an aura of factuality that the moods… seems uniquely realistic" (Geertz 1993, 90). Rather than merely facing west, one can *know* one is "facing Mecca." Rather than just feeling bad, one can *know* one has "sinned." These aspects of one's experience are intelligible within the lifeworld unfolded by myths. Myths do not lack reference to the ordinary world but destroy the given world by refiguring it or even producing a new world on its ruins in light of mythic possibilities (see Ricoeur 1974, 80). They are not like Post-It note labels stuck on the forehead of some God or some set of spiritual facts. Instead, myths "participate" in that which they symbolize. As Tillich explains, myths open up dimensions of both the self and the world that are only experienceable by virtue of them (Tillich 2001, 48). A myth is not a label for a transcendent reality, as if we could remove the label and experience that purported reality without distortion. Instead, I want us to see myths this way: they open up *an eminently immanent refiguration of our reality.*

The "unconditioned" or "ultimate" is the crucial ground for why we use religious language, or myths and symbols, at all. Epistemologically, we recognize our perspectives are limited. Simply recognizing this limit stimulates our imagination about the other side—the *un*-limited. Any concepts of it are essentially symbolic since we can only use limited concepts for it. Limited concepts cannot be used to grasp what is inherently unlimited. Moreover, our reason is like a toddler who incessantly asks, "Why?" We quest after reasons for why things are the way they are (see Kant 2007, 294). This leads us to seek a fundamental support for other things but is not itself in need of support, the ultimate ground. The European Enlightenment philosopher Immanuel Kant calls this "the unconditioned." As Anderson elaborates, this ontological unconditioned functions as a regulative ideal by which we try to integrate ourselves despite pulls of disintegration (see Anderson 1998). Ontologically, we feel pulled apart by a number of polarities, such as individuation and participation (Tillich 1951, 168). Under conditions of finite existence, these are pressurized to the point where we break down. We long and strive for an alternative state of being. This alternative state of being is an ideal, where—as Tillich explains—we are pulled by an "infinity" to transcend our finite selves (Tillich 1975, 191). I want us to note that this is *transcendental*, not metaphysically transcendent. The unconditioned orients us *immanently.* That is, we are not trying to transcend our human life to some other nonhuman or superhuman realm. This is instead a religious humanism.

We can similarly isolate a critical notion of "history," alluded to by the popular phrase that "history is written by the victors." This phrase suggests there is an unadulterated set of facts that victors distort to serve their interests and, through propaganda, oppress others who might see the "actual" facts and thereby challenge their dominance. A subtler issue at stake can be brought out through examining the position of the historian relative to the historical narrative they tell. Audiences and readers compliment historians by saying that they are "good story-tellers." When we look closely at the temporality of narration, though, we can notice that the position of the narrator is always "after" that which is being narrated (see Ricoeur 1985b). That is, just as myth is about an inaccessible "unconditioned," histories are about something else we cannot access directly, namely, the past. Historians tell stories about this past, and as such, are "the voice[s] of authority," the critical historian Hayden White points out (White 1982, 12). According to White, the reader or listener stands "in a position of voluntary servitude regarding what will be revealed and when" (White 1982, 12). Such a voice and position buttress the narrator's vision of the world (see Ricoeur 1988, 117). Yet this vision claims probability and reliability through a number of methods, such as corroborating written eye-witness accounts, tombstone inscriptions, artifacts, or other remains (see Ehrman 2013, 37–42). Whereas fictional narrative can turn to the imagination as an archive for world-production, the worlds produced through modern historical studies—on the whole—are bound to corroborating documentary archives (see Ricoeur 1995, 244).

A crucial problem with taking such a historical disposition, a historicist attitude, toward the past is the implication that we are somehow above or outside the vicissitudes of historical processes. Past events reverberate beyond our present and into our futures. A historicist attitude transforms past events into mere events of the past as if they are over and done with (see Moltmann 1995, 76). That is, we in the contemporary world are the "victors" over the past, believing that we are done with it even if it is not done with us. Our critical disposition liberates us from mere subjection to historical forces. If we do not learn from history, we will likely just repeat it. Nevertheless, small freedoms like this are always within broader contexts and conditions keeping us bound to the unfolding of history. As Gadamer writes,

> History does not belong to us; we belong to it. Long before we understand ourselves through the process of self-examination, we understand ourselves in a self-evident way in the family, society, and state in

which we live. The focus on subjectivity is a distorting mirror. The self-awareness of the individual is only a flickering in the closed circuits of historical life. That is why the pre-judgments of the individual, far more than [one's] judgments, constitute the historical reality of [one's] being.

(Gadamer 2013, 288–9)

The rational subject of historical criticism purports to stand above prejudice, which contrasts with romanticist naturalism celebrating passion, myth, and nature. At issue is not whether a historical narrative is accurate or inaccurate. At issue is not the truth of "history," but the *use* of "history." As we know from Nietzschean-influenced genealogies and archeologies, the very notion of "history" is a site of contestation and is caught up in strategies for consolidating institutional hegemony. As the Chan (Zen) studies scholar Morten Schlütter illustrates through examining the Dunhuang manuscripts—the numerous editions of Zen transmission records discovered in Central Asia in the early twentieth century—historical genealogic lineages tracing through masters all the way back to "the historical Buddha" are fluid (Schlütter 2008; see also McRae 2003, 60–8). By claiming historical precedence, they consolidated and legitimized their political power. The very notion of "religion," as another example, gets applied anachronistically to people of the past when we are not self-critical about its emergence in service of European colonialism (see Masuzawa 2005).

My point is that religious narrative is neither mere myth nor mere history, and that we need to be critical of how both "myth" and "history" are often politically contested terms (see Kafer 2013, 8–9). In addition to those attempts above to rehabilitate and situate both myth and history existentially, others have attempted to specify the unique quality of religious narrative as "history-like." Ricoeur writes, "It is an indisputable trait of the basic stories of [religions] that they are history-like, with the exception of intended fictions such as parables" (Ricoeur 1995, 244). Religious narratives, emerging before the modern era, made no distinctions between mere myth and accurate history. That is, the question of positivistic (in)accuracy is *our* question, not theirs. It is anachronistic to project this concern onto ancient writers as if it were also an issue for them. A number of approaches can help us isolate distinctive features of religious literature as a kind of fiction preceding the categories of myth and history.

One modern genre that is like history, yet distinct, is biography. An ancient style of biography dating to the turn of the first millennium in Hellenistic culture is "aretology," stories presenting virtues of a master for disciples to emulate (see Cox 1983; and Smith 1993). When Greek philosophical traditions splintered into various schools, each school centered on their founder, who in their eyes both taught and embodied wisdom. Followers used biographies of their heroes as guides to the good life, as regulative ideals to orient their lives. As Alter writes, "We learn through [narration] because we encounter in it the translucent images the writer has cunningly projected out of an intuitively grasped fund of experience not dissimilar to our own, only shaped, defined, ordered, probed in ways we never manage in the muddled and diffuse transactions of our own lives" (Alter 1981, 194). Writers of these aretologies like Diogenes Laertius took license freely to adapt oral traditions and other source materials to bring out virtuosity of the heroes with utmost vividness (see Burridge 1992, 205). Ancient aretologists did not completely make up their narratives. However, they took liberty imaginatively to construct truths about their subjects to reveal the way "it must have been" (Burridge 1992, 174). As Wolterstorff puts it, "Not that things *did go* thus and so, but that, whether or not they did, they *might well have gone* thus and so—given such and such" (Wolterstorff 1995, 257). Aretologists composed plausible images and meanings of central figures to disseminate to readers for their emulation. A similar genre emerged in the Song dynasty (960–1279 CE). As the Chan studies scholar Albert Welter explains, the production and proliferation of the sayings of classical Chan masters involved a retroactive reshaping of them (Welter 2008, 143). Song Buddhists were religiously inspired and ideologically interested in making specific classical masters, such as Mazu and Linji, into outstanding models of radical teachings and strategies for immediate enlightenment—but in such a way that was especially attractive to Song court literati and patrons. This sort of literary genre is called *chuanqi*, literally translated as "the transmission of the marvelous" (Welter 2008, 154). As Welter writes, this literary tradition "might be termed 'believable fiction,' fantasy parading as history" (Welter 2008, 143). As the Chan studies scholar Alan Cole elaborates, the Chan authors during the Song dynasty were aware that they were writing a distinctively religious literature and were deliberate in their efforts to reshape tradition (see Cole 2016). The New Testament studies scholar Matthew Larsen provides a further alternative approach to examining the Gospel of Mark in particular (Larsen 2018). We can approach this Gospel as less a finished book with an "author" and "publication date," and more a set of working notes available to anyone wanting to compose their own gospel tailored to a specific community. This genre is called *hypomnemata*, a less finished set of notes available for others to use in the creation of more finished compositions. There is in *hypomnemata*, Larsen writes, an "openness left in the text for another to rework them and attach their name to them as 'author'" (Larsen 2018, 36). In this way, our contemporary questions about "book, author, and publication" as well as questions about historical (in)accuracy are "foreign to the earliest centuries of the Common Era" (Larsen 2018, 149).

By extension, many religious narratives are compositions of plausible images of central characters to serve communities as regulative ideals, ideals giving them orientation and purpose (see Alter 1981, 24). These narratives, according to Alter,

> are not, strictly speaking, historiography, but rather the imaginative reenactment of history by a gifted writer who organizes his materials along certain thematic biases and according to his own remarkable intuition of the psychology of the characters. He feels entirely free, one should remember, to invent interior monologue for his characters; to ascribe feeling, intention, or motive to them when he chooses; to supply verbatim dialogue (and he is one of literature's masters of dialogue) for occasions when no one but the actors themselves could have had knowledge of exactly what was said. The author of the David stories stands in basically the same relation to Israelite history as Shakespeare stands to English history in his history plays.
>
> (Alter 1981, 40)

By approaching religious narrative in this way, we can resist the temptation to ask questions informed by modernist interests, such as whether or not a religious narrative is factually accurate. We can instead ask questions such as, what plausible image—however irreverent and radical—might Dharma heirs construct of Bodhidharma for emulation (see Faure 1986)? Is it even *plausible* to read deific voices as asking sincere and genuine questions?

I want to approach the plausibility of deific voices in terms of the social fabric that binds religious communities together in a camaraderie of shared values and regulative ideals for what constitutes a meaningful life. Disputes over plausibility of images can lead to tears in the social fabric, as we seem to observe with religious sectarianism. This fabric is essential for both support of and orientation for our spiritual aspirations. Yet why has "fabrication" turned into an accusation, an accusation of falsehood? It seems to be a result of a modern preoccupation with discovery (history!) over invention (myth!). Religious communities manufacture fabrics of plausible images to give concrete orientation to their spiritual aspirations (cf. McCutcheon 2003). My emphasis on fabric here is deliberate because it helps bring out how I want us to think of the world of the text, where "text" is situated properly in its etymological relation to the textile industry. Texts weave together sentences into narrative wholes. A religious story is a "good yarn," not in some dismissive sense but in the sense of versatile clothing. Some clothing is versatile—giving us warmth in the cold, matching with any other color, stretchable for pregnancy, wearable with or without a tie, and more. Rarely do we hear people say that clothes are *mere* fabrications. In fact, Cotton Inc. claimed that cotton is the fabric of our lives. How much more are texts the fabric of our lives? Rather than approaching them as either historical or mere myth, let us approach religious narratives as giving orientation to our existential strivings for meaningful lives. Moreover, as Alter emphasizes,

> It seems to me perfectly plausible to assume... that the makers of [religious] narrative gave themselves to these various pleasures of invention and expression because, whatever their sense of divinely warranted mission, they were, after all, writers, moved to work out their vision of human nature and history in a particular medium, prose [narration], over which they had technical mastery, and in the manipulation which they found continual delight.
>
> (Alter 1981, 194)

Producing religious narrative, as well as reading religious narrative, can be fun, beautiful, interesting, and captivating. Readers weave themselves into the social fabric produced via religious narratives through the dialogical process of interpretation, the process of exchange of questions and answers.

I have argued in this chapter that religious texts should not be approached and read as if they represent some reality external to them. I also argued that a critical notion of "fiction" can be useful for navigating between the demands that a religious narrative either be historically accurate or is mere myth. Let us turn to examine this logic of question and answer in interpretation with more specification.

3

What Is at Risk with Questions in Deific Discourse?

As we examined in Chapter 1, it takes shared questions to transfer meanings or complete thoughts between speakers. Only if we ask the question to which someone responds can what they say make sense to us. Just because we share a question, though, does not entail that we take their answer as "the" answer or appropriate their answer as our own. We pointed out that sharing questions situates us to consider their statements as possible answers. In Chapter 2, we examined that just as we can share questions with other people in face-to-face dialogue, we can also share questions with texts—asking those questions to which the narrative voice responds. Questions, while not operative between writer and reader, are operative in sometimes silent reading between the reader (giving voice to the text itself) and the one read to (the reader oneself). If we do not find and ask the questions to which the written work responds, then what is said will be lost on us, like when we "read" a page in a book but have no idea what is going on. As Gadamer writes, "We understand the sense of a text only by acquiring the horizon of the question—a horizon that, as such, necessarily includes other possible answers" (Gadamer 2013, 378). As we discussed, it is not merely that texts respond to implicit or explicitly stated questions that readers must share so that what a text means can be transferred to readers for understanding. A further crucial feature of reading texts is that texts themselves pose questions to readers. Texts put questions to readers, and active readers respond to those questions. All these layers of questioning, spanning from readers asking the questions to which each line of text responds to readers responding to questions texts themselves ask of readers, shape the way readers' lives are woven into the fabric of a text's possible meanings. Sharing these questions makes possible readers' existential appropriation of meanings. When it comes to uniquely religious texts, such questioning enables readers to be enveloped within a religious community where matters of ultimate concern are at stake.

In this chapter, I argue that there are four discrete layers of questioning in interpretation. This chapter will undertake laying out these layers of questioning in discrete detail. What differentiates my approach from many other hermeneutic theories is that it is informed by literacy pedagogy. While we can understand that shared questions are crucial for transferring meanings, it seems that—on the whole—questions do not occur as often as this axiom seems to suggest. That is, when we observe our own acts of reading, we do not seem explicitly to ask questions for each sentence, and writers do not seem to preface every sentence with a question as that which each sentence answers. When we neglect using empirical research in literacy pedagogy with children, we risk being so theory-driven that we force reading into our model of question and answer when in actuality it might not apply. It may seem as if we are saying, "I have a hammer. Everything better be a nail!" Research in teaching children how to read can help slow down the process of interpretation, where we can lay out layers of questions explicitly. That is, literacy is demonstrated by readers' ability to ask and answer different kinds of questions. I want to organize these kinds of questions in alignment with the exegetical and existential hermeneutic circles. These distinctions will help us be precise when we move to examine questions attributed to deific voices.

Some hermeneutic theories bypass questioning altogether. The literary critic E. D. Hirsch, for example, emphasizes projecting hypotheses to test them for reliability against information in a text and data external to the text itself, like cultural context or the writer's psychology (see Hirsch 1967, 170). The presumption is that we already understand the information, that we already understand what is being said, and interpretation is simply a matter of how reliable our way of holding the information together is. Hirsch focuses primarily on writer intention as having priority for interpretation or the criterion definitive for the probability of an interpretation (see also Plummer 2010, 130). My approach, aligned with Gadamer and Ricoeur, rests on the axiom that we do not have any relevant information unless we ask the questions that the information answers. Questioning has hermeneutic priority, not authorial intent. The literary critic Stanley Fish, alternatively, seems to render texts themselves practically vacuous, emphasizing that reading communities themselves legitimate some interpretations over others through conventions and canons of acceptability (see Fish 1980, 349). It is institutions, not texts themselves, that—via consensus of readers—determine what is "in the text." Fish gives a version of reader-response the priority in interpretation. Again, for us, questioning has hermeneutic priority. Both of these extremes—of authority resting solely in writer intentions and of the sovereignty of reader communities—downplay semantic autonomy of texts themselves (see Ricoeur 1976, 30). We can only come to understand what is said through dialogue with the voice of the text, through the layers of logic of question and answer. Recall, however, that questioning is not completely in our power. It is as much a passion as it is an action, in the sense that questions occur to us above our willing and choosing. Thus, reading communities cannot be the sovereign factor in determining a text's meaning. Yet we also know that readers do not engage with writers themselves, but the voice of the text. The author and narrator—in the dialogue of interpretation—are semantic beings, not entities standing behind the book.

Others have tried to isolate discrete layers of reading, in alignment with kinds of questions (see, for example, Adler and Van Doren 1972). Ricoeur develops a three-tiered framework for analyzing reading. He relegates logics of question and answer to what he calls the "rereading" of a text as this is distinct from what he calls "preliminary" reading (Ricoeur 1988, 175; see also Ricoeur 1976, 87). For Ricoeur, without a preliminary reading, there is nothing about which to ask questions. Preliminary reading opens, Ricoeur writes, "a space of meaning in which the logic of question and answer will subsequently unfold" (Ricoeur 1988, 174). According to Ricoeur, this is a perceptive reception of information about the world of the text, an acquisition of what is given in this world, with suggestions of meanings that a "rereading" will thematize for interpretation through historical-critical questions such as those about original audiences or authorial intent (see Ricoeur 1988, 174). Yet the properly hermeneutical questions go above and beyond these receptions in preliminary reading and historical constraints in rereading. For Ricoeur, this *third* reading involves properly hermeneutical questions, and these have the formal character of, "What does the text say to me and what do I say to the text?" (Ricoeur 1988, 175). The insight I want to take from Ricoeur here is that *this properly hermeneutical layer of questioning governs other layers of reading by giving order to them*, in that the other two layers serve the purpose of providing conditions within which to realize a dialogue with the text itself. Acquiring information and putting information in context are not merely rote activities to repeat without further significance, as some historicist readings do. Doing this just explains the book away as an artifact rather than interprets the text. Acquiring information and putting it in context are incomplete by themselves. It is the hermeneutical layer of questioning whereby we actually succeed at reading. Otherwise, we are merely "regurgitating" information without understanding, without placing the information within a web of existential relevance.

Ricoeur overlooks, though, just how pervasive questioning is in literacy, even at the layer he believes is mere perceptive reception. Turning to reading pedagogy can help us bring this implicit ubiquity of questioning out more explicitly. One of the most influential literacy strategies in reading comprehension instruction over the last forty years is literacy education specialist Taffy Raphael's "Question Answer Relationships" (QAR)

(Raphael 1986; see Vacca, Vacca, and Mraz 2017, and Wilson, Grisham, and Smetana 2009). Raphael's goal in developing QAR is to provide a practical starting point for addressing four problems (see Raphael and Au 2005, 208). First, there is a general need for a shared terminology to make explicit largely implicit processes in reading and listening comprehension. Second, there is a need for a way to organize questioning practices and instruction across grades and subject matters. Third, there is a need for reform of literacy instruction to orient it toward "higher level thinking" (Raphael and Au 2005, 208; cf. Dickman 2009b). Fourth, there is a need to empower students by preparing them for high stakes standardized testing without sacrificing "higher level thinking." I set off the phrasing of "higher level thinking" because, as I have argued elsewhere, the very distinction between higher- and lower-level thinking—especially as these pertain to organizing questioning interventions—does not play out in research on classroom questioning (see Dickman 2009b). Any sort of question can prompt excited student engagement, and simple questions are sometimes crucial for shy students. The point is less about using some superficial hierarchy of question types and is more about ensuring our questions are invitational for shared asking or ensuring that we affirm students' own questions.

Despite my taking issue with this technicality, QAR has nevertheless had remarkable staying power in literacy pedagogy. In light of studies with various populations from third graders to adult learners to readers with learning disabilities, there is general consensus that exposure to and use of QAR improve readers' comprehension of what they read (see Cummins, Streiff, and Ceprano 2012). Even merely a ten-minute orientation in the QAR strategy seems to improve the performance of skilled adult readers (see Raphael 1981). While QAR is often recommended to educators for use to help students with reading (see, for example, Knight 2017), empirical results from QAR interventions on elementary and junior high students in particular are mixed (see Davidson 2017). The mixed outcomes, however, are due to small sample sizes in some studies and poor quality of procedural fidelity with proctors in others. Despite this reservation, further research in QAR seems hopeful, where further studies continue to suggest its positive impact on readers. For us, the important part is that it has been researched empirically and has in many cases benefited children learning to read. My goal is to refine QAR more thoroughly in alignment with the hermeneutic priority of questioning.

The QAR taxonomy of questions is provided to readers as a coordinated strategy for comprehension of texts and is used by teachers to shape literacy instruction. The taxonomy is organized around where answers can be found, either "in the book" or "in my head." Some questions related to texts and their subject matters can be addressed by looking at specific sentences in the text, and hence can only be answered by looking at what is "in the book." Other questions related more so to the subject matter need to be answered not by looking at specific sentences in the book but by reflecting on one's own experiences and background knowledge, and hence need to be answered by looking at what is "in my head."

Each of these broad categories is subdivided into two further specified categories. Questions that can be answered by looking in the book can concern what is "right there" in lines of the text, and other questions can concern what is implied by what is right there in multiple sentences requiring readers to "think and search." Answers to questions about what is "right there" can be located in one sentence, where readers can put their finger directly on it, and the questions use words that are in the same sentence as the answer. A "right there" question about, say, the *Three Little Pigs* could be, "What did the big bad wolf do?" The answer would then be, "He huffed and puffed." A "think and search" question, alternatively, requires readers to put together multiple sentences, perhaps from disparate sections of the book, to draw out an implication not explicitly stated. In typical English versions of Aesop's fable about the tortoise and the hare, there is no sentence that attributes "concentrated" to the tortoise. Yet a reader could be asked, "What is a character trait of the tortoise?" Readers can draw out this implication that the tortoise is concentrated on the task through combining numerous sentences about the tortoise. Both sorts of "in the book" questions require readers to reread, look for keywords, highlight important information, and more.

The "in my head" questions have two divisions as well. Questions can concern how an author's perspective might compare with one's own perspective in "author and you" questions, but other questions can concern solely a reader's perspective that can only be answered "on my own." In both types, the answers cannot be found in the book itself. The "Author and You" questions prompt readers to anticipate and apply what an author might say about a topic. For example, we might ask, "How would Aesop feel about performance enhancement drugs in sports and education today?" The reader cannot find an answer explicitly or implicitly stated in the text but must construct a plausible answer based off of the text and other information they might have about the writer while also bringing to bear the reader's own knowledge about performance enhancement drugs. An "on my own" question prompts a reader to reflect on one's own knowledge, experience, and perspective, perhaps recalling other texts one has read. Again, the reader cannot find an answer explicitly stated in the text but must construct a plausible answer based on one's own background. For example, in light of the

Three Little Pigs we might ask, "How does it feel to lose your home to natural disasters or financial difficulty?" Neither of these kinds of questions can be addressed by explicit or implicit information in a book.

For the rest of the chapter, I want to refine QAR in terms of my semantic approach to questions, where sentences perceived are transformed into complete thoughts understood only via asking the questions to which those complete thoughts answer. While I hope this reformulation will prove beneficial for future research on QAR with students, my goal is not to rank questions from lower-order to higher-order thinking skills. Rather, my goal is to clarify what we identified above as properly hermeneutic questions, because these are the questions readers must answer to in their engagement with deific voices of religious texts. Coordinating the QAR taxonomy with the hermeneutic priority of questions will give more precision about what readers are to do with lines of text. Four distinct levels of reading can be correlated to four orientations of questioning exercised by a reader (see Brownlie, Close, and Wingren 1988; Porter and Stovell 2012; and Dickman 2014):

1. "On the line(s)" questions focus attention on explicit information stated in sentences, like Raphael's "right there" questions.
2. "Between the lines" questions focus attention on implicit information based on what is explicitly stated in sentences, like Raphael's "think and search" questions.
3. "Behind the lines" questions focus attention on elements shared by both of Raphael's "in your head" types of questions, where readers move into details about a writer's life, or historical context of either the book or the content of the book, or even the economic conditions under which a book is published. Notice how such orientations for questions can concern either what is between "author and me" or what one can know "on my own."
4. The fourth coordinate for questioning lines of text I want to call "beyond the lines." Questions concerning what is "beyond the lines" again can be either "on my own" or "author and me" questions. Questions about what is beyond the lines have to do with ways a reader's life might be refigured in light of a text, or ways communities might authorize some readings of a book rather than others.

These four coordinates of questions and what to do with lines of text will provide organization in our analysis of HaShem's, Mazu's, and Jesus' questions.

Questions on the Level of Story: On and Between the Lines

Weaving together and manufacturing the fabric of a world of the text occurs primarily in the exegetical hermeneutic circle, where parts of a text are coordinated with its entirety. As we said above, words in a sentence only make sense in light of the whole sentence and vice versa. Chapters only make complete sense in light of the whole book and vice versa. This is part of what makes the process circular, moving back and forth between part and whole, between elements of a complete thought and a complete thought as a whole. Since our project here is about religious narrative, we will focus primarily on narrative wholes. While structural analysis of narratives gives us a technical vocabulary for isolating some parts of narratives, what our hermeneutic priority of questioning helps us isolate is ways these structures open questions for answers in a reader's manufacturing of the textual world. Some questions, as the literary critic Wayne C. Booth urges, are "insisted upon by a text" and some questions "the text declares 'inappropriate' or 'improper'" (Booth 1979, 238). For example, a fairy tale beginning with "Once upon a time…" demands a reader ask, "And then?" Every detail supplied by a story answers such questions. This does not mean that readers cannot ask "improper" questions instead, and thus refuse to play along with the text. As Booth writes, "To refuse might be the very best thing in the world for us to do; there is no guarantee that a text, taken in terms of its own demands, will be either interesting or harmless" (Booth 1979, 239). In light of the hermeneutic priority of questioning, however, if we do not ask the questions to which the text answers, then we can hardly be said to be reading the text. Even to begin reading, we need to ask these proper questions.

These first questions and answers deal with individual sentences. They are "on the line(s)" questions. Who did HaShem speak to as a burning bush? What did Mazu's master try to polish into a mirror? What did Jesus do to the fig tree? Each of these questions can be answered by looking at specific sentences in the texts. These are sincere questions, where a reader lacks the information and gains that information through the act of questioning. With beginning readers, we can only tell if they are starting to read by answering these sorts of questions. Without answers to these sorts of questions, we cannot tell if they have the basic threads with which to weave together the textual world. Some toddlers' books use a mixture of repetition and pictures to help them acquire this skill. For example, in the book *Brown Bear, Brown Bear, What Do You See?* (Martin and Carle 1967), the reader can anticipate answers to questions by glancing at pictures. Moreover, the questions are explicitly stated. What does the brown bear see? A red bird. What does the red bird see? And so on. These answers provide the basic parts of the narrative whole, the building blocks on which the world of the text is built. Through these questions, readers acquire and retain details of a specific story, such as the characters' names, what they do, the quality of the atmosphere, and so forth. Each sentence contains determinant information consisting of a subject and a predicate, and each bit of information is an answer to this kind of question.

Yet texts are concatenations of multiple sentences, so readers need to gather together what needs special attention but might not be stated explicitly in a single sentence. This information is acquired through answering questions about what is "between the lines." Through "between the lines" questions, readers combine details given in specific sentences into larger wholes, such as the construction of a character trait. Such a trait might not be "on the lines" as explicitly stated in a sentence, but nevertheless it is, as Ricoeur puts it, "of" the text (see Ricoeur 1995, 221). Implications left unwritten are brought into the foreground by these questions. Perhaps there are inconsistent details that require resolution, incongruities that stimulate active readers to ask, "How do these details fit together?" At an early spot in the Genesis narrative, the God appears transcendent and all-knowing by having an absolute perspective over all of God's creation as if nothing is lost on this God, judging each day as "good." Yet this same God asks of the primordial human beings just a few sentences later, "Where are you?" The active reader needs to bring these incongruities into some sort of harmony of meaning. Determining implicit details is something readers do regularly. For example, Frodo performs timid behaviors early in his journey, but later performs brave ones. Readers attribute a growth in courage to him. Readers are led, Alter explains,

> through varying darknesses that are lit up by intense but narrow beams, phantasmal glimmerings, sudden strobic flashes. We are compelled to get at character and motive, as in Impressionist writers…, through a process of inference from fragmentary data, often with crucial pieces of narrative exposition strategically withheld, and this leads to multiple or sometimes even wavering perspectives on the characters. There is, in other words, an abiding mystery in character as [religious] writers conceive it, which they embody in their typical methods of presentation.
> (Alter 1981, 158)

Already at this level of questioning, readers can start to diverge in their interpretations. We come up with different inferences based on the explicit information we have.

These two sets of questions—on and between the lines—allow for the world of the text to emerge. Against Ricoeur, this preliminary understanding is not merely a perceptive reception but a set of answers to questions. If it were merely perception as in a collection of sensations or imaginations, then what we see would just be of the book as an artifact. As we discussed above, a text is a work that emerges in the reading process of dialogue, not a mere artifact or book we can put on the shelf. In reading, we employ the hermeneutic reduction, a bracketing out of mere sensations and questions about what is or is not real, so possible semantic fields are brought into the foreground. This can be illustrated by analogy to "magic eye" images. Looking at the image in a typical way, one only sees a two-dimensional repetitive pattern. Yet when one "suspends" one's normal vision by, say, crossing one's eyes slightly or looking through rather than at the image, the two-dimensional image yields to a three-dimensional shape—perhaps a rocket, or coffee cup, or schooner. Is this shape "in" the image? It is, at the very least, "of" the image. It is a virtual apparition that emerges only in the interaction of the artifact (image) with the audience. The shape that emerges is objective—we can make true or false statements about it that others can falsify or verify. Moreover, once an audience "sees," say, the coffee cup, the audience can begin to ask questions such as, "Whose cup is that?" That is, with the emergence of the virtual world, the audience is liberated to explore it imaginatively. Without this preliminary understanding, there would be nothing about which to ask further questions.

My proposed division of questions, like Raphael's division of them, suggests that they belong to clear and distinct categories. Before moving to elaborate on our further two kinds of questions, I want to note some complications with this categorization. I note this *not* to bring out the failure of my framework but to show how all the question kinds are interconnected. On the lines questions are incomplete without beyond the lines questions, and vice versa. This is, in part, what grounds Fish's point that what counts as a correct interpretation is what is legitimized by a reading community. Allow me to explain. Consider what appears to be a clear example of an "on the lines" question: Who were Jesus' disciples? Here we start to get into more complicated questions because in addressing such a question, we realize that different Gospels have conflicting information and even the same Gospel might have different information at different moments in the narrative. Which Gospel will a reader privilege over the others? How will the reader integrate the Gospels (as parts) into a greater whole, if this is even possible? Notice just how quickly we drift into questions of what's behind and beyond the lines. The father of modern philosophical hermeneutics Friedrich Schleiermacher helps us see that it is more difficult to divide these domains than we might imagine given our modification of QAR's framework. The reader's attitude affects what they anticipate as the "whole" or complete meaning of a text or affects how the reader empathizes (or does not) with the voice of the text (see Schmidt 2006, 16–18). As Schleiermacher develops, though, a book—as a part—is situated in a language and culture—as an even broader whole (see Schleiermacher 1977, and Schmidt 2006). What we realize is that on the lines and between the lines questions are incomplete without the further levels of questioning. Parts and whole apply to questioning layers as well. Let us turn to elaborate on behind the lines and beyond the lines questions.

Questions on the Level of Discourse: Behind and Beyond the Lines

One worry some people have about choosing an alternative to "authorial intent" as the primary criterion for determining the correct meaning of a text is that readers will capriciously make a text mean whatever they feel like making it mean (see Plummer 2010, 128–9). Wolterstorff proposes "authorial discourse interpretation" as a more subtle form of writer intent as governing what counts as a correct interpretation (see Wolterstorff 1995, and Wolterstorff 2006). He describes reader caprice with regard to religious texts as the "wax nose" problem, where interpreting them, he writes, "is directly at the mercy of the vagaries of human belief" (Wolterstorff 1995, 226). In contrast, Barthes is sometimes interpreted as celebrating the "death of the author" to justify reader (mis)readings (see Barthes 1977). We should be hesitant to attribute this to him, though, since it may instead be best read as performative irony (see Carlier 2000). As Fish writes—aligned with the death of the author orientation to interpretation and seeming to support rejection of writer intent as the principal criterion for correct interpretation—"no reading, however outlandish it might appear, is inherently an impossible one" (Fish 1980, 347). What a text means cannot merely be reader caprice, can it? Would not this lead to relativistic chaos in interpretations? How will we argue some interpretations are correct and others are not? Consider, for example, discussions of the US Constitution. If readers can make it mean anything they want, how can we trust governing officials *not* to be tyrants?

Recall that our main constraint on reader caprice is that we are emphasizing the priority of questioning, something that is not entirely in the reader's power. It is important to note that constraints are not necessarily a restriction of one's freedom. In fact, many constraints or boundaries or rules enable and empower our freedom. Consider, for example, taking away all the rules to a game, like basketball. Without the rules or the boundaries, we are not freed to play it and no field of play is set off for the game. Consider driving. If we took away all the rules, we would not be able to get anywhere within the chaos of automobiles. Consider religious institutions and practices. Shariah law, for example, enables people to be free to be Muslim. Thus, state legislation proposals to ban Shariah law actually restrict religious freedom despite claiming to uphold religious freedom (see Shanmugasundaram 2018).

Let us keep focused on reading and interpretation, though. The constraint of the hermeneutic priority of questioning does not restrict a reader's freedom, but instead sets people free actually to read. Without it, we cannot even start to read; we are just projecting our desires or interests or fears. Reading and projecting are two distinct activities. There are other boundaries and constraints that make reading possible. While it is possible to interpret a text in more than one way, a text, writes Ricoeur, "presents a limited field of possible constructions" (Ricoeur 1976, 79). Part of what limits the field are the specific questions and the sentences that address those questions. Another boundary is the genre of a work, as we noted above (see Ricoeur 1974). Implied author and ideal reader, as structural elements of a text, also provide boundaries for the limited field within which to be freed to read a book. One crucial boundary for text interpretation is historical context, and this helps us move into the third layer of questioning, questions about what is "behind the lines."

As we noted above, "behind the lines" questions focus attention on elements shared by both of Raphael's "in your head" types of questions, but also some aspects of "author and me" questions, where readers move into details about a writer's life, or historical context of either the book or the content of the book, or even the economic conditions under which a book is published. Some word choices, for example, can reveal that a text is a product of a particular historical era or culture, such as when authors refer to humankind as "mankind." This is another dimension of the exegetical hermeneutic circle. Just as a sentence (part) in a text must be understood in light of the text itself (the whole), so also is a text a part of a broader culture and historical context. As Schleiermacher puts it, "The vocabulary and the history of the period in which an author [writes] constitute the whole within which [their] texts must be understood with all their peculiarities" (Schleiermacher 1978, 10). As Western readers, we know we are at a particular cultural and historical distance from the *Mazu yulu* and transmission of the lamp literature of the Tang and Song dynasties more broadly. Readers without fluency in classical Chinese rely on translators to put the literature into words we can understand but also require extended commentary and explanations of allusions, geography, unfamiliar names, and more. Kierkegaard illustrates this gap between context and understanding with a dramatic description of a lover painstakingly translating a love letter term-by-term from a beloved who does not speak the same language, when a friend of this translating lover asks, "How goes reading the letter?" Kierkegaard describes this lover as getting furious at the friend, exclaiming that the translating is merely preparatory to be able to read the beloved's letter (see Kierkegaard 1990).

In fact, as the literature forming the origins of the contemporary phenomenon going by the name of "Zen," contemporary readers are especially prone to miss asking "proper" questions demanded by Dharma transmission texts. Moreover, as we will examine in closer detail, "encounter dialogues" are particularly subject to readerly caprice because they are brief and seemingly contextless interactions between masters and students. Zen has become a peculiar Western cultural phenomenon, where we can find books with "Zen" in the title where writers themselves explain in the preface that they have no expertise in or knowledge of Zen (see Pirsig 2000). In popular contexts, we accuse people who do this of "cultural appropriation." It is known as the critique of orientalism in academic circles, where what is perceived as "other" from the perspective of Eurocentric imperialism is distorted in two directions: demonization and eroticization or mystification (see Said 1979). The critical historian of religions Tomoko Masuzawa, for instance, explains how this polarized and distorted perception of the other negatively prejudiced Western notions of "Islam" and positively prejudiced Western notions of "Buddhism" (see Masuzawa 2005). This shows up even in popular phenomena like *Star Wars*, where the Jedi are modeled on Buddhist monastics and, more insidiously, the Tusken Raiders or "Sand People" are based off of nomadic Arab tribes. On the one hand, orientalism opens a way for people to appropriate things out of context. On the other hand, it merely projects what the appropriator wants to see. Another way this has been described is the "pizza effect," where US tourists seek out "authentic pizza" in Italy but savvy Italian entrepreneurs serve Americanized pizza to satisfy their customers—to such an extent that Italian cuisine itself changes. Just as with pizza, so also with Buddhist phenomena like "Zen"—the Zen US citizens pursue is tailored to sell to them (see Jenkins 2002). For us, all questions concerning such factors have to do with what is "behind the lines."

While questions about what is behind the lines are particularly clear in cases of translations from one language to another, this also happens when writers' words become archaic for contemporary readers or when their figures of speech, topics, and jokes do not age well. If a reader notices the use of "Moslem" for Muslim or "mankind" for humankind in a book published in the US, the reader knows they are likely reading something either from well before the Civil Rights movement or from a writer who has ignored social progress since then. Another way to think about this is the problem of anachronism, where contemporary readers project their vocabularies and concerns onto texts from earlier historical eras. For example, the question of what Christian Bibles teach about "homosexuality" projects onto a culture a notion that first century Palestinians simply did not use. The very notion, like "heterosexuality," was coined and medicalized in the last century, where both terms indicate a pathological obsession with either the same or the opposite sex. Only through what the legal philosopher Martha Nussbaum refers to as "the politics of disgust," did certain communities come to politicize and change the meanings of these two words (see Nussbaum 2010). To project contemporary notions onto past cultures overlooks how forces change meanings of words, even though we clearly recognize the phenomena with words like "awful" changing from something filling us with awe to something tasting disgusting or like "gay" changing from a synonym for happy to a term reclaimed by a community striving to take public pride in themselves. When we ask questions about the vocabulary and grammar of a text, we are asking questions about what is "behind the lines," even if in the QAR system these particular issues would be located in the "think and search" category.

There are a lot of other ways to get "behind the lines." Sometimes it is necessary to develop an idea of how the "original audience" would take a text or narrative. Levine, for example, exposes how a lot of Christian preaching in the United States is either explicitly or implicitly anti-Jewish (Levine 2015, 20). There is a pernicious repetition and reinforcement of Jewish stereotypes, where Jesus' parables in particular are taught often as if it is a battle between Jesus and "the Jews," as if Jesus accepts all sinners and Jews reject sinners (Levine 2015, 23). What is particularly interesting is that Gospel writers themselves try to domesticate Jesus' parables into anti-Jewish allegories, where Luke, for example, frames the parables of the Lost Sheep, the Lost Coin, and the Prodigal Son as about sinners who repent. It is not as if coins and sheep can ask for forgiveness, and it is not as if the notion of forgiveness was somehow a new idea to Jews (Levine 2015, 30–40). The point is that emphasizing how original audiences would have taken Jesus' parables serves as an antidote to pernicious anti-Judaism. Jesus' Jewish audience would not have taken the parables as somehow about the superiority of Christianity over Judaism, especially since Jesus himself was Jewish. As Alter puts this, "Reading any body of literature involves specialized mode of perception in which every culture trains its members from childhood. As modern readers of [religious texts], we need to relearn something of this mode of perception that was second nature to the original audiences" (Alter 1981, 74). Yet we need to be cautious about the role the notion of an "original audience" plays in interpretation, just as we have seen that "writer intent" cannot serve as the primary criterion to determine whether an interpretation is correct. As Gadamer points out, we cannot confuse empathizing with an original audience with understanding and interpretation (Gadamer 2013, 200). Like translation, this is merely a pre-condition for interpretation, and is not separated easily from the process of interpretation itself—as we will elaborate below with regard to the existential hermeneutic circle and "beyond the lines" questions. As Gadamer writes,

> The horizon of [interpretation] cannot be limited either by what the writer originally had in mind or by the horizon of the person to whom the text was originally addressed. It sounds at first like a sensible hermeneutical rule—and is generally recognized as such—that nothing should be put into a text that the writer or the reader could not have intended. But this rule can be applied only in extreme cases… The idea of the contemporary addressee can claim only a restricted critical validity… The idea of the original reader is full of unexamined idealization… The reference to the original reader, like that to the meaning of the author, seems to offer only a very crude historico-hermeneutical criterion that cannot really limit the horizon of a text's meaning… Normative concepts such as the author's meaning or the original reader's understanding in fact represent only an empty space that is filled from time to time in understanding.
>
> (Gadamer 2013, 412–13)

The notion of the original audience can help constrain reader bias in interpretation, but it will not replace actually reading and interpreting a text. Moreover, it only enters consideration in developing interpretations on particularly troubling occasions such as Levine's concern to rehabilitate anti-Judaism out of Jesus' parables. Most of the time, however, the original audience and writer intent do not enter into our interpretive process, like when we successfully discover the virtual pattern emerging from a magic eye image, we do not consider questions of authorship or original audience, such as "What did the designer of the magic-eye image intend by this?" Or, "Is this how people saw it in the 1990s?"

Note that questions about writer intent and original audience do not arise with "on the lines" questions or questions about what is "between the lines." Constructing the world of the text in front of the book through questions on the level of story or content comes first. As Ricoeur writes, "reconstructing the expectations of a text's first receivers in order to restore to the text its original otherness—these are already steps in rereading, standing [secondarily] in relation to a primary understanding that allows the text to develop its own [structure]" (Ricoeur 1988, 174). Readers who take up historical reconstruction and contextualization can resist narcissistic satisfaction in sheer aesthetic pleasure or contemporary stereotypes. The main direction of inquiry "behind the lines" of a text requires readers to appeal outside the world of the text, perhaps to such an extent that such readers have to interrupt or discontinue their hermeneutic reduction, to suspend their suspension, or stop reading altogether. The questions about a writer's psychology, the perspectives of original audiences, the political and economic divisions of the era, and more are reducible to what Ricoeur calls an "explanatory attitude," an attitude that inhibits a text's fulfilment in present dialogue between the voice of the text and the reader (Ricoeur 1991, 118). As the hermeneutic philosopher Wilhelm Dilthey points out, explanation merely breaks things down into parts, but—as we have seen—interpretation also involves integrating these parts into a meaningful whole (see Dilthey 1972; Dilthey 1988; and Ricoeur 1991). In the explanatory mode, readers can attempt to situate a book in specific historical contexts, rendering its "present speech" innocuous. At times, such as those identified by Levine, this antidote is necessary to help make our world a safer place for persecuted and oppressed peoples. In the academic study of the Hebrew Bible, source criticism and redaction criticism are examples whereby a book is reduced merely to constituent parts like the JEPD sources, and those parts are shown to belong to often contesting cultures (see McKenzie and Haynes 1999; cf. Holstein 1975). Even inquiry about the psychology of the writer can be merely explanatory in this way. The logician Jakko Hintikka, for example, explains the philosopher of language Ludwig Wittgenstein's enigmatic writings are a result of dyslexia (Hintikka 2000, 6). Whether in the form of historical-criticism of books as a whole or in the form of mere psychological explanations about the writer, such an explanatory attitude dislodges itself from the hierarchical integration that coordinates multiple sentences into a great whole. In other words, such methods change the topic. What is being talked about is no longer the world of the text emerging in front of the text but the historical (or purportedly metaphysical) realities behind the book. The methods and attitude can let us say we have explained a book, but using them and going no further indicates that we have not yet interpreted the text (see Ricoeur 1976, 84; and Gadamer 2013, 412). They get us "behind the lines," and they refer us to some physical or metaphysical reality.

There is another way to conceive of questions about what is "behind the lines," an attitude and orientation that preserve the hermeneutic reduction necessary for reading a text. Hermeneutically sensitive critical questioning does not exhaust itself in some reality outside the world of the text. Instead, such questions need to be situated as one moment without the broader unfolding of the text. Ricoeur names this process the hermeneutic arc, where a reader moves from (1) a sense of the text, through (2) explanatory critique of it, to (3) a post-critical appropriation of its meanings in an interpretation (see Ricoeur 1976, 74–94). It is not that we should avoid explanatory methods but that we need to put them in their place as preparatory for interpretation, like translation is preparatory for reading. Through these questions about what is "behind the lines," we lay out further boundaries and limitations to free us for interpretation. In this case, we free ourselves from reader caprice, because caprice is a way we *inhibit* our own freedom to interpret. We are not free to read if we are at the whims of inherited stereotypes or reactive immediate emotions. Historical reading, writes Ricoeur,

> continues to be guided by the expectations of [primary] reading and by the questions of [further] reading. The merely historicizing question— what did the text say?—remains under the control of *the properly hermeneutical question*—what does the text say to me and *what do I say to the text*?
>
> (Ricoeur 1988, 175 my emphasis)

Laying out sets of interpretive constraints, inquiry behind the lines ideally plays a purifying role, allowing readers to isolate a voice in the text and what this voice asks of them.

Properly hermeneutic questions concern what is "beyond the lines." This fourth category of questioning is the most important in our refinement of QAR. Such questions can be either "on my own" or "author and me" questions. Questions about what is beyond the lines have to do with ways a reader's life might be refigured in light of a text, or ways communities might authorize some readings of a book rather than others. These questions govern the process of interpretation and give shape to the existential hermeneutic circle. Recall that the exegetical hermeneutic circle relates parts and wholes— from words to sentences, sentences to chapters, chapters to texts, and texts to historical eras. In the existential hermeneutic circle, however, readers' anticipations of meaning are revised in light of what a text says (see Gadamer 2013, 278–310). This is most apparent when readers are surprised by what a text says to them. As Gadamer emphasizes, "Every experience worthy of the name thwarts an expectation" (Gadamer 2013, 364). How can this happen if a reader or reading community just projects onto a text what they want it to mean? Recall above how we explained that the same text can say different things to readers at different moments in their lives. It is not merely because readers' perspectives change. More importantly for us is that the text itself "listens" to what readers say in response, and thereby changes or adds to what it has to say to those readers in subsequent rereadings. Only one kind of questioning belongs to the properly hermeneutical dimension of reading whereby a dialogue is realized with a text that speaks and listens. Only these questions bring a listener into the foreground, a listener who is *not in* but is *still "of"* the text itself, the narrator or implied author grafted to the reading voice of the reader.

Recall our earlier mention about how notions like "original audience" and "implied author" are empty in themselves, and the process of getting behind the lines is not separated easily from the process of interpretation itself. Another way to conceive of this is that *the exegetical hermeneutic circle is governed by the existential hermeneutic circle*. Anticipations or prejudices lead readers to put parts and wholes together in different ways, yet they also transform the readers themselves as an understanding of a story is achieved. That is, answers to questions about what is on the lines, between the lines, and behind the lines are affected by answers to questions about what is beyond the lines. I seem to be suggesting here that reader projections determine the meaning of a text. This is not so. Recall that questioning is not solely in our own power; questions occur to us. The circularity of hermeneutic circles is not a vicious logical circle (see Heidegger 2010, 144–61). Circular reasoning in logic is a formal fallacy where someone argues to a conclusion that already is assumed as a premise anyway. Just because we revise our anticipations of meaning in light of what a text says that surprises us does not mean we stop anticipating meanings. We cannot escape this in our efforts to understand and interpret. As the feminist hermeneutic philosopher Georgia Warnke explains, we need to enter the circle in a fitting way, where some projections enable rather than inhibit understanding (see Warnke 1997). There is, like face-to-face dialogue, an incompleteness to every interpretation. Just like dialogues can always be resumed and taken further, so also can every interpretation be taken further. Every "completion" opens to an incompletion.

Only "beyond the lines" questions facilitate the dialogical process of interpretation. Not all our questions unfold a virtual listener before the text. Through beyond the lines questions, readers experience the text as raising certain questions of significance and power that engender a pathos in which readers "hearken" to the text speaking *with* them (see Ricoeur 1974, 153; and Heidegger 2010, 157). If a power endures through submission to the exegetical hermeneutic circles and boundary setting questions, then the text (as grafted to the voice of the reader) and the reader (as the one read to) can be said to engage in dialogue. A reader might reflect upon reading a text and hearing what it has to say by asking for its existential and practical applications: "How will I live differently in light of what is being said?"

Ricoeur calls this "mimesis3," or the reconfiguration of one's life in light of a story (Ricoeur 1984, 70–87). Through sustained dialogue with this partner, the reader's world comes to be refigured in various applications. By way of these questions the reader realizes a "fusion of horizons," bridging between the virtual world of the text and the existential world of the reader (Ricoeur 1986; and Iser 1972). Such questioning is not deficit-driven in need of one particular settled answer, but surplus-driven and more in awe at the predicative possibilities before any specific possibility is appropriated. It is by virtue of the shared question that I can try out these predicative possibilities for a specific subject, and when I find a predication or coordination of predicates that works, it expands my horizon and enriches my world.

The formal quality of beyond the lines questions or properly hermeneutical questions implies an ontological duality within oneself: not only do we receive what a text says by way of grafting it to our own reading voice, *we also respond to this voice as if it were itself listening to our responses.* These ontologically discrete speakers and listeners integrate as participants in a dialogue. We need to posit under the aegis of the metaphor that a text speaks that this speaker is also listening. It is through this additional impertinent predication of texts "listening" that we can open up a different response to the theme of how a text can have different things to say to the same reader in different readings of the same text. Not only do "texts speak," they also "listen" to what we have to say in response and thus change what they have to say in turn, and so on.

This virtual dialogue unfolds the differently radiating aspects of subject matters (see Dickman 2014). Consider an example such as Plato's *Lysis*. The ancient Greek philosopher Socrates is Plato's first-person narrator, often saying, "I said" or "I think," yet when readers graft their reading voice to the voice of the text, they too say, "I said" or "I think." By the end of the dialogue, Socrates (or "the I" as the voice of the text) leaves open the question of what constitutes true friendship. Indeed, in the *Crito*, Socrates says, "I do not convince Crito that I am this Socrates talking to you here and ordering all I say, but he thinks that I am the thing which he will soon be looking at as a corpse, and so he asks how he shall bury me" (115d). It is not that readers should identify with Socrates but the I who speaks. What happens as a consequence is that the reader, not as the one giving voice to the text but as the one read to, is empowered to address questions for and from oneself. Who are my true friends? Do I agree with Socrates' considerations and arguments? These are properly hermeneutical questions, questions that go beyond the lines. Do religious texts similarly speak with readers, raising questions to which readers themselves need to respond, where their response will be heard?

Questions Asked by Deific Voices Stand in Need of Demythologization

What is at risk with questions posed by deific voices? Not only are figures of ultimate authority depicted asking questions of others in religious narratives but readers also themselves must ask questions of religious texts to read them successfully. Moreover, religious texts—as we have seen—ask questions of readers and readers respond to those questions. These interlocking circles of questions and responses in reader engagement with religious narratives, what does it all mean? My goal is to interpret these questions within the framework of Bultmann's mission of demythologization (see Congdon 2015). Demythologization has been associated with complete rejection of religious narrative in light of modern science. For Bultmann, however, demythologization is what can help preserve transformative power of religious narratives despite the archaic worldviews presupposed in them. Bultmann writes,

> Experience and control of the world have developed to such an extent through science and technology that no one can or does seriously maintain the New Testament world picture. What sense does it make to confess today that "he descended into hell" or "he ascended into heaven," if the confessor no longer shares the underlying mythical world picture of a three-story world?
>
> (Bultmann 1989, 4)

What Bultmann says of the New Testament applies as much to worldviews presupposed in the *Mazu yulu* and the Torah. We cannot make use of electric lights, modern medicine, and smartphones and at the same time believe in spiritual and mystical powers that shape religious worlds (Bultmann 1989, 4). It is not merely that our notion of the universe has changed. Our views of psychology have too. On the one hand, through Romanticism, we have a view of our individuality as a subject of experience empowered to make meaning for ourselves trekking through the wilderness of life. On the other hand, through psychiatry, we diagnose people with disorders, such as those who have a heightened sense of paranoia, a grandeur of feeling persecuted by devils and demons, with schizophrenia. Despite these developments in the modern world, demythologization resists picking religious texts apart, where people only keep those parts that still have credibility. Religious narratives strike contemporary readers as incredible when readers are expected to believe in religious worldviews forming the setting within which the narratives take place. This would be to stop "behind the lines" with some historical and metaphysical reality. The transformative power in religious narratives comes not from their description of some physical or metaphysical reality or atmosphere but from their concern to address human capacities for responsibility (see Bultmann 1962, 97). As Levinas underscores, our condition of suffering in a chaotic world "reveals a God Who renounces all aids to manifestation and appeals instead to the full maturity of the responsible individual" (Levinas 1990, 143).

Let us turn briefly to an illustration from pop culture. Did you know that George Lucas credits ideas for his original *Star Wars* trilogy to the evangelist for comparative mythology and literature, Joseph Campbell? Campbell is practically a cult figure for many English and creative writing teachers and students, where his models like "the hero's journey" are formative both for videogame producers and novice creative writers. Campbell describes religious myths and symbols as having existential power for people, and Lucas tries to transpose this power from ancient mythological contexts to contemporary science fiction. As a cultural phenomenon, Campbell and his popular influence might be interesting in its own right. Despite his popular influence, we need to recognize Indigenous scholars' critique of Campbell's orientalist imposition of notions that distort their grassroots narrative traditions (see Fear-Segal and Tillet 2014). However, I want to focus on and expand upon one specific illustration he makes in passing in an interview with Bill Moyers, collected and published as *Joseph Campbell and the Power of Myth* (Campbell 1991, ch. 4).

Amid weaving together Indigenous American coming-of-age practices, Buddhist meditation rituals, ancient Indian epic narratives, Christian passion stories, what he calls "vegetation traditions," and more, Campbell moves into a conceptual analysis of the notions of duality and unity, particularly with regard to Christian communion practices. He describes the act of communion as a way a practitioner overcomes separation or duality by taking in their deity so that their deity may work within them. The particular image I want to focus on is how Campbell describes this: "Jesus is the fruit of eternal life which was on the second tree in the Garden of Eden" (Campbell 1991). Whereas the tree of the knowledge of good and evil symbolizes dualities such as life/death or male/female, the tree of life symbolizes unity. Campbell exclaims, "And this is exactly the tree under which the Buddha sits… the Buddha under his tree, and Christ hanging on his tree are the same image [for reunification]." That is, the Christian acts of communion of eating the bread and drinking the wine seem, in Campbell's model, parallel to Buddhist acts of meditation as ritual emulations of the Buddha's seated meditation and enlightenment experience. This should strike readers as odd. Would not Christian prayer be a more fitting form of comparison for seated meditation? We can elaborate a further coordinate of comparison here. Consider that Torah scrolls are bound on wooden rollers or staves, with decorative knobs often resembling fruits like apples or pomegranates, symbolizing the tree of life. Indeed, some wooden casings for the entire scrolls are called the tree of life. Working within Campbell's model, then, we could say—surprisingly—that the act of reading the Torah is one's eating from the tree of life. Let me draw this out explicitly in case we miss the potential methodological application of this model for comparative study of religions. Torah study in modern Judaisms is not the same as Christians reading their Bibles or Buddhists reading their sutras. Moreover, Buddhist meditation is not like Jewish or Christian prayers or other contemplative practices. The surprising result of this model is that comparative study would necessitate looking at Christian communion practices, Buddhist meditation rituals, and Torah study in Judaism as symbols of the same attempt by the human being to overcome duality. That is, inasmuch as human beings share a universal or general structure of yearning for transcendence and growth, or what Campbell calls the "monomyth" of the "hero's journey," then these seemingly disparate elements of different religions—elements that on the surface do not seem to correspond to one another—all symbolize this same underlying thing: the effort to integrate despite pulls of disintegration (see Tillich 2000, 90). Hearing these stories, reading the texts within these symbolic orders, putting them into practice—all these help transform the readers.

I provide this extended illustration because it shows how existential interpretation of religious symbols and myth already permeates contemporary culture as well as shows a way comparative phenomenology of religions might go. We are already primed to appreciate Bultmann's approach to philosophizing about religions as mythic structures because of this. I do not want to give the impression that Bultmann is just doing the same thing as Campbell, however. I sometimes tell colleagues and students who are Campbell fanatics that "Campbell is just Bultmann with training wheels." That is, Campbell presupposes Bultmann's sophisticated ontology and epistemology in "discovering" (or, really, *imposing*) his patterns like the hero's journey in diverse myths and symbols. How is it possible to derive existential empowerment through experiences of symbols and myths? Can such empowerment come from questions posed by deific voices? The crucial thing for Bultmann is a myth's kerygmatic core, what a myth proclaims as a decisive intervention of some ultimate dimension of human existence (Bultmann 1989, 8–9 and 24). How does the Buddha's Dharma or Paul's "good news" reach human beings in their everydayness? This approach preserves the hermeneutic reduction necessary for reading religious narrative. To ask questions about whether some feature of Gautama's life or Jesus' death is historically accurate is to exhaust reading at the level of "behind the lines" questions. Only questions going beyond the lines open readers for transformative understanding of kerygmatic meanings.

My approach, however, raises a wonder about whether the *kerygma* or proclamation is a declarative statement or a genuine question. That is, *having something proclaimed at or stated to you is quite different from being asked a question that invites you to speak up too.* Even if we allow that religious texts call readers into question, recall that there are two fundamental kinds of questions: sincere typical interrogatives and genuine questions. Typical interrogatives are always reducible to imperatives. Thus, even if the kerygma reaches readers in the form of a sincere question, this is to call readers out (see Dickman 2018b). Is the question asked of readers a deficit-driven or surplus-driven one? When Mazu asks questions of students, when the God inquires about the whereabouts of the primordial human beings, when Jesus questions his disciples, are these deficit or surplus ones? If the questions are solely typical interrogatives, what can this tell us about religious existential ontologies? Do they just make human beings subordinate to authoritarian supernatural demands? Might some or any of the questions be genuine? We can only address these issues by examining and interpreting specific religious narratives.

I have argued throughout this chapter that interpretation of texts presupposes four discrete layers of questioning. These layers reflect different qualities of engagement with a text. And I have specified that historical criticism is subordinate to properly hermeneutic questioning. Let us turn to specific religious narratives.

Part Two

The Exegetical Hermeneutic Circle: Questions in the Direct Discourse of Deific Figures

Chapter 4: *HaShem* Asks, "Where Are You?"   85
   Preliminary Clarification: Choosing Anthropomorphism over the Omnibeing   86
   Questions on the Lines: HaShem Is Often, if Not Always, an Interrogator   91
   Questions between the Lines: Does HaShem Seek Understanding with Others?   95

Chapter 5: Ancestor Ma Asks, "Why Are You Seeking Outside?"   101
   Preliminary Clarification: Classical Chan Masters Are Constructed as Buddhas   102
   Questions on the Lines: Provocations Often, if Not Always, Occur in Encounter Dialogues   107
   Questions between the Lines: Does Mazu Seek Understanding with Others?   113

Chapter 6: Jesus Asks, "Who Do You Say I Am?"   117
   Preliminary Clarification: Gospel Portraits of Jesus Conflict   119
   Questions on the Lines: Jesus Often, if Not Always, Asks Rhetorical Questions   121
   Questions between the Lines: Does Jesus Seek Understanding with Others?   124

The following three chapters will look at specific religious texts and how deific figures are depicted therein. We will focus on questions concerning what is on and between the lines, or the exegetical hermeneutic circle. Part III will turn to engage the "voice" of these texts, looking at questions about what is behind and beyond the lines, or the existential hermeneutic circle. My primary goal is to apply what we have developed in Part I about the nature of questioning, the fabric of religious narrative, and the layers of questions necessary for reading religious texts. Recall that shared questioning facilitates the transfer of complete thoughts from one person to another. We need to ask the question to which our conversation partners respond so what they say will make sense to us. Recall, too, that religious texts are semantic fabric structures before they somehow represent historical or metaphysical facts. That is, religious texts weave communities together in a social fabric of meaning and relevance. Finally, recall that we isolated four layers of questions necessary for reading, noting only one as the properly hermeneutic layer: on the lines, between them, behind them, and beyond them. On, between, and behind the lines questions give shape to the exegetical hermeneutic circle and questions that go beyond the lines give shape to the existential hermeneutic circle.

In Chapters 4–6, I will move through one deific figure at a time, with an aim at isolating questions in their direct discourse. Chapter 4 will focus on the God depicted in the Tanak. Many questions are attributed to this figure. For example, in the book of Job, this figure asks sixty-eight questions in a row. Chapter 5 will focus on Mazu, a classical Chan (Zen) master who often is identified as the progenitor of the most irreverent forms of Zen. Mazu uses many different tactics to elicit awakening from his followers, but questions are among the most predominant tactics. Chapter 6 focuses on Jesus of Nazareth. Sometimes Jesus is depicted as using questions to lament or even sigh with disappointment at those around him. For all of these figures, my goal is to figure out whether we can interpret any of their questions as genuine questions. This would prove to be exceptional. Here I want to briefly provide some preliminary clarifications about our case studies.

Some of my readers might wonder why I choose to put HaShem first, Mazu second, and Jesus third. Does that suggest Christian superiority, as if—by putting Jesus last—I in some way see Jesus as more significant to the previous figures? I am not out to do that deliberately or inadvertently. I have made a few assumptions about my likely potential audience. You probably are already familiar with both HaShem and Jesus, whether directly through participating in Christian practices or indirectly through Christianities permeating US culture. I want to create some hermeneutic distance, returning the texts to their originary otherness, making what seems familiar to us into something a bit stranger. That is why I want to start with HaShem. Surely readers are familiar with the ubiquity of ideas of "god," particularly of some supreme being of philosophical theology who is said to be all-knowing and all-powerful. I want to disorient us with this idea by returning to the anthropomorphic locus in the Torah, emphasizing Jewish (rather than Christian) approaches to this deity. I assume most readers are unfamiliar with Chan masters, which means that readers should be able to follow my methodological application to Chan texts best. This serves two purposes. First, Chan texts help us get even more distance from naïve assumptions we might have about deific figures. Second, it will help us see more clearly how my method applies to religious narrative, which means if we can do an analysis of Chan masters comfortably, then we should be able to transfer similar methods and findings to texts readers may hold onto as "more" sacred. The hermeneutic productive distance created by starting with the God of the Torah as anthropomorphic in the narratives and the compounded distance by turning to unfamiliar Chan literature will help us see narratives starring Jesus in a properly critical light. Even though HaShem is among the most mysterious figures in world literature, and even though US readers are likely unfamiliar with Chan masters, I believe Jesus will be the most difficult case study because readers in the United States—with a predominantly Christian-influenced populace—will likely have more invested in their version Jesus. We have more stereotypes and representations we need to overcome to hear what the text says.

I believe comparative hermeneutic work is crucial because—as a scholar of comparative questions in the academic study of religions—it is surprising how little impact discoveries in the study of different religions have on one another (see Freiberger 2019). For example, the Dunhuang manuscripts discovered in China over the last century have proven essential for clarifying editorial license in revisions of Huineng's *Platform Sutra* (Schlütter, forthcoming). Through the different editions and dates, we can track contestation over lineage superiority, where different groups attempt to garner patronage and leadership in monasteries. Parallel contestations have been pointed out about the different noncanonical gospels discovered in the last century (see King 2003, and Pagels 1989). The writer of, for example, the Gospel of Mary challenges leadership transmission from Jesus to Peter. Source-text analysis of the Hebrew Bible helps show how different uses of language throughout a small set of verses in Genesis reflect different cultures and how the different groups vie for governing what the text means (see McKenzie 1999). While there may be some discussion between scholars of the Hebrew Bible and scholars of the New Testament in select professional organizations, such as the Society of Biblical Literature, scholars of Chan, too, study religious literature. I want my work to be a step in the direction of putting these seemingly disparate groups into better conversation.

I should provide one further note about how I will organize each case study. Given the four layers of questions I delineate in Chapter 3, I follow that structure—looking at on the line details first, then between the lines details. Part III will take up the structure of behind the lines details and beyond the lines ones. However, in each case, I first provide some preliminary clarifications about the deific figure at issue or the nature of the texts at issue. I want to use this to first alienate us from the texts for productive distance, to serve as an antidote to what Levine calls "auditory atrophy" (Levine 2015). This way we can approach the texts with fresher and more sensitive ears, without imposing our typical stereotypes and biases. In phenomenology, as we discussed above, we call this "bracketing" our natural and naïve attitude. It is a first step in performing our hermeneutic reduction. Let us turn to look at HaShem and questions this figure asks.

4

HaShem Asks, "Where Are You?"

What is going on in the passage below?

> They heard the sound of the Lord God walking in the garden at the time
> of the evening breeze, and the man and his wife hid themselves from the
> presence of the Lord God among the trees of the garden. But the Lord
> God called to the man, and said to him, "Where are you?" He said, "I
> heard the sound of you in the garden, and I was afraid, because I was
> naked; and I hid myself." He said, "Who told you that you were naked?
> Have you eaten from the tree of which I commanded you not to eat?"
> The man said, "The woman whom you gave to be with me, she gave me
> fruit from the tree, and I ate." Then the Lord God said to the woman,
> "What is this that you have done?" The woman said, "The serpent
> tricked me, and I ate."
>
> (Gen. 3:8-13)

In this quotation from Genesis, there is a deity and primordial human
beings, and—despite what seems to be an earlier depiction of this God as
cosmically omniscient and powerful (Genesis 1)—the God asks a number of
questions that at least on the surface seem to be sincere and, perhaps, even
genuine. I want to know whether it is a "fact" of the story, whether it is "right
there in the text," that this God asks a genuine surplus-driven question. I
am also curious about whether it is in the text that this God asks a sincere,
but deficit-driven, question. Note, however, Fish's criticism that asserting
what is right there in a text is one of the best games in town within canons
of interpretive acceptability (Fish 1980). Our development of semantic
autonomy from both writer intent and reader caprice helps us isolate
interpretive possibilities within respectable constraints. In what follows, I
want first to clarify our focus on the God who emerges before the text rather
than some metaphysically transcendent God behind the book, choosing
scriptural anthropomorphism over the abstract omnibeing of philosophical
theology. This step will prepare us to survey a number of questions attributed
to this God to develop traits of character inferable from them—addressing
what is "on the lines" and "between the lines," and to focus in on one peculiar

and exceptional question, the first question posed to the primordial human beings, "Where are you?" We will save questions about what is behind the lines and beyond the lines for Chapter 7.

In this chapter, I argue that there is at least one exceptional case where HaShem might be asking other characters a genuine question. I argue this is exceptional because, as we will see, this God usually uses questions to interrogate others or overwhelm others. Before examining HaShem's questions, I need to isolate—for more thorough contextualization and interpretive parameters—that the anthropomorphic deity in biblical narrative stands in contrast to the abstract omnibeing of philosophical theology.

Preliminary Clarification: Choosing Anthropomorphism over the Omnibeing

One might be tempted to speculate about the nature or being of "god" given the question "Can God ask a genuine question?" This would distract us from how HaShem is characterized in narratives throughout the Torah and rabbinic traditions. Such a temptation seems unavoidable, though, so we need to take time to provide an antidote to it here. In both popular and academic contexts, the word "god" often is taken as unproblematically referring to a transcendent metaphysical entity, a supernatural being or the so-called higher power. For example, a Pew Research study found that the majority of US citizens claim to believe in "god" or some higher power, with roughly half stating they believe in the God depicted in the Christian Bible (Pew Research 2018). Perhaps a surprising result:

> In the U.S., belief in a deity is common even among the religiously unaffiliated—a group composed of those who identify themselves, religiously, as atheist, agnostic or "nothing in particular," and sometimes referred to, collectively, as religious "nones." Indeed, nearly three-quarters of religious "nones" (72%) believe in a higher power of some kind, even if not in God as described in the Bible.
>
> (Pew Research 2018, 5).

That is, on a popular level, even people who describe themselves as "not religious" tend to believe in some notion of a God as a higher power, presumably much like the God of institutionalized philosophy of religion. In academic circles, particularly in most publications about philosophy of religion, the word "god" is taken to refer to what we can call, with the "friendly" atheist philosopher of religion William Rowe, the "omnibeing" of philosophical theology or "traditional theism" (see Rowe 2006; see also Schilbrack 2014). This entity is said to be omniscient (all-knowing), omnipotent (all-powerful), omnibenevolent (all-loving or all-good), immutable (unchanging), perfect, and more. Numerous questions seem to arise in light of this notion of a God. Is human free will compatible with this God's knowledge? If this God is both all-powerful and all-good, how can egregious suffering or evil exist? An entire academic publication industry revolves around such questions. Even critical or postmodern philosophical theologians who purport to move away from institutionalized theism centered on this omnibeing, such as the philosophical theologian John Caputo, emphasize the word "god" as a name (see, for example, Caputo 2006). These social norms make it seem natural and sensible to ask questions like the following: Does God exist? What is the nature of God?

In such questions, people take the word "god" uncritically. That is, the word "god" starts to take on the veneer of a proper name. We can see this happen in other contexts. For example, many Buddhists come to use Siddhartha Gautama's title, "the Buddha," as a nickname, a practice that is so predominant that the word "Buddha" gets used as a name without the definite article (see Thich 2007). The complete thought really is, "Siddhartha Gautama is the Buddha." The same thing happens in Christian circles when Jesus is called "Christ" without qualification or a definite article, to such an extent that some people see it as Jesus' last name. The complete thought really is, "Jesus of Nazareth is the Christ" (see Tillich 1975, 97–8). Grammatically speaking, words like "the Prophet," "the Christ," "the Buddha," and "the God" belong to the predicate rather than sentential subject side of complete thoughts. The point here is that questions in philosophy of religion such as those about whether "god" exists are so normalized and institutionalized that asking "*which 'god'*" they might be talking about is met with deer-in-headlights reactions. That is, writers and speakers within this framework will say, "God exists" or "God does not exist." The question we should always have on the ready for such statements is "Which 'god'?" They respond, "What do you mean 'which god'? *The* god, of course!" In this way, the boundaries of this institution are policed and reinforced. The personal name of the God in scriptural narrative is not just any god but that which "HaShem" replaces, as we noted in the Introduction. As this God is depicted in Torah narratives, however, the figure does not seem to match up with the broad concept of the omnibeing. At least in terms of most of the stories, this God goes through numerous changes—even the simple act of walking through a garden in our selected passage. People bring their assumptions about the institutionalized theistic notion of an omnibeing to bear on their reading of the Torah, not interpreting what is said (*exegesis*) but projecting what must be the case (*eisegesis*) to preserve commitment to their notion of this omnibeing.

Such interpretation is nothing new. The medieval Jewish philosophical theologian Moses Maimonides, for example, argues that all scripture needs to be interpreted allegorically (see Maimonides 1995, 58). This is for two related reasons. On the one hand, the monotheistic God is known through rational inquiry and logical principles, and is—as Maimonides inherits from Plato and Aristotle—best conceived as the unmoved mover or first cause, a profound unity (Maimonides 1995, 67–8). On the other hand, the majority of people do not have sufficient training in rigorous rational inquiry either due to their lack of privilege for the life of study or due to their natural abilities, and so scriptures use images and myths to make divine truths accessible to as many people as possible (Maimonides 1995, 58). Maimonides's partition of philosophy (and science) from religious language is preserved in later Jewish philosophies, such as the modern philosopher Benedict Spinoza's critique of religion (see Spinoza 2001). We can know, for example, that since the divine being is "perfect," it also cannot change because any change would have to be toward some imperfection; there is nowhere to go but "down." The Torah is not against reason, however, but also shows a keen awareness of human limits. Like his Muslim contemporary Ibn Rushd, Maimonides cautions against making metaphysics or philosophical theology publicly available to the majority of people (see Averroes 2012; see also Strauss 1988). The topic of divine being is extremely subtle and takes a long preparatory education before one is capable of philosophical theology. Moreover, even if someone is capable of it, they still might not actualize their potential (see Maimonides 1995, 59).

Despite this, Maimonides believes that all readers of the Torah need to be taught to reject any hints of anthropomorphism, any treatment of the divine being with human attributes like "holding the whole world in his hands" or "walking in the garden" (Maimonides 1995, 63). The divine being, according to Maimonides, is not and does not have a body, is so different from human beings that human predicates cannot directly apply to the divine being (Maimonides 1995, 63). He believes this aligns with the Torah's prohibition of idolatry (Maimonides 1995, 178). Maimonides inspired a current in medieval philosophical theology across dominant monotheisms of Christianity, Judaism, and Islam, a movement that has come to be called "negative theology." The fundamental position is that human beings, even with capable intellects, cannot make positive assertions about the omnibeing (see Maimonides 1995, 18). Hence the list of this God's qualities takes on negative prefixes, such as "in-finite," "un-limited," "un-conditioned," or even "im-mortal." Even the ascription of "unity" or "existence" to this entity involves the ascription of human notions, which, in principle, cannot apply to this utterly transcendent yet metaphysically real entity.

We might even ask whether it makes sense to believe that this omnibeing is a person. We should also notice how this inspires Bultmann's and Tillich's approach to symbols and myth, where positive terms for the divine should be taken symbolically and not literally. This theological trajectory, through Tillich, also inspired the 1960s phenomenon of "death of God" theologians, such as the Jewish death of God theologian Richard Rubenstein, who goes so far as to say that "Omnipotent Nothingness is the Lord of all creation . . . It is impossible to affirm the loving and the creative aspects of God's activity without also affirming that creation and destruction are part of an indivisible process. Each wave in the ocean of God's Nothingness has its moment, but it must inevitably give way to other waves" (Rubenstein 1992, 305–6). Similar to the ultimate negativity of terms like "infinity," Rubenstein approaches this God as a nothingness, or literally "no-thing," in part inspired by Lurianic Kabbalah's notion of *tzimtzum* (the divine self-contraction in creation).

Of course, if we picture Gods in too personalistic of terms, we seem to reduce Gods to mere human beings and verge on idolatry. However, this influential notion of some omnibeing does not prove any less anthropomorphic than more tangible anthropomorphic notions of a God (see Cherbonnier 1962). While it seems that basic human actions ascribed to a divine being are problematic if such divine beings are intrinsically transcendent, even ascriptions of profound predicates like "infinite" or "unlimited" as Hume points out can be just as much a projection of human wish fulfilment (see Hume 1998). For example, teleological arguments that use some analogy with human designed artifacts such as a clock ascribe intelligence to the omnibeing, where just like we know an organized clock requires a clockmaker, we also know that the universe is organized and requires an intelligent universe-maker. Even if our notion of intelligence is expanded or intensified by calling it "infinite intelligence," it is still deriving from a human notion of intelligence.

In contrast, narratives about HaShem do not maintain consistency with attributes of the omnibeing. Promoters of the omnibeing will say this God is completely unknowable. Yet even in passages where the God of the Tanak is described as "unknowable" (see Isa. 55:8-9 or Prov. 1:28), this is not because HaShem is in principle not knowable through human categories. It is instead that HaShem, like us, can refuse to disclose oneself to others (Cherbonnier 1962, 195). That is, like human beings, HaShem can act unpredictably. While the omnibeing resists all predication in being intrinsically unlimited, HaShem seems to be described as unlimited in the sense of completely free to accomplish one's intentions. As the religious studies scholar Edmond Cherbonnier writes,

The gods of Canaan and Babylon were at least good imitations. The prophets do not charge [these other gods or their devotees] with being anthropomorphic, but with being frauds… The ineffable "Ground of Being" is a god in chains. Zeus, Baal, or Ishtar, on the other hand, if they really existed, would be something to reckon with.

(Cherbonnier 1962, 192)

Only an anthropomorphic God can take action, specifically an action such as asking a question. Only this sort of God speaks (see Wolterstorff 1995).

Before turning to HaShem's questions, I want to note one more point about focusing our attention on the anthropomorphic HaShem in the Torah rather than the abstract omnibeing of institutionalized philosophy of religion. If we hold rigorously to the fundamental grammatical distinction between sentential subjects and predicates, and as long as we know that the word "god" belongs to the predicate rather than the subject class of words, then we need to develop some consequences for institutionalized debates about whether or not "God exists." Arguments for or against "God's existence" are neither valid nor invalid; the conclusion that "God exists" is neither true nor false. Arguments for or against "God's existence" are meaningless. As Tillich states, "If 'existence' refers to something which can be found within the whole of reality, no divine being exists" (Tillich 2001, 54). This is not to promote atheism, or the belief that "God does not exist." The reason why validity cannot apply to the arguments and why truth cannot apply to the conclusion is that making "god" the subject of a sentence is simply ungrammatical. Consider the following comparisons. Does "hero" exist? It is difficult to know how to answer this question except to change the presuppositions within the question—the specific presupposition that "hero" refers to something specific that either exists or does not. A better question is: "Who will be my hero?" Consider this example. Does "president" exist? Now we can see some absurdity to the grammar of the question. Perhaps the institutional role of "president" exists, but the real question is: "Who is the president?"

Rather than trying to use the Torah to access indirectly some omnibeing who exists behind the book, we are approaching narratives where HaShem plays a role, with positive predicates constituting a personality. In a way, the omnibeing God behind the lines must die so that the interpersonal and communicative HaShem before the lines can live, can engage readers in living dialogue (see Dickman 2014). Let us turn to look at questions on the lines ascribed to this God and develop characteristics of this personality implied between the lines.

Questions on the Lines: HaShem Is Often, if Not Always, an Interrogator

As I just mentioned, arguments for or against the existence of a "god" probably are not the best place to start in philosophy of religions. More important is that Gods have personal names, in this case, HaShem. A better question is, then, does HaShem exist? Or—perhaps even better—who is HaShem? I have no pretense to address that question exhaustively or with finality. However, we can use our theory of narrative and hermeneutic priority of questioning detailed in previous chapters to flesh out some aspects of HaShem's personhood. As Alter emphasizes, biblical narration always directs readers' attention to character dialogue (Alter 1981, 82). That is, within biblical narratives, our attention really is drawn to interactions between characters where they ask questions of one another. Rather than approaching this God as an entity that really does or does not exist, this God is foremost a figure in narrative and HaShem uses questions to express HaShem's self. Regardless of whether HaShem is all-powerful and all-knowing, this God speaks. Note that this God—unlike the metaphysical God of ontotheology lurking behind the book as an authorizer of the discourse—is a god on or between the lines of text (see Dickman 2014; cf. Wolterstorff 1995). Let's look at some general features of this God's speech and then focus on questioning in particular.

A series of cumulative covenants determine the personalistic depictions of HaShem throughout the Tanak, especially the Torah. HaShem's covenant with Abraham and his descendants is realized concretely with Moses at Mt. Sinai, where Israel is established as HaShem's people and where they should do this God's will in reciprocity for HaShem's protection (Neusner 1993, 27). Approaching HaShem in some sense as a person or personality is requisite for making sense of this narrative, a person communicating with others in a variety of speech acts, from commands, to promises, to declarations. The Jewish studies scholar Jacob Neusner notes that a conception of this God as a full-fledged person or "incarnation" did not emerge in Jewish traditions until the end of the sixth century CE with the redaction of the *Bavli* or Babylonian Talmud (Neusner 1988, 165). Before then, texts portray this God as the creator of the universe and deliverer of the Torah, and as a person to whom prayer is addressed (Neusner 1988, ix). The Talmud moves beyond personhood to incarnation because HaShem exhibits emotional traits like human beings, performing actions like humans do in the way they do them (Neusner 1988, ix). The point I want us to grasp here is that—while it might be explained in later Jewish tradition—*how* this God communicates with other figures in the covenants and narratives is a question that Tanak narrative suspends. But *that* this God communicates is granted.

HaShem's use of language to communicate is both performative and creative. This God brings things into existence by way of speech, but also issues commands, makes promises, confers blessings, and even asks questions. In the first division of the creation narrative in *Bereshit* or Genesis, HaShem uses speech to "initiate each stage of creation" (Cherbonnier 1962, 192–3). Alter writes, "Each day begins with God's world-making utterance" (Alter 1981, 143). "No performative could be purer," writes literary studies scholar Michael Hancher (Hancher 1988, 27). It may seem as if this God issues commands or directives for entities to exist. As Hancher states, "directives are supposed to influence the actions of a hearer—and of course there is no hearer present at the beginning of Genesis" (Hancher 1988, 28). Declarations, rather than commands, bring about changes in referenced objects solely in light of successful performance of them. Commands, alternatively, can result in failure if the listener does not accomplish what they are commanded to do. Declarations, however, do not admit of this contingency. By way of their very performance, they are successful. This is a dynamic of discourse presupposed throughout Semitic conceptions of the "built-in efficacy of the uttered word" (Vawter 1977, 41).

The God of the Torah makes promises or covenants, too. As with HaShem's creative utterances, covenant discourse establishes "extralinguistic conventions and institutions" (Alster-Elata and Salmon 1993, 27). These instances of discourse change the world as such. Covenants differ from promises. Promises are unilateral, where one person commits herself to future action and fulfills (or fails to fulfill) the promise. Covenants, as literary scholars Gerda Alster-Elata and Rachel Salmon note, "always involve mutuality as a necessary condition" (Alster-Elata and Salmon 1993, 27). It requires both parties to the covenant to maintain the speech. When a person does not live up to their share of the commitment, the covenant is rendered null and void. When it comes to covenants with the God, however, they are not dissolved if one party (namely, fallible human beings) fails to live up to their part. Divine covenants bring about permanent changes in the world (see Alster-Elata and Salmon 1993, 28). Yet a surprising feature of such covenants is that they are initiated by the God. In all human-to-human covenants, where people "cut a deal" with one another, it is the weaker party who initiates and requests the agreement. Typically, a sort of asymmetry exists between the covenanters, where one is a foreigner to the land, such as Abraham is to Abimelech in Gen. 21:22-34, and "the party which feels threatened initiates the covenantal process" (Alster-Elata and Salmon 1993, 29). It seems, then, that *HaShem occupies the structurally weaker position in initiating covenants.* The first one, with Noah, depicts human beings as only passive. The rainbow, for instance, is not really a sign for human beings but a reminder for HaShem as indicated in Gen. 9:14-15. "When I bring clouds over the earth, and the bow appears in the sky, *I will remember* my covenant between me and you and every living creature among all flesh, so that the waters shall never again become a flood to destroy all flesh" (emphasis added). The sign communicates the remembrance to human beings, bestowing on them a sign and therewith the capacity for sign use and language in general. That is, they can use this sign, and signs, to communicate with HaShem (Alster-Elata and Salmon 1993, 35). HaShem and human beings thus share a universe of discourse.

Human beings play a more active role in the second covenant. The God of the Torah initiates it through the call to Abraham to leave his motherland, and HaShem offers a number of promised incentives if Abraham follows the call. Abraham grows suspicious after the promises seem to go unfulfilled, and HaShem reiterates them. Abraham asks, "O Lord God, how shall I know that I am to possess it?" (Gen. 15:8). Abraham's question transforms HaShem's promises into a genuine covenant, by challenging HaShem (see Alster-Elata and Salmon 1993, 37). In answer to the question, HaShem gives Abraham a sign: a "flaming pot" passing between a hallway of severed carcasses Abraham prepared. Abraham literally "cut" a covenant with the God. This ritual practice in the ancient world indicated that the one who passes through the hallway will end up like the carcasses if they do not follow through on their commitments. That is, HaShem conveys to Abraham that Abraham (or his descendants) can kill HaShem if HaShem does not live up to the covenant. What else were human beings doing in building the tower of Babel except to storm the heavens? This stands in stark contrast to the immortal omnibeing of philosophical theology. Can human beings attempt to kill the omnibeing? For Alster-Elata and Salmon, this "cutting" underscores the performative rather than merely referential quality of HaShem's making a covenant, where the act brings about the convergence between divine discourse and human discourse (Alster-Elata and Salmon 1993, 37).

This God's discourse is similarly performative in questions asked. An especially fascinating question asked in Job, however, is HaShem's to HaSatan (the adversary), "Where did you just come from?" (Job 1:7). This seems like a paradigmatic sincere question requesting information that the questioner does not yet have. There are many more questions ascribed to HaShem in Job, over sixty-eight rhetorical questions in a row in reaction to Job's lament, such as "Were you there when I laid the earth's foundation?" The Hebrew Bible scholar Michael V. Fox claims that this God uses such questions to establish and exploit a "special intimacy" between interrogator and listener (Fox 1981, 58). According to Fox, such questions purportedly ask for something which both the questioner and listener know, and the listener knows that the questioner knows the listener knows. This spiral of knowledge underlies these questions and binds the interlocutors. According to Fox, rhetorical questions establish intimacy because they make the listener accept the questioner's claims "out of his own consciousness rather than having the information imposed on him from the outside" (Fox 1981, 58). This God appears to pile up questions so as to elicit an "about-face" from Job's lament. Many of these questions revolve around the interrogative word "who," as in Job 38:5: "Do you know who fixed [the earth's] dimensions, or who measured it with a line?" For Job, the seemingly irresistible and inevitable "answer" to these questions is "you, HaShem." In these questions, HaShem "reminds" Job that Job himself already knows who made the universe, who is in charge of it. The God of the Tanak overwhelms Job with the obvious "by opening his eyes to what he already knows" (Fox 1981, 59). Even if we disagree about rhetorical questions establishing a "special intimacy," we can nevertheless see that this God's use of questions is an important discursive strategy.

Using questions to elicit consent from another person is neither a sincere nor genuine use of questions in our senses of those terms. A sincere question would require that the questioner does not know the information and uses the question to acquire it. A genuine question is open-ended such that one's understanding and horizons might be broadened through considering what another person has to say. For a genuine question, HaShem would need to be open to understanding things in a new light. And this would presumably happen in dialogue with another person. Does HaShem change HaShem's mind? While the God of the Torah does not bend on already issued decrees, the Hebrew Bible scholar Robert Chisholm argues that many of this God's statements of intention are not decrees (Chisholm 1995, 389). As Chisholm asks, "Under what conditions does [HaShem] retract a statement or deviate from an intended course of action? Under what conditions does [HaShem] refuse to do so?" (Chisholm 1995, 389). Decrees are unconditional, binding "the speaker to a course of action" (Chisholm 1995, 389). Mere announcements of intent have a conditional element and "do not necessarily bind the speaker to a stated course of action" (Chisholm 1995, 389). Jacob, for example, requires Esau to swear an oath to give Jacob his birthright in Gen. 25:32-33. Whereas Esau's first response—in the form of a rhetorical question—announced his intention, swearing an oath made the transfer unconditionally binding. The same distinction applies in Joseph's promise to bury Jacob (now renamed Israel) in Canaan in Gen. 47:28-30. Israel requires Joseph to swear an oath, not merely express an intention.

This distinction applies within HaShem's discourse, too. On the one hand, this God's covenant with Abraham in Gen. 22:16-18 unconditionally binds them, though the timing of fulfilment is indeterminate. On the other hand, in Gen. 12:1-2, the God of the Torah calls to Abraham, and asks him to leave his family and home while promising to make his name great. The fulfilment of the promise, though, is contingent on Abraham's performance. The point here is that any ascription of absolute unchanging state of mind to HaShem is specific only to those unconditional decrees, but not to HaShem's announcements of intent more generally. This God changes their mind, for example, in Exod. 32:10, where HaShem angrily expresses the intent to destroy all the Hebrews in the wilderness and generate a new nation solely out of Moses. Were this a decree, HaShem would seemingly have to follow through on it. Moses persuades HaShem to change course, however, by appealing to HaShem's reputation, pleading, and reminding HaShem of the unconditional covenant they made with the Patriarchs in Exod. 32:11-14. An additional example can be noted in the book of Jonah, where Jonah pronounces HaShem's intention to destroy Nineveh. The people's response to avert the God's judgment and destruction is appropriate. Indeed, HaShem's change of mind as a result elicits Jonah's criticism of HaShem's choosing mercy over justice.

As these examples illustrate, the God of the Torah is capable of taking into consideration what another person says or does. On the whole, however, HaShem seems to ask mainly rhetorical questions and a few merely sincere questions to request information. Is HaShem capable of having their horizon expanded through sharing a genuine question with another?

Questions between the Lines: Does HaShem Seek Understanding with Others?

I want to return to our selected passage within the second version of the creation story (Gen. 2:4b-2:25). The third instance of discourse uttered by the God is a question, following a directive ("Don't eat of the tree") and expression of concern ("It's not good that Adam is alone"). We can develop the argument that this God is the first figure in the entire Tanak to have a genuine interrogative statement ascribed to them. That is, HaShem seems to be the first figure to ask a question in the Hebrew Bible. I am interested in whether this first question is either a sincere one or a genuine one.

It is not readily apparent in English translations that HaShem asks the first question, though. In most English translations, the serpent apparently asks the first question (Gen. 3:1): "Did God really say You shall not eat of any tree in the garden?" The statement in the Hebrew, however, is not a question. The question seems to be implied, as the religious studies scholar Hugh C. White writes, "by the interjectional use of the conjunction אַף (indeed, even, really)" (White 1991, 130). The serpent is not asking a question but is attempting to provoke *Isha*, or Eve, to put her on the defensive through deliberate overstatement of the God's prohibition. In this way, the serpent is trying to draw out her reaction. Alter revises the serpent's statement like this: "Though God said, you shall not eat from any tree in the garden—" (Alter 2004, 24). Isha then interrupts the serpent to correct them. We should note that HaShem's prohibition was said to Adam, so Isha probably only had knowledge of it second-hand. Is her knowledge and interpretation reliable? Regardless, deliberate provocation is not a sincere or genuine question. Rather than the serpent, the God seems to pose the very first question in the text ("Where are you?"), and perhaps this first question is itself a genuine one. Let us try to make a case that this is an exceptional instance where this God asks a genuine question at least once.

This question occurs in one of the most mysterious and enigmatic episodes in the Torah, an episode concerning the origins of the human condition. The primordial human beings hide from HaShem upon hearing HaShem moving through the garden. What they hide, though, is that they have covered themselves with makeshift clothing. That is, they hide that they are hiding parts of themselves in light of the apparently sexual knowledge gained from eating "fruit" from the tree of knowledge of good and bad. They hide their breech of HaShem's prohibition, the content of which they could not really understand—that if they eat of it, they will die (see Kierkegaard 1980).

The God calls out to Adam and Isha, asking, "Where are you?" This is the question that is on the lines. The original Hebrew of Gen. 3:9 is: וַיִּקְרָא יְהוָה אֱלֹהִים אֶל־הָאָדָם וַיֹּאמֶר לוֹ אַיֶּכָּה (The Lord God called out to the man and said to him, "Where are you?"). Is it a sincere question or a genuine question or merely a rhetorical question? What aspect of the human condition is this episode about, though? In juxtaposition with Qoheleth's lament about death rendering life meaningless, for example, this episode seems to be an argument in favor of death making life meaningful (see Forman 1960). At issue for us, however, is the philosophical interest in this God's capacity to reach an understanding with others through genuine questions.

We seem to be able to read the question as a genuine one. In the Midrash on Genesis, the *Aggadat Bereshit*, the interrogative word *ayeka* (אַיֶּכָּה) troubles the Amoraim or rabbis. It challenges their conception of the divine as omniscient. They interpret the question as an expression of wonderment. They say, "God wonders about man and says, 'Pull yourself together and tell me what happened to your former high stature'" (see Shuchat 2006, 365). For the rabbis, this question can only mean that, as the rabbi Wilfred Shuchat writes, "God wanted Adam to explain his behavior and to confront the nature of the situation in which he found himself. Thus, from the sages' view, the plain translation could not be 'where are you,' but instead, 'Where do you stand?'" (Shuchat 2006, 11–12). Rashi, the medieval French scriptural commentator, reiterates this precedent. In his commentary on Genesis, he adds that *the purpose of the question is so HaShem and Adam can enter into dialogue.* He writes, "He knew where he was, but [he asked him this] *in order to enter into conversation with him*" (Rashi 2008; my emphasis). Rather than approaching the interrogative word as indicating a sincere question or typical interrogative statement, the rabbis read *ayeka* as expressing a genuine question. It is, as the Torah scholar Avivah Zornberg explains, "a conversation opener" (Zornberg 2006, 207). By way of this question, Adam and Eve's responses are "courted by God" (Zornberg 2006, 209).

Adam appears to respond to it as if it were a genuine question, explaining and attesting to what has happened—that he and Isha believed they should hide their hiddenness. Further questions and responses unfold from there. While the question might seem like it is merely a sincere question for information, the way Adam and Isha respond locates it closely within the possibility of being a genuine question. The dialogue becomes complicated— in the sense of needing further dialogue—immediately. The question and response are not so disarmingly simple (cf. White 1991, 139). Rather than responding with what eventually becomes the customary "Here I am" in later divine and human interactions such as with Samuel, Adam recounts why he hid: "I was afraid because I was naked" (Gen. 3:10). However, as we noted, Adam and Isha are *not* naked. What they hide is not their nakedness but their clothing or covering, the covering that represents one's hiding one's nakedness. To put this differently, Adam and Isha hide their explicit markings of their change in perspective to where they now divide the world into what is permissible to show and what must be concealed (see White 1991, 139).

Adam does not evade the question, though. He does not merely confess, either. Adam's response counts as an explanation and focus on the conditions that make HaShem's question a live possibility. What makes it possible for HaShem to ask the question? It is because Adam has gained a new perspective on things and has acted in accord with that new perspective, and thus can be asked for it. Adam and Isha's actions have disturbed the pristine order into which HaShem has divided the world, and this disruption seems to disorient HaShem. Their actions provide the conditions of the possibility of HaShem's posing a genuine question. Adam takes more initiative upon himself than is required if HaShem's question is merely a sincere one. Not only does Adam imply where he is—hiding—he also goes beyond that by explaining why he is hiding.

On this possible reading, HaShem hears Adam's response but does not completely understand what Adam has said, and so HaShem poses further questions (3:11): "Who told you... did you eat of the tree?" It does not make any sense that Adam would be afraid to be naked before the creator of that very body. The questions indicate trouble with orientation, with what is going on, and request that Adam be even more specific, especially with regard to the causal chain that has led all involved to this point. These questions can be described as "penetrating communication barriers to bring to light that which is hidden" (White 1991, 140). These questions point to an alienation between the dialogue partners, a breakdown and need for repair of the relationship. Yet rather than merely "penetrating" the subject matter or "repairing" the communicative process, they actually facilitate it, as Rashi explains. By means of the question, HaShem and Adam and Isha begin to reach a new understanding and fusion of horizons.

Adam responds to the further questions by saying, "The woman You put by my side—she gave me of the tree and I ate" (Gen. 3:12). The Hebrew Bible scholar Joel Rosenberg describes this as a denial or evasion of culpability, pointing away from himself to Isha (see Rosenberg 1984, 52). The religious studies scholar W. Lee Humphreys describes this as an excuse that shifts blame to Isha and, indirectly, to HaShem (Humphreys 2001, 46). White describes this as a defensive shield behind which Adam further hides and uses it to deflect the "thrust" of interrogation to Isha (White 1991, 141). What leads so many to caricature Adam as merely evasive and escapist is that they all read the God's questions as sincere interrogations rather than as genuine questions. Are we really to believe that Adam defensively implicates Isha and HaShem by merely relaying the facts of what transpired? It is not as if Adam asked to have the trauma of Isha being created out of his "rib" while under a kind of divine anesthesia. That is, HaShem said that it was not good for Adam to be alone. Adam did not express loneliness and did not ask to be ripped apart. Is Adam's "At last..." (Gen. 2:23) an expression of satisfaction or a gesture to have HaShem stop? Moreover, Isha *did* give him the fruit. Again, it seems that Adam can be read as going above and beyond what is asked in a sincere question for information. Moreover, HaShem seems to show that HaShem hears what Adam says. HaShem does not express disagreement, nor does the later "curse" mention anything about Adam's speaking evasively. Is Gen. 3:14-17 really a curse or just a description of what life is going to be like for human beings under the conditions of death? Reading the God's question as genuine helps readers to make sense of HaShem with regard to the surrounding direct discourse, the dialogue that ensues between HaShem and the primordial people.

Some authors believe that the Hebrew Bible can be integrated into the question, "Who is the Lord?" (see Ricoeur 1995, 185). On this reading of the God asking a genuine question, instead we can say the question is, "Where are you?" When HaShem calls to Abraham, Jacob, Samuel, and others, HaShem always seems to begin with asking (explicitly or implicitly), "Where are you?" As such, a divine and human dialogue is constitutive of the world of the text of the Torah. There seems to be sufficient warrant to read this question as a genuine question.

I have argued throughout this chapter that there seems to be at least one exceptional case where HaShem asks another character a genuine question. This God usually interrogates or overwhelms others with questions, which makes this instance exceptional. It seems ambiguous, though. This ambiguity is really only resolvable on the level of narration, where the reader engages with the text in the determination of the plot. The meaning this can have for the reader, then, depends on the larger dialogue about the plot within which this option fits as a "fact" or "on the lines" within the story. We will turn to this aspect of engaging the text in Part III of the book. For now, let us turn to look at other deific figures to whom questions are ascribed.

Ancestor Ma Asks, "Why Are You Seeking Outside?"

What is going on in the passage below?

When Ta-chu [Dazhu] came to see the Patriarch for the first time, the Patriarch asked him, "Where are you coming from?" "I am coming from Ta-yün [Dayun] Monastery in Yüeh-chou [Yuezhou]." replied Ta-chu. The Patriarch asked him, "What is your intention in coming here?" Ta-chu said, "I have come here to seek the Buddhadharma." The Patriarch said, "Without looking at your own treasure, for what purpose are leaving your home and walking around? Here I do not have a single thing. What Buddhadharma are you looking for?" Ta-chu bowed, and asked, "What is Hui-hai's [Huihai's] own treasure?" The Patriarch said, "That which is asking me right now is your own treasure—perfectly complete, it lacks nothing. You are free to use it; *why are you seeking outside?*" Upon hearing this, Ta-chu realized the original mind without relying on knowledge and understanding. Overjoyed, he paid his respects to the Patriarch and thanked him. After this he stayed with him for six years and served him as his disciple. Later he returned [to Yüeh-chou] and composed a treatise entitled *Essentials of Entering the Way Through Sudden Awakening* in one chuan [juan]. When the Patriarch saw the text, he said to the assembly, "In Yüeh-chou there is a great pearl (ta-chu); its perfect brilliance shines freely without obstruction."
(Cheng Chein 1992, 69–70, emphasis added; see also Jia 2006, 128–9)

In this quotation, there is an enlightened master whose Dharma equals that of the historical Buddha and a novice disciple, and—despite what seems to be an earlier depiction of this master as sitting on the throne of pronouncements—the master asks a number of questions that at least on the surface seem to be sincere and, perhaps, even genuine. I want to know whether it is a "fact" of the narrative, whether it is "right there in the text," that the Chan master Mazu asks a genuine surplus-driven question (see Dickman 2020). I am also curious about whether it is in the text that this master asks a sincere, but deficit-driven, question. Again, recall Fish's criticism that asserting what is right there in the text is one of the best games in town within the canons of interpretive acceptability. And again, our development of the concept of semantic autonomy from both writer intent and reader caprice helps us isolate interpretive possibilities within respectable constraints.

In this chapter, I argue that there is at least one exceptional case where Mazu might be asking other characters a genuine question. I argue this is exceptional because, as we will see, Mazu usually uses questions to interrogate others or overwhelm others. In what follows, I want first to provide some context of Buddhist traditions to help develop ways the *Mazu yulu* frames Mazu as equal to Gautama Buddha through mind-to-mind transmission of the Dharma. In such literature, masters emerge in front of the text as social and virtual constructions rather than historical descriptions of past people behind the book. This step will prepare us to survey a number of questions attributed to Mazu and other classical Chan masters to develop traits of character inferable from them. We will primarily address what is "on the lines" and "between the lines," and to focus on one peculiar question, the last question posed to a disciple who realizes enlightenment in response to the question, "Why are you seeking outside?" This is the exegetical hermeneutic circle. We will save questions about what is behind and beyond the lines, or the existential hermeneutic circle, for Chapter 8.

Preliminary Clarification: Classical Chan Masters Are Constructed as Buddhas

Chan, or Zen as it is better known in Western popular culture, is one among many traditions in the broad movement of Mahayana Buddhism (see Williams 2009). The Mahayana movement was opened by the first-century philosopher Nagarjuna's radical critique and developments in Madhyamaka philosophy (Nagarjuna 1995; Westerhorff 2009). Just as there is no such thing as "Christianity" or "Islam," there is no such thing as "Buddhism"—because all such labels within the world religions paradigm reify complex and highly differentiated cultural phenomena. As Masuzawa explains, the world religions paradigm, expediently inaugurated in the mid-1800s, serves the interests of European empire and colonialism (Masuzawa 2005). If someone asks, "What do Muslims believe?" the first response should be "Which Muslims?" The same applies when someone asks, "What do Buddhists believe?" Our first response should be "Which Buddhists?" While "Buddhism" is often characterized as atheistic by Westerners, even

Theravadin Buddhist texts such as Jataka tales about the historical Buddha's past lives include many references to *devas* or Gods and Goddesses, many from the ancient Indian milieu within which Buddhisms emerged (see Faure 2009, 59). In broad terms, the issue is that even Gods need to realize nirvana or awakening. In Mahayana, celestial Buddhas and Bodhisattvas take some precedent over Gods and Goddesses because like all other beings in samsara or cyclical existence, they too require enlightenment through realization of the Buddhist Dharma or ultimate truth. All things possess an inherent Buddhanature, or the potential to be a Buddha. Chan Buddhism picks up on this theme, claiming that—through "mind-to-mind" or direct, immediate, and wordless transmission of the Dharma—Chan masters, like Mazu, are equal to Gautama Buddha (Wright 1998, 140–1). Given this doctrinal backdrop, it is possible to read Mazu as not just a historical person but as a deific figure.

Mazu is among the most notorious of classical Chan masters. Mazu Daoyi (馬祖道一, 709–788 CE) and multiple generations of his successors, collectively referred to as the Hongzhou School, set the norms for Zen practice. As the Chan studies scholar John R. McRae writes,

> This is when Chan appears to have become really Chan, when Chan masters seem to have really behaved like Chan masters... Here the locus of religious practice was firmly removed from individual effort in the meditation hall and replaced by a demanding genre of interrogation that sought to destabilize all habitual, logical patterns.
>
> (McRae 2003, 19)

Rather than using direct expository language in order to elaborate and explain the ultimate truth, or Dharma, the classical literature depicts masters such as Mazu attempting to "demonstrate it by means of paradoxical replies and inexplicable counterquestions, gestures and physical demonstrations, and even the shocking and painful tactics of shouts and blows" (McRae 2003, 76). The standard version of Mazu's life and teaching is the *Jiangxi Mazu Daoyi chanshi yulu* (江西馬祖道一禪師語錄, "Record of the sayings of Chan Master Mazu Daoyi of Jiangxi," referred to as the *Mazu yulu*), first published as part of the *Sijia yulu* ("Records of the Sayings of Four Masters") during the Northern Song dynasty from 960 to 1126 CE (Poceski 2004, 44–5; and Jia 2006, 53). The *Sijia yulu* also includes the records of three generations of Mazu's Dharma heirs: Baizhang Huaihai (749–814 CE), Huangbo Xiyun (d. 850 CE), and Linji Yixuan (d. 866 CE). However, the earliest extant version of this collection is an edition from the late Ming dynasty, which lasted from 1368 to 1644 CE (Poceski 2004, 55). The compilation date of the collection is nonetheless verifiable with probability by the preface date, preserved in the Ming edition, corresponding to November 20, 1085 CE. While this may not tell us much, it does suggest that the text probably circulated before this time—though the preface may have just been recycled into the compilation from a text that bore few similarities to this compilation. There is no independent documentation suggesting that Mazu's discourse records existed as an integral whole prior to its inclusion in the collection. As the Chan studies scholar Mario Poceski points out, "That means that the [*Mazu yulu*] was compiled almost three centuries after Mazu's death," where Mazu and his Dharma heirs flourished during the Tang dynasty which lasted from 618 to 907 CE (Poceski 2004, 55).

The *Mazu yulu* abides by the convention and standards of the "records of sayings" genre. *Yulu*, as Schlütter defines it, "refers to sermons and talks given by a master, and sometimes addresses encounters and dialogues he had with others, which purport to have been recorded and written down by someone who was present at the occasion" (Schlütter 2004, 183). *Yulu* proper center a specific master. Poceski compares the *Mazu yulu* to a quilt in that it consists of a patchwork of various literary genres, some of which preexisted the final edition of the text and others that were contemporaneous with its consolidation (Poceski 2004, 64). Mazu's *yulu* has three main parts: a biography, a collection of sermons, and a collection of encounter dialogues. Most episodes in *yulu* depict enlightened masters in rhetorical occasions where the master *says* something assumed to manifest their Buddhahood—hence the *yu* ("discourse") of the *yulu* ("discourse records"). These rhetorical interactions, or *jiyuan wenda* ("encounter dialogues"), involve both a master and a student or some other foil where the master often tests the state of mind of the student, tries to solicit awakening from the student, or transmits their Dharma to the student. The phrase "*jiyuan wenda*" literally refers to "a question-and-answer [full of] karmic potentiality" (see Yanagida 1983). Can genuine and ordinary questions have explosive potential?

The biographical sketch is traceable to a stele inscription and a short stone inscription, both composed in 791 CE, only three years after Mazu's death, written by renowned literati on familiar terms with Mazu and his disciples. The sermons are corroborated by numerous quotations or allusions in the earlier material by Baizhang and Huangbo, as well as the parallel structures to their own sermons. The writings of a famous Chan historian, Guifeng Zongmi (780–841 CE), display familiarity with Mazu's sermons, indicating that they were read in the early ninth century. Despite hagiographic embellishments of the biographical sketch and the mere circumstantial evidence surrounding the sermons, it seems reasonable to assume that these two sections of the *Mazu yulu* provide readers with a roughly accurate historical image of Mazu as a fairly traditional teacher of Chan Buddhist doctrine. The main elements of his biography, sermons, and dialogues are also depicted in the *Zutang ji* ("Anthology of the Patriarchal Hall"), compiled by 952 CE, and the *Jingde chuandeng lu* ("Record of the Transmission of the Lamp [from the] Jingde [Imperial period of the Northern Song]"), presented to the Song court in 1004 CE. Through a system of patronage, Mazu's style of Chan came to dominate all other forms of Buddhism in China for nearly 100 years (McRae 2003, 109).

Every era constructs its own "classics," where what is currently considered classical is projected into an idealized past (see Amoros et al. 1994). We need to distinguish between early Chan on the one hand, spanning roughly from 700 to 900 CE, and "classical Chan" on the other hand, as early Chan is constructed in the *Zutang ji* and the *Jingde chuundeng lu* (see McRae 2003, 16). We should call Mazu's era "classical Chan" because of the way it is "remembered" or reconstructed in this later transmission literature. Through this distinction, we can pay greater attention to the role language and rhetoric play in classical Chan—which is not a historical period but a genre of Chan literature. These texts purport to be *recordings* of eighth- and ninth-century Chan masters like Mazu and their interactions with students. Yet however much these texts might appear as if they are accurate records of originally spontaneous oral interactions, the basic problem with this literary veneer is the fact that they were not completed until well after the early Chan masters flourished. In other words, however much the works bear marks of orality and realism, they are texts and must be approached as literary constructions rather than accurate historical records (see Faure 1986, and Berling 1987). This problematic rhetoric of "records" of spoken discourse is compounded by the texts' historical inaccuracy. For example, in the *Jingde chuandeng lu*, Bodhidharma leads a sect of Chan that did not exist until centuries after his lifetime, and ancient Buddhas speak in Chan riddles (see Wright 1998, 110).

The case of the encounter dialogues is our clue to the constructed quality of classical Chan and masters like Mazu who are equal to Gautama Buddha. None of the Tang period sources have encounter dialogues in them. The *Zutang ji* contains versions of five dialogues of the thirty-two in the *Mazu yulu*. The *Jingde chuandeng lu* contains a larger amount of the dialogues with only minor differences. These "transmission histories" served as, Schlütter points out, "a kind of who's who of Chan masters—and anyone in the Song interested in Chan would have been very familiar with these lists" (Schlütter 2008, 9). The radical and iconoclastic image of Mazu in the dialogues is a construction of the Chan imaginary of the Song dynasty. At least for the most part. The Chan studies scholar Jinhua Jia argues, for instance, that some of the dialogues can be authenticated historically (Jia 2006, 55). These dialogues are our main focus since it is here that Mazu asks most of his questions.

Encounter dialogue is a notoriously difficult concept to determine. As McRae remarks, "No clearly stated definition of encounter dialogues appears in the scholarship on Chinese Chan... The very nature of the subject matter militates against concise definition" (McRae 2003, 77). McRae's proposed definition can be summarized as follows: encounter dialogues are written transcriptions of what were presumably originally spoken exchanges, a peculiar type of oral practice where masters use various verbal and physical methods to facilitate the enlightenment of students (McRae 2000, 47–8). McRae intentionally excludes in his definition "questions that seek to elicit explanations about Buddhist doctrine or the spiritual path in general, as well as answers that seek to provide information" (McRae 2000, 48). Such descriptive or referential discourse falls outside the scope of the encounter dialogue subgenre because they lack the performative quality where masters attempt to "speak to the needs of an actual seeker in the immediate present" (McRae 2000, 48).

At the basis of the subgenre is the seeming spontaneous and immediate exchange between an enlightened master and an aspiring disciple, where the master uses a number of discursive devices, such as punning or paradox, and particularly exaggerated nonverbal gestures, such as twisting a disciple's nose or kicking them (Heine 2000, 139). "The impression of vivid immediacy," writes McRae, "is primarily a literary effect, a direct result of [the subgenre's] rhetorical style" (McRae 2003, 77). One convention of the genre is to omit the level of functions, to relay little to no circumstantial information. Thus, the context lacks texture, so much so that the dialogues appear to take place within a vacuum. Moreover, this convention serves to bring the level of action into the foreground by emphasizing the contrast between the locale in which the action takes place and the interaction between the master and disciple. In other words, the reader's attention is caught up straightaway in the action and the relationship between the speaking agents. Just like Alter's claim that narrative in the Torah emphasizes dialogue, this convention too focuses attention on dialogue. It is, then, primarily the actions and speech acts that define the subgenre.

The depiction of these rhetorical interactions between characters is understood in modern Western scholarship to bear characteristics of illocutionary language and *non sequitur* responses, responses that—according to Chan self-understanding—indirectly manifest enlightenment (Schlütter 2008, 92). McRae argues, however, that encounter dialogues represent a kind of interaction between master and student required by the genealogical structure of the Chan transmission tradition and genealogical lineage

(McRae 2003, 97). They are, in a sense, an instance of the Chinese transformation of the Indian *mārga* ("spiritual path"), the individual's progression from ignorance to enlightenment (see Hershock 2009, 36–7). This makes sense given the dynamically interactive cosmology and ontology presupposed in pre-Buddhist Chinese culture (see Mair 1983). Rather than the psychological journey of a solitary individual making gradual progress toward the *telos* of enlightenment, Chan spiritual cultivation and practice forced students into rhetorically engaged interaction. As the Buddhist studies scholar Robert Sharf writes, "[Chan] *mārga* treatises are not so much maps of inner psychic space as they are scripts for the performance of *an eminently public religious drama*" (Sharf 1995, 269; my emphasis). Thus, in Chan traditions, solitary spiritual progression shifts to interpersonal collaboration (McRae 2003, 98). We can isolate general patterns of the collaborative intersubjectivity of Chan spiritual cultivation in encounter dialogues, patterns that can help us isolate uses of questions in particular.

Questions on the Lines: Provocations Often, if Not Always, Occur in Encounter Dialogues

Encounter dialogues often read as spontaneous interactions and the exchange of *wenda* appears to be pre-reflective—in that the interchange, especially the responses of the master, flows back and forth without hesitation and reflection (Wright 1993, 36). Indeed, "immediacy" and "directness" are some of the highest forms of praise for the rhetorical practices of masters in transmission literature. Given that according to Buddhist doctrine a master has no self and thus no premeditated intentions, the Chan studies scholar Dale S. Wright argues, the master's role in dialogue reflects in a selfless way whatever is manifest or can become manifest in the moment (Wright 1998, 101). Consider the following example of prereflective response on the part of Mazu's peer, Shitou:

> A monk asked, "How does one get emancipated?" The Master [Shitou] said, "Who has ever put you in bondage?" Monk, "What is the Pure Land?" Master, "Who has ever defiled you?" Monk, "What is nirvana?" Master, "Who has ever subjected you to birth-and-death?"
> (quoted in Suzuki 1978, 105–7)

This excerpted example from transmission literature shows up as an isolated event, where it opens and closes in this brief span. After Shitou's question, the scene ends, then moves to the next encounter. Shitou's responses to the monk just bounce back, apparently without hesitation or reflection. This example of Shitou's agility and capacity to respond without hesitation illustrates the general virtuosity of masters to speak words well-suited to exposing the power of the present moment (Hershock 2009, 117). Hesitation or faltering as a consequence of premeditation would divulge a failure to attend undividedly to the contingencies of the situation (see Wright 1993, 37). In classical Chan self-understanding, the character and discourse of masters are functions of the *Dao*, or Way, rather than the premeditated acts of individuals.

Encounter dialogues also often depict masters comporting their behavior to contingent and situation specific circumstances. Consider the following example of the master Dongshan interacting with a student:

> One time when the master [Dongshan] was washing his bowls, he saw two birds contending over a frog. A monk who also saw this asked, "Why does it come to that?" The Master replied, "It is only for your benefit, Āchārya."
>
> (quoted in Foster and Shoemaker 1996, 122)

The contextual information referring to birds fighting over a frog, as well as the lament of the student, provides readers with knowledge of the contingent situation to which Dongshan responds. Encounter dialogues present masters as unhesitating and unflinching in the face of the central Buddhist realization of the impermanence, emptiness, and groundlessness of every contingency. As Wright characterizes such situational sensitivity of Chan masters, "The [Chan] master is the one who no longer seeks a solid ground, who realizes that all things and situations are supported, not by firm ground and solid self-nature, but rather by shifting and contingent relations" (Wright 1998, 100). Insofar as these characters are depicted as engaged in some form of dialogue, the meaning of their words also depends on the context, a context including not only words but also gestures, vocal inflection, and the entire existential setting in which spoken words occur (see Faure 1993, 227). In essence, the thinking of the masters is depicted as situational as opposed to categorical or principled.

Because of the conventions of the transmission literary genre, encounter dialogues arrange the characters hierarchically with regard to one another, though there are rare exceptions illustrating those instances where former students have themselves achieved mastery over Chan rhetoric (or "achieved enlightenment"). Consider the following two examples involving the master Linji and two different interlocutors, where the second example represents an instance breaking the norm of hierarchy establishment while simultaneously illustrating it:

1. Someone asked, "What was Bodhidharma's purpose in coming from the west?" The Master [Linji] said, "If he had a purpose, he wouldn't have been able to save even himself!" The questioner said, "If he had no purpose, then how did the Second Ancestor manage to get the Dharma?" The Master said, "Getting means not getting." "If it means not getting," said the questioner, "then what do you mean by 'not getting'?" The Master said, "You can't seem to stop your mind from racing around everywhere seeking something. That's why the Ancestor said, 'Hopeless fellows— using their heads to look for their heads!' You must right now turn your light around and shine it on yourselves, not go seeking somewhere else. Then you will understand that in body and mind you are no different from the Ancestors and buddhas, and that there is nothing to do. Do that and you may speak of 'getting the Dharma'" (Sasaki 2009, 28 and 265–6).
2. The Master [Linji] said to Xingshan, "How about that white ox on the bare ground?" Xingshan said, "Moo, moo!" The Master said, "Lost your voice?" Xingshan said, "How about you, Reverend?" The Master said, "This beast!" (Sasaki 2009, 38 and 302).

On first reading, these two encounter dialogues might appear unrelated because, on the one hand, a student consults Linji and, on the other hand, a student appears to rebel against him. Whereas a student seeks doctrinal clarification from Linji in the first example, Linji—insofar as he plays the role of master—is hardly consulting Xingshan for doctrinal clarification. Yet the difference between the stories is less important than their similarity here. As a result of the conventions of the genre, Linji in both cases usurps the role of commentator, judging the level of understanding of the student. In these kinds of interactions, the master represents the standpoint of enlightenment as heir to the lineage, and thus speaks from the position of authority. Is it authoritarian? In the case with Xingshan, it is not clear that Linji judges Xingshan as inferior—that is, his final words on the matter do not have the same condescension as when he discourages the questioner in the first case.

Encounter dialogues are often agonistic in nature. They are referred to as "Dharma battles" (Faure 1993, 213). The interactions between the characters exhibit the hierarchy because the interactions typically produce winners and losers. The method of the masters is often to pose an inescapable quandary and then to demand an immediate response—a game at which one can only expect to lose (see Wright 1993, 33). Masters pressure their students for response, a response that must be given under their judging gaze. Consider the following example involving Shitou and his student, Yueshan Weiyan:

> Yueshan... an enlightened monk, was doing [Chan meditation]. His master Shitou asked him, "What are you doing [Chan meditation] for?" Yueshan answered, "Not for anything." "That means you are sitting idly," said Shitou. Yueshan countered, "If this is sitting idly, then that would be for something." The master then said, "What is it that is not for anything?" The monk answered, "A thousand sages wouldn't know."
> (quoted in Sheng-yen 1988, 43)

Shitou is engaged here in a Dharma battle with his student, posing impossible questions demanding immediate responses to be subjected to his judgment. Yet, the student appears to have succeeded in demonstrating enlightenment, however inferior, insofar as the dialogue ends without the master's judgment and commentary. The orality of these interactions situates awakening and knowledge in the context of struggle and negotiation (see Faure 1993, 226).

A further convention is that the interchanges, especially on the part of the master, flow back and forth without hesitation and reflection (Wright 1993, 36). Closely related to this convention is the depiction of masters as comporting their behavior to the contingencies of the interaction, adapting themselves by "skillful means" to the actions of their interlocutors. The general virtuosity of masters involves speaking words well-suited to exposing the power of the present moment (Hershock 2009, 117). As Mazu claims, "The very words I now speak are nothing else but a function of the Way [*Dao*]" (Pas 1987, 40). Insofar as these characters are depicted as engaged in some form of dialogue, then, the meaning of their words also depends on the situation, a context including not only words but also gestures, vocal inflection, and the entire existential setting in which the spoken words occur.

Just as with any other discursive practices, the rhetoric of masters such as Mazu also bears the marks of performative language. A reader could, if so inclined, map out the various utterances according to the standard speech act taxonomy. However, as Fish points out, such an endeavor provides merely trivial information in interpreting a text (see Fish 1976). Encounter dialogues include illocutionary acts in that students often express their deluded states and masters declare judgments. And the rhetorical interactions are perlocutionary in that masters attempt to produce affects in their students. The performative character of the interactions seems to give privilege to formal positioning between the characters, where masters put students in their place, at the expense of semantic content, though masters often make numerous puns and references to various sutras. Moreover, the utterances of masters are not simply propositional acts asserting "truths" but are also attempts to impress those "truths" upon their interlocutors as well as to gain the upper hand (Faure 1993, 202). The speech is not representational but also illocutionary insofar as it is disruptive, transgressive, and throws the compulsive grasping of students into question (Wright 1992b, 128). The rhetorical practice of Chan masters like Mazu calls into question normal states of mind through undercutting and disrupting interlocutors engrained in the posture of a grasping subject, and this evokes disorientation in the student, which Wright suggests is essential to orienting oneself (Wright 1993, 31–2).

Within this genre of literature, and in the *Mazu yulu* specifically, questions appear to have a number of specific roles: on the one hand, as sincere questions or typical interrogatives in the hands of students; and on the other hand, as disruptive tactics in the hands of masters. Mazu initiates nine of his thirty-two dialogues by asking students a question. And in all, he poses over thirty-five questions in a small amount of space. For every action, there is an agent. However, the master is in many ways determined, McRae writes, "by the kind of interaction he had with his students" (McRae 1986, 95). Students are highly differentiated in that there is not simply one kind of student. The master often assumes the superior role by commenting on his interlocutor's action and speech. In these interactions, the master represents the standpoint of enlightenment as heir to the lineage, and thus speaks from the position of authority. The student interlocutor represents, as Foulk writes, "abject delusion, striving for awakening, or awakened insight rivaling that of the master, but always in the inferior position of being evaluated by the voice of the master" (Foulk 2000, 33).

There are three kinds of student questions corresponding to three kinds of students: the utterly lost, the halfway enlightened, and the enlightened rival. Nanquan Puyuan, one of Mazu's Dharma heirs, represents an enlightened rival in the second encounter dialogue in the *Mazu yulu*:

> Once, as Nan-ch'üan [Nanquan] was serving gruel to the community of monks, the Patriarch asked him, "What is in the bucket?" Nan-ch'üan said, "This old man should keep his mouth shut. What is all this talk about?" The Patriarch did not respond.
>
> (Cheng Chein 1992, 69)

Both Nanquan's challenging question and Mazu's lack of commentary show that Nanquan is a serious rival, a fact ultimately revealed in Nanquan's being an heir of Mazu, listed in the transmission genealogy.

The utterly lost and, at times, the halfway-enlightened students often ask typical interrogatives or sincere questions and presuppose that all syntactically correct interrogatives have cognitively significant answers (Rosemont 1970, 119). These students demand an answer, as one is liable to do with typical interrogatives, and so also attempt to subject the master to their demands—as is implicit in typical interrogatives. Baoche Magu, for example, asks two typical interrogatives in Mazu's ninth dialogue:

> One day as Ch'an Master Pao-ch'e of Ma-ku [Baoche of Magu] was accompanying the Patriarch for a walk, he asked, "What is the Great Nirvāna?" "Quickly!" exclaimed the Patriarch. "What quickly?" asked Pao-ch'e. "Look at the water," said the Patriarch.
>
> (Ching Chein 1992, 73)

We can generalize from these examples to the description that the performative character of student questions is often sincere, though their challenging questions break with this structure.

Some of Mazu's questions seem to be sincere, where he asks a question and receives information. This description is contestable, though. It could be the case that masters are always testing their students or potential students, even with those seemingly simple questions. This possibility is grounded firmly on a constellation of expectations cultivated by both elements of the genre and familiarity with a specific interpretive community, expectations that are not universally shared. Going by what is merely "on the lines," some of Mazu's questions appear to be sincere questions though the subgenre simultaneously challenges this reading of them. For instance, Mazu initiates dialogue thirty-two by asking, "Where are you coming from?" His interlocutor answers with, "I am coming from Hu-nan (South of the lake)" (Cheng Chein 1992, 73). Most questions posed by Mazu, however, break with the structure of sincere questions. They do not bear the marks of typical interrogatives because they neither dictate an answer nor reduce their listeners to a mere means for the acquisition of information. In the twenty-first dialogue, Mazu asks the following of a challenger:

> Someone asked, "What is the meaning of [Bodhidharma's] coming from the West?" "What is the meaning of your asking at precisely this moment?" replied the Patriarch.
>
> (Wright 1998, 215)

The Asian philosophy scholar Henry Rosemont, Jr., explains that the perlocutionary dimension of masters' questions such as the one above has the specific intent to elicit a particular response from students, to shock students out of their ordinary thinking and catapult them into enlightenment (Rosemont 1970, 117). Rather than interrogating others in order to settle things with answers, Mazu's questions often unsettle things and open them up (Wright 1993, 32). For another example, speaking with Shigong Huicang when Shigong was a hunter, Mazu asked, "How many deer can you shoot with a single arrow?" He then proceeds to criticize Shigong for his inability to shoot the entire herd with a single arrow (Cheng Chein 1992, 71). Eventually, Shigong becomes one of Mazu's Dharma heirs.

Questions between the Lines: Does Mazu Seek Understanding with Others?

The comparative religions scholar Judith A. Berling claims that the masters use language in a peculiar way to destroy any final meaningfulness of language. In so doing, she thinks, they point beyond themselves to a state that must be experienced to be understood; this state can at best be momentarily glimpsed through experiencing the master (Berling 1987, 62). The aim is to facilitate the other's self-realization, not to acquire information. The questions do not call for information but call forth the students themselves. Even though utterly lost and halfway-enlightened student questions are typically interrogative, masters are characters in the drama who can neither be commanded by nor subjected to the intentions of those who seek to reduce them. The questions masters themselves pose are rarely interrogative, and instead are somehow disruptive of the grasping implicit in typical interrogatives. Thus, students continually reinforce the "ontological difference" or dualism between themselves and masters, and the masters continually call that duality into question, presumably to reveal the inherent Buddhanature of all things—including the students themselves.

These norms of the dramatic discourse, however, do not entail that the masters can never be read as speaking in *ordinary* language—as in posing genuine questions, for these too, as we have seen in Part I, disrupt the implicit grasping of typical interrogatives. Excluding this kind of question from their repertoire would seem to reinscribe the idolization that their discourse clearly attempts to suspend. While they indeed employ a number of disruptive and transgressive strategies to elicit the self-realization of students—such as yelling and hitting—genuine questions too can preserve this basic orientation while simultaneously defending against the strong temptation to idolize the masters.

Rather than the flamboyant and ferocious actions of masters, in this one exceptional case it may be a genuine question that insinuates the presence of a shared horizon between the ordinary and the extraordinary and so allow for the transmission of the Dharma. A candidate for a genuine question occurs in Mazu's fourth dialogue. It takes place between himself and Dazhu Huihai, one of his Dharma heirs, on what appears to be their first encounter:

> Ta-chu bowed, and asked, "What is Hui-hai's [Huihai's] own treasure?" The Patriarch said, "That which is asking me right now is your own treasure—perfectly complete, it lacks nothing. You are free to use it; *why are you seeking outside?*" Upon hearing this, Ta-chu realized the original mind without relying on knowledge and understanding. Overjoyed, he paid his respects to the Patriarch and thanked him. After this he stayed with him for six years and served him as his disciple. Later he returned [to Yüeh-chou] and composed a treatise entitled *Essentials of Entering the Way Through Sudden Awakening* in one *chuan*.
>
> (Cheng Chein 1992, 69–70; Jia 2006, 55)

The central question at issue for my reading is Mazu's asking, "Why are you seeking outside?" For the original reads: 何假向外求觅。(*he jia xiang wai qiu mi*). The interrogative word, "*he*" (何) means "why." Mazu asks five questions in this encounter dialogue, and they form a crescendo that climaxes with the question that appears to trigger Dazhu's realization of the Chan thesis—shared by various other Mahayana traditions—of radical nonduality between who one is and one's Buddhanature. In his sermons accompanying the encounter dialogues in his records of sayings, Mazu expounds upon the Mahayana promotion of inherent Buddhanature of all sentient beings, derived from the notion of the *tathāgatagarbha*, as it pertains to the individual striving for enlightenment (Poceski 2007, 168–79). He teaches there that, for instance, "All of you should believe that your mind is Buddha, that this mind is identical with Buddha" (Cheng Chein 1992, 62). Upon posing a question to his student, Mazu appears to elicit realization of this. Here, the connection between an interrogative act and a broader event of understanding obtains.

Each question builds upon the preceding ones in the sequence. The first question is merely a typical interrogative, a request for information. The second question is also a typical interrogative, but more intense and personal in that it asks about an intention. The third and fourth questions are what we can call "examination questions." These are among the most common questions posed by Chan masters. The following encounter dialogue provides further illustration of this kind of question:

> Once Hsi-t'ang [Xitang], Pai-chang [Baizhang], and Nan-ch'üan [Nanquan] accompanied the Patriarch [Mazu] to watch the moon. The Patriarch asked, "What shall we do now?" Hsi-T'ang said, "We should make offerings." Pai-chang said, "It is best to practice." Nan-ch'üan shook his sleeves and went away. The Patriarch said, "The sūtras enter the treasury, meditation returns to the sea. It is P'u-yüan [Puyuan] alone that goes beyond all things."
>
> (Cheng Chein 1992, 69)

Poceski (aka Cheng Chein) notes that Mazu's use of the word "treasury" refers to part of Xitang's Dharma-name, and that "sea" refers to part of Baizhang's Dharma-name. Puyuan is Nanquan's Dharma-name. Here Mazu poses a question to his students and assesses their responses, and in his assessment, he puns on each of the students' names. In other words, he uses a question to examine them and to determine an "appropriate" response to their answers. Going back to the former illustration, the further two examination questions build on the early questions and thereby further intensify the encounter.

What about Mazu's final question? Its transformative power comes from a reversal or inversion of the intensification. It releases the tension. One might expect a question that elicits enlightenment to possess mystical power. But none of the other kinds of questions we have examined seem to be capable of performing this feat. Mazu reorients Dazhu's quest for the Dharma back toward Dazhu himself, implying that the most important "answers" to Dazhu's quest can only be realized in a self-conscious relation to the "who" of questioning (Wright 1992a, 45). Mazu gets Dazhu to share his question. Imagine Dazhu asking, "Huh. Why *am* I seeking outside myself?!" Huihai means "treasure," and so Dazhu is literally seeking himself in this dialogue.

If we can read this as a genuine question, as an exception, Mazu presents it at precisely the right moment when, through prior cultivation by way of intensified questioning, Dazhu's self, the "I," "is prepared to emerge into self-awareness" (Wright 1998, 215). If we keep in mind Mazu's emphasis on radical nonduality, implying that ordinary life is not different from the realization of the Dharma, then perhaps it is not unreasonable to read that question as a genuine one. *What could be more ordinary than just asking another person what they think?* This reading accounts for the rest of the story, where the student Dazhu continues to converse with the master. This is implied by his remaining at the monastery with Mazu as well as his composing a straightforward treatise on sudden enlightenment (see Blofeld 1962).

This question can be interpreted as a genuine question. If so, then Mazu is capable of engaging others in dialogue. Mazu's question appears to be *the* question of Chan: Why are you seeking outside when you already are that which you seek? I have argued throughout this chapter that Mazu might ask another character at least one genuine question. Since Mazu typically uses questions to interrogate or overwhelm others, this one instance is exceptional. What this means for the reader is resolvable ultimately only on the level of narration, however, where reader and narrator engage in dialogue about the plot of the story and the way in which specific actions fit into the word of the text. This will be addressed in Chapter 8.

Jesus Asks, "Who Do You Say I Am?"

What is going on in the passages below?

Jesus went on with his disciples to the villages of Caesarea Philippi; and on the way he asked his disciples, "Who do people say that I am?" And they answered him, "John the Baptist; and others, Elijah; and still others, one of the prophets." He asked them, "*But who do you say that I am?*" Peter answered him, "You are the Messiah." And he sternly ordered them not to tell anyone about him. Then he began to teach them that the Son of Man must undergo great suffering, and be rejected by the elders, the chief priests, and the scribes, and be killed, and after three days rise again. He said all this quite openly. And Peter took him aside and began to rebuke him. But turning and looking at his disciples, he rebuked Peter and said, "Get behind me, Satan! For you are setting your mind not on divine things but on human things." He called the crowd with his disciples, and said to them, "If any want to become my followers, let them deny themselves and take up their cross and follow me. For those who want to save their life will lose it, and those who lose their life for my sake, and for the sake of the gospel, will save it. For what will it profit them to gain the whole world and forfeit their life?

(Mark 8:27-36)

Now when Jesus came into the district of Caesarea Philippi, he asked his disciples, "Who do people say that the Son of Man is?" And they said, "Some say John the Baptist, but others Elijah, and still others Jeremiah or one of the prophets." He said to them, "*But who do you say that I am?*" Simon Peter answered, "You are the Messiah, the Son of the living God." And Jesus answered him, "Blessed are you, Simon son of Jonah! For flesh and blood has not revealed this to you, but my Father in heaven. And I tell you, you are Peter, and on this rock I will build my church, and the gates of Hades will not prevail against it. I will give you the keys of the kingdom of heaven, and whatever you bind on earth will be bound in heaven, and whatever you loose on earth will be loosed in heaven." Then he sternly ordered the disciples not to tell anyone that he was the Messiah. From that time on, Jesus began to show his disciples that he must go to Jerusalem and undergo great suffering at the hands of the elders and chief priests and scribes, and be killed, and on the third day be raised. And Peter took him aside and began to rebuke him, saying, "God forbid it, Lord! This must never happen to you." But he turned and said to Peter, "Get behind me, Satan! You are a stumbling block to me; for you are setting your mind not on divine things but on human things." Then Jesus told his disciples, "If any want to become my followers, let them deny themselves and take up their cross and follow me. For those who want to save their life will lose it, and those who lose their life for my sake will find it. For what will it profit them if they gain the whole world but forfeit their life? Or what will they give in return for their life?"

(Matthew 16:13-26)

Once when Jesus was praying alone, with only the disciples near him, he asked them, "Who do the crowds say that I am?" They answered, "John the Baptist; but others, Elijah; and still others, that one of the ancient prophets has arisen." He said to them, "*But who do you say that I am?*" Peter answered, "The Messiah of God." He sternly ordered and commanded them not to tell anyone, saying, "The Son of Man must undergo great suffering, and be rejected by the elders, chief priests, and scribes, and be killed, and on the third day be raised." Then he said to them all, "If any want to become my followers, let them deny themselves and take up their cross daily and follow me. For those who want to save their life will lose it, and those who lose their life for my sake will save it. What does it profit them if they gain the whole world, but lose or forfeit themselves?"

(Luke 9:18-25)

In these quotations from Mark, Matthew, and Luke, there is a leader of a movement and an unnumbered gathering of eager disciples, and—despite what seems to be an earlier depiction of this leader as rhetorical genius teaching in parables—the leader asks a number of questions that seem at least on the surface to be sincere and, perhaps, even genuine. I want to know whether it is "fact" of the story, whether it is "right there in the text," that Jesus asks a genuine surplus-driven question (see Dickman 2016). I am also curious about whether Jesus asks a sincere, but deficit-driven, question. Again, recall

Fish's criticism that asserting what is right there in the text is one of the best games in town given the canons of interpretive acceptability. Also recall our development of the concept of semantic autonomy, navigating between the extremes of writer intent and reader caprice. This helps us isolate interpretive possibilities within respectable constraints.

In this chapter, I argue that there is at least one exceptional case where Jesus might be asking other characters a genuine question. I argue this is exceptional because, as we will see, Jesus usually uses questions to interrogate others or overwhelm others. In what follows, I first provide some constraints for interpretive possibilities of the Gospels, concerning the different Gospel portraits of Jesus. This step will prepare us to survey a number of questions and dialogues attributed to Jesus, addressing what is "on the lines" and "between the lines," or the exegetical hermeneutic circle. This all will help us focus on one peculiar question, a gravitational center of the major plot in the Gospel writers' development of Jesus into the Christ, where he asks, "Who do you say that I am?" We will save questions for what is behind and beyond the lines, or the existential hermeneutic circle, for Chapter 9.

Preliminary Clarification: Gospel Portraits of Jesus Conflict

We need to approach Jesus as a deific figure because his actions and words are imbued with cosmic significance in Christian traditions. The fundamental Christological paradox is that Jesus the Christ is thought to be both completely human and completely divine. Numerous theologians have attempted to philosophize the complex ontology here. The medieval Christian theologian Thomas Aquinas, for example, uses an analogy between putting thought into concrete words as illuminating the relation between the intelligible divine and the tangible human being (see Aquinas 2010, 737–9). We are less concerned about the philosophical underpinnings that clarify the Christological paradox with ontological precision, and more concerned with how Jesus is depicted in literature centering him. Many early Church fathers, such as Irenaeus and Titian, sought to harmonize the four canonized Gospels of Matthew, Mark, Luke, and John. Yet, as the New Testament studies scholar Stephen Barton emphasizes, these cannot be harmonized on the literary level (Barton 2001, 176). They each develop a distinctive portrait of Jesus that stand in contrast—sometimes starkly so—with one another. John's Gospel, for example, presents a cosmic messiah, where Jesus as the Christ is conceived of as the pre-existent *logos*, or word. We will focus here on the synoptic Gospels, keeping in mind the broad Christian notion in

Christology about Jesus the Christ being fully human and fully divine, and thus is a deific figure.

The writer of Mark shapes Jesus into a figure with a primary pattern of suffering in service to others (see Miller 1997, 105). Jesus' death is his service. Martyrdom ought not to be confused with suffering as an act of selflessness. Mark's depictions of Jesus performing healings and exorcisms are eschatological acts focused on his power, not his love. As Jesus is depicted here, he is full of mystery and paradox, creating fear and trembling (Barton 2001, 175). This means discipleship requires martyrdom for Mark. The writer of Mark focuses criticism primarily on the twelve disciples, who do not understand Jesus' life and teachings (Crossan 1995, 17–18). This pattern is obsolete today in a world where forms of Christianity predominate (Miller 1997, 108). It is impossible to be a martyr for Christianity under global Christian hegemony.

The writer of Luke, alternatively, does not develop a picture of a servant-martyr dying *for* his people but of a prophet-martyr who is killed *by* his people (Miller 1997, 113). For Mark, the cross is a sign of success. For Luke, it is a sign of failure—particularly a failure of Jesus' fellow Jews to repent and reorient their lives around the God of Judaism. Thus, Jesus' death benefits no one (Miller 1997, 113). This framing on Luke's part results from his writing for a Greek audience, and Luke triangulates with his audience against Jews and Jewish Christians (see Levine 2015). That is, Luke (or at least standard receptions of this text) predominantly makes Jews—especially Pharisees and Sadducees—look bad in order to make Jesus look good. We must be careful, though, because Luke does not blame Jews as a whole (see Miller 1997, 113).

The writer in Matthew, however, patterns Jesus not as a martyr but as a prophet-teacher (Miller 1997, 110–12). Jesus reveals the kingdom, calls disciples to a mission, and represents the God being present *with* humanity. Martyrdom is only part, and a minor part, of the picture. For example, the Sermon on the Mount provides textual allusion to Moses with the Decalogue on Mt. Sinai. The point is not merely to serve and suffer but to teach and recruit more disciples (Miller 1997, 111). Matthew stands in contrast to Luke, because Matthew is a Jewish author writing for the Jewish Christian community. This is crucial for noting different intensities of anti-Jewish content (see Crossan 1995, 16–17). Matthew focuses criticism not on most Jews, like in Luke, but on apparently corrupt Jewish leadership manipulating others.

The point here is that the three evangelists configure the details of Jesus' story according to their own patterns, and thus endow the story and main character with new and different meanings. So, we must consider the image of Jesus developed in the Gospel narratives—and in the traditions that ensued from them—as constructions of latter social imaginaries rather than as historical works documenting the life of a person named Jesus (see King 2003, 110). The figure of Jesus developed in the Gospels is a construction, a character, an element of a narrative. Thus, when we investigate Jesus asking questions, we are asking about this construction and character, not about the historical person. Let us turn to focus attention on details of Jesus' direct discourse.

Questions on the Lines: Jesus Often, if Not Always, Asks Rhetorical Questions

Jesus asks roughly seventy-five questions per Gospel. In Luke's version, Jesus even asks questions at a noticeably young age (Lk. 2: 46-47). Jesus' use of questions is nested within depictions of conversation between characters, and these sequences are themselves embedded within stories incorporating a variety of genres of discourse, from genealogy to sermons. We can look at Jesus' use of parables to illustrate the performative aspect of his discourse. As Levine notes,

> What makes the parables mysterious, or difficult, is that they challenge us to look into the hidden aspects of our own values, our own lives. They bring to the surface unasked questions, and they reveal the answers we have always known, but refuse to acknowledge. Our reaction to them should be one of resistance rather than acceptance.
>
> (Levine 2013, 3)

As the New Testament theologian Ernst Fuchs explains, Jesus does not use parables merely to convey concepts but also in the very uttering of them he calls, promises, demands, or gives (see Fuchs 1964). The Christian theologian Anthony C. Thiselton elaborates on this: "Cleary this is very different from merely talking about actual or possible promises, or actual or possible gifts. The language of Jesus effects a change in the situation; it enacts an event" (Thiselton 1970, 438). Jesus draws his hearers into a "world" created by the parabolic discourse, not as spectators but as participants (see Levine 2013, 12–15). This world of the parable, however, is not oriented toward some future place or state of affairs. The words interpret the present. Fuchs illustrates this point through the parable of the vineyard workers (Mt. 20:1-16), where the last to be hired are paid the same as everyone else, and the impact of this on hearers both "effects and demands a decision" about equitable distribution of money independent of labor (Fuchs 1964, 212)

Jesus seems to have attracted many followers by speaking to them at their core in this way. Jesus uses imaginative shock or surprise to draw listeners' attention to the whole background and foreground of an event (see Funk 1966, 204). As Levine illustrates with the parable about the helpful Samaritan, the original audience would have been shocked to see one of their enemies offering help to a member of their community (Levine 2013, 103). The audience would expect an Israelite to help the person wounded near the side of the road, but instead it is as if they were told that a terrorist or colonialist stopped to help them. The parables paradoxically describe commonplace events in such a way as to force the listener to compare the world in which they live to the "world" of the parable and thus come to a decision that resolves the tension (Sandifer 1991, 288). As the Jesus Seminar cofounder Robert Funk writes, "Since that other world deforms the received world, the parable constitutes nothing less than an invitation to live in that other world, to see the received world in a new way, to take up one's abode in a referential totality different from the everyday world" (Funk 1966, 205). Parables disclose a world that Jesus invites his listeners to inhabit, provoking and transforming response, bringing "the Kingdom as such into the history of [humanity]" (Funk 1966, 206). At the same time, parables have a degree of open-endedness that allows for a variety—though not an infinite variety—of interpretations (see Levine 2013). They raise genuine questions for the audience, though they are not themselves genuine questions shared by both Jesus and his interlocutors.

There is an abundance of studies on Jesus' discourse in parables, yet to date little work has been done on his use of questions (see Estes 2012; and Dickman 2016). In one study of Jesus' use of questions in Matthew's Gospel, the Christian ethics scholar Ian McDonald claims that Jesus' aim is to enable his audience to "discern truth" through "rhetorical" questions (McDonald 1998, 333). As McDonald writes, "Such an aim is not achieved without the sharing and exploring of horizons with his audience and an attempt to push back the limits of these horizons until new perspectives on truth—or the way things are—emerge more clearly" (McDonald 1998, 333). We can see this precisely parallels the above noted studies on Jesus' parabolic discourse. McDonald believes that rhetorical questions are disparaged and dismissed unfairly, when to be successful they presuppose a shared horizon of understanding (McDonald 1998, 339). Rhetorical questions, in McDonald's framework, are briefer than enthymemes, those categorical arguments that leave out a premise or the conclusion and require the audience to supply them. Like enthymemes, rhetorical questions enable identification between speaker and listeners, and suggest irresistible conclusions. Rhetorical questions facilitate three different goals: communion between speaker and audience, confrontation of the audience by the speaker, and discernment elicited from the audience by the speaker. A communion is achieved because rhetorical questions orient the speaker and audience around a shared topic, including an assumed agreement about this topic. When an audience "responds" to such a question, they ultimately affirm this implicit agreement (McDonald 1998, 341). We can look at a sequence of such rhetorical questions attributed to Jesus in Matthew's Gospel. In Mt. 5:46-47, Jesus asks, "For if you love those who love you, what reward do you have? Do not even the tax collectors do the same? And if you greet only your brothers and sisters, what more are you doing than others? Do not even the Gentiles do the same?" McDonald claims that Jesus is here maintaining communion with his audience while leading them to a new perspective (McDonald 1998, 342).

Jesus also uses rhetorical counter-questions to confront others. One pattern of Pharisaic or rabbinic rhetoric in Jesus' day is what can be called "forensic interrogation" (Daube 1956, 151). In this sequence, an adversary first poses a loaded question to a teacher, seeming to corner them. Rather than answering, the teacher responds with a counter-question, and the naïve adversary answers it. This answer exposes a vulnerability—conceptual or existential—in the adversary's position, and the teacher uses this to refute the original challenge (Owen-Ball 1993, 4). Jesus uses this method of forensic interrogation when challenged about his authority in Mt. 21:23-27. He asks, "I will also ask you one question; if you tell me the answer, then I will also tell you by what authority I do these things. Did the baptism of John [the Baptist] come from heaven, or was it of human origin?" It is not as if Jesus is seeking information here. Jesus uses these rhetorical tactics to confront others. Whereas statements admit of being true or false, rhetorical questions and forensic interrogation lend themselves to discerning truth and falsity (see McDonald 1998, 343).

We can further illustrate Jesus' use of such questions to elicit discernment in other passages. Consider an episode where John the Baptist's disciples ask Jesus whether he is the one about whom John prophesied, in Mt. 11:2-17. After their interrogation of him, he turns to others gathered nearby him, and asks a number of questions in a row. Most of them are modifications of the basic question: "What did you go into the desert expecting to see?" The final question, though, introduces an allegory or parable, where Jesus compares his contemporaries to children at the marketplace. He asks, "But to what shall I compare this generation?" While the people might have gone into the desert with grandiose anticipations, they were overturned by witnessing instead John's imprisonment and execution. Jesus' questions require his listeners reflect on their own expectations and perceptions, what they naïvely hoped for and what they actually saw. This cognitive dissonance affects a change in them. Jesus resists providing anyone in the episode a direct answer to their questions, but instead provides them guidance through questions to, as McDonald writes, "an interpretive framework and discerning frame of mind" (McDonald 1998, 344). The episode depicts Jesus helping his listeners to "discern the finger of God in their own history and experience" (McDonald 1998, 344). The questions transform their perspectives. Consider, too, Jesus' rhetorical question in Lk. 11:13, where—after speaking about how fathers treat their children—Jesus asks, "If you then, who are evil, know how to give good gifts to your children, how much more will the heavenly Father give the Holy Spirit to those who ask him?" This sort of question requires listeners to change their perspective in response (see Thiselton 1970, 439, fn. 2).

Just like his use of parables, Jesus' questions seem to be oriented toward transforming or at least promoting the transformation of his listeners' perspectives. However, do any of Jesus' questions indicate an attempt to reach an understanding with his listeners? That is, are any of his questions genuine ones, where he asks the question for the sake of taking seriously what another person thinks? Does Jesus speak *at* or *with* others in his questions? While the above approach to rhetorical questions requires that Jesus and his listeners share a horizon of understanding, it neglects the building or establishment of shared horizons that occurs in dwelling together in genuine questions and dialogue. Does Jesus ask the kind of questions whereby he fuses horizons with others? Let us turn to look for this possibility.

Questions between the Lines: Does Jesus Seek Understanding with Others?

I want to open up this exceptional possibility through two preliminary steps. I want to pinpoint first a few places where Jesus asks sincere questions, and then turn to an instance where Jesus appears to change his mind based on listening to what another person has to say. A number of questions Jesus asks are patently typical interrogatives, implying that he lacks the requisite information and needs that information in order to determine the best way in which to proceed with a course of action. Some of his questions are sincere requests for information. For instance, in Mk. 6:38, where Jesus' disciples struggle with how to go about feeding a crowd that has gathered around them, Jesus asks his disciples, "How many loaves do you have?" Jesus asks two more such questions in Mk. 9:16-21, where some of his disciples have been arguing with a crowd of people about a demon-possessed boy. First, he asks his disciples, "What are you arguing about with them?" Then he asks the father of the boy, "How long has he been like this?" Within the famous story of a hemorrhaging woman who touched Jesus' robe in order to be healed (Lk. 8:45), Jesus asks, "Who touched me?" Perhaps surprisingly, Jesus is depicted as asking a sincere question even in John's Gospel. In Jn 11:34, Jesus asks the people of Bethany about the location of Lazarus' body: "Where have you put him?" All these questions illustrate that Gospel writers do not seem to hesitate to depict Jesus asking sincere questions, using them to acquire information.

Recall, however, that more needs to be in place and more needs to happen for a genuine question. Genuine questions go beyond sincere ones. The questioner needs to use the question to listen to what the other person has to say. There has to be an attempt to learn from another, to understand another person's perspective. It seems that at least in one episode of Mt. 15:21-28, Jesus takes what another says into serious consideration, to such an extent that Jesus changes his mind. In his encounter with the unnamed Syrophoenician woman, Jesus' horizons expand (see Scott 1996):

> a Canaanite woman from that region came out and started shouting, "Have mercy on me, Lord, Son of David; my daughter is tormented by a demon." But he did not answer her at all. And his disciples came and urged him, saying, "Send her away, for she keeps shouting after us." He answered, "I was sent only to the lost sheep of the house of Israel." But she came and knelt before him, saying, "Lord, help me." He answered, "It is not fair to take the children's food and throw it to the dogs." She said, "Yes, Lord, yet even the dogs eat the crumbs that fall from their masters' table." Then Jesus answered her, "Woman, great is your faith! Let it be done for you as you wish." And her daughter was healed instantly.

While Jesus—like classical Chan masters—typically plays the role of commentator and victor in debate or dialogue, in this case *the woman persuades Jesus*. Bultmann identifies this episode as a unique "controversy dialogue" (an encounter dialogue?) where "on this occasion Jesus proves not to be the victor" (Bultmann 1963, 38). Bultmann highlights the main point as being "the change in Jesus' behavior as the dialogue goes on" (Bultmann 1963, 38). Jesus' mind is broadened through the exchange with the woman. As the Christian scholar Martin Scott concludes,

> In the end Jesus' rudeness towards this woman allows *her* to play the role which the reader had by now come to expect of *Jesus*. By taking on the role of humbly bearing the mockery of his attack, she enables him to see that his boundaries are set too narrow.
>
> (Scott 1996, 42)

My point with this case is that not only does Jesus ask sincere questions at times but he also listens to what others have to say in such a way to be open to having his horizons broadened—at least this one time. A genuine question brings together sincere questions and an openness to having one's horizon broadened. Does Jesus ever ask one of these sorts of questions?

The New Testament studies scholar Bart Ehrman claims that Jesus' *final* question is a genuine one (Ehrman 2000, 72). Yet we also know that Jesus is repeating the call of the writer of Ps. 22:1. In Mk. 15:34, Jesus cries out, "My god, my god, why have you forsaken me?" Is this a genuine question? Perhaps. We would need to theorize discourse appropriation, though, such as when by sharing a Tweet, one might be seen as endorsing the content of the Tweet as one's own position. Kierkegaard's pseudonym, Johannes Climacus, interprets as genuine the question John (in 21:16) attributes to Jesus: "Do you love me?" Climacus tries to read this question as a loving one, one that displays utter human vulnerability in which the "god-man" situates himself to achieve a genuine equality between the God and human beings. Climacus writes, "What wonderful self-denial to ask in concern, even though the [other person] is [in truth] the lowliest of persons: Do you really love me?" (Kierkegaard 1985, 33). By way of such vulnerability, Climacus thinks, the God descends from their role as "the omnipotent one who performs miracles" to a servant "who humbled himself in equality" (Kierkegaard 1985, 33). However, if one examines the larger passage in which Jesus poses this question three times to Peter, the reader will notice that precisely the opposite of Climacus' contention occurs. Jesus asking this question three times alludes to Peter's three denials, which in their turn pre-figure Jesus' questions, of knowing who Jesus is. It is difficult to interpret this sequence of questions as anything other than a reprimand. It probably is not, as Climacus seems to think, a genuine question.

I want to turn to a possibility that seems less controversial—from our specific passage excerpted at the start of this chapter. Jesus explicitly asks his disciples for both the perspective of the people and for their own perspective on who he is in asking (Mk. 8:27-29; Mt. 16:13-15; Lk. 9:18-20), "What are people saying about me?" and "What about you, who do you say I am?" The Greek reads: καὶ αὐτὸς ἐπηρώτα αὐτούς· ὑμεῖς δὲ τίνα με λέγετε εἶναι; ἀποκριθεὶς ὁ Πέτρος λέγει αὐτῷ· σὺ εἶ ὁ Χριστός. We can translate this literally as: But he continued to press them, "What about you, who do you say I am?" Peter responds to him, "You are the Anointed!" (see Aland et al. 1993, 116). The interrogative word is τίνα ("who"). Especially in Mark's Gospel, these questions are the culmination of a crucial and pivotal moment (Ehrman 2000, 67). These questions are not merely attempts to acquire information. They are focused, rather, on what other characters in the narrative think. While Jesus appears to address these questions to his disciples as a whole, his disciple Peter (or Simon Peter) responds to the second question by saying (Mk. 8:29), "You are the Anointed!" Matthew has Simon Peter continue, by adding (Mt. 16:16), "…, the Son of the living God!" Luke's Peter says something different (Lk 9:20), "God's Anointed!" In Mark and Luke, readers are not given Jesus' exact words in response to what Peter says, but instead are merely told that Jesus requested of the disciples that they tell no one about him or who he is. In Matthew, however, Jesus responds to Simon Peter's claim by blessing him and renaming him or at least punning on his name "Peter" (meaning "rock"). He says (Mt. 16:17), "You are to be congratulated, Simon son of Jonah, because flesh and blood did not reveal this to you but my Father in heaven. Let me tell you, you are Peter."

Shortly thereafter, in all three synoptic Gospels, Jesus speaks about the imminent persecution and suffering of the "Son of Man" (*not*, significantly, the "Son of God" or the "Christ of God"). Some Christian theologians believe that Jesus' prediction of the "Son of Man" suffering is the proper continuation of the narrative in Mark and Luke's Gospels, whereas Jesus' seemingly self-congratulatory statements to Peter in Matthew interrupt the narrative flow (see Gundry 1964). Jesus' reservations about the title "Christ" suggest this incongruity. Jesus' later rebuke of Peter—calling him "Satan" after Peter contradicts Jesus' predictions—is even more evidence to the lack of fit for the congratulatory passage in Matthew (Gundry 1964, 5; cf. Ehrman 2000, 67). Drawing a connection between these elements of the story, Ricoeur writes, "If Peter is Satan, as we are told in the episode at Caesarea Philippi, is this not so because all the figures, when confronted by the enigma of Jesus, reply to the question 'Who do you say that I am?' with comparable withdrawal?" (Ricoeur 1995, 197).

This sequence is often referred to as "Peter's Confession" within Christian traditions. Bultmann believes that the entire passage is patently myth, and that the questions in particular are merely a literary device for the authors to draw out a "confession" from the readers or hearers in the early Church (Bultmann 1963, 257–8). As Bultmann explains, the questions are neither Socratic nor pedagogical because such questioning was "as foreign to the Synoptic as to Jewish dialogues. Besides it is the disciple, not the teacher who poses the questions in Rabbinic dialogues" (Bultmann 1963, 257 fn 5). He writes,

> The fact that Jesus takes the initiative with his question itself suggests that this narrative is secondary… as does the content of the question altogether. Why does Jesus ask about something on which he is bound to be every bit as well informed as were the disciples?
>
> (Bultmann 1963, 257)

For Bultmann, the disciples here function as a medium for the people of the Church, serving as a representation of the Church and giving expression "to the specific judgment which the Church had about Jesus" (Bultmann 1963, 258). The questions are not actions of a historical person for Bultmann, but literary devices for oral performance in communal liturgy. Jesus purportedly already knows both what the people in general are saying about him and what the disciples think of him. Ricoeur adds—in alignment with Bultmann— that the story of Peter's ambivalence (embodied in the conjunction of his confession and his later denial) "becomes a source of uncertainty for the reader insofar as the reader is invited to proffer an affirmation of faith with such a force that it will cut the ambiguity of everything that has gone before" (Ricoeur 1995, 197). Others have similarly claimed that the questions are not genuinely open but that "Jesus is obviously trying to draw out ... a confession by His questions to the twelve—and his purpose is just so that He can begin the task of remolding their concept of Messiahship. [The questions are] leading questions, not questions designed primarily for getting information" (Gundry 1964, 6). The New Testament studies scholar Robert Gundry points out that Bultmann's analysis may be off target here because the disciples probably are better informed than Jesus about others' opinions about Jesus, since they were the ones mingling with people (Gundry 1964, 6).

Recall that our concern is not with questions that the historical person Jesus actually asked. That is going to what is behind the lines. *We are looking on the lines and between the lines for what unfolds in front of the text through the reader's engagement with it.* What is Jesus' character as it is constructed via the narrative? I want to note that Jesus is not asking, "Who am I?" He asks, "Who do *you* say that I am?" He is inquiring about another person's perspective about him. Perhaps this is for the pedagogical purpose of making their perspective explicit so he can correct it. However—and this is what I want us to see as plausible—perhaps he is asking it for the purpose of reaching an understanding with them. Is Bultmann claiming that Jesus is in a better position to know what the disciples think than the disciples themselves? No. Bultmann is saying Jesus is in a better position to know his perspective on himself than they are. At least in the case of the people gathered, the disciples have a proximity with them that Jesus does not, and thus they are in a better position to know what people are saying about him. In the case of the disciples themselves, however, even granting the fallibility of self-understanding, the disciples need only to introspect or to recall what they have already said about Jesus to determine what they think about him. To say, as Bultmann does, that Jesus was in a better position than the disciples to know the answer to his own question projects onto Jesus a precise omniscience that lacks sufficient textual evidence.

One way of reading Jesus' questions about what others think of him is to read them as genuine, not merely rhetorical and not merely pedagogical. In such a reading, Peter's answer matters, not because he is being tested but *because Jesus takes what Peter thinks seriously.* If Jesus poses a genuine question to Peter, it implies that what Peter has to say is also relevant to the unfolding of the subject matter, the issue at stake in Jesus' question. The elliptical endings in Mark and Luke's Gospels, where Jesus invokes "messianic secrecy," leave the subject matter in suspense. We do not know how the conversation unfolded afterward. So, these two do not exclude the possibility that Jesus asks a genuine question here. What if they debated the political or spiritual meaning of the concept of "messiah"? Even in Matthew, where Jesus seems to congratulate Peter for his answer, the question can still be considered a genuine question, especially since readers learn of Peter's differing perspective in his response to Jesus' prediction of his imminent death. Peter's response contributes to the unfolding of the subject matter (the identity of Jesus). Fuchs' statement with regard to Jesus' use of parables seems all the more pertinent here, with regard to Jesus' use of genuine questions: "Is this not the way of true love? Love does not just blurt out. Instead, it provides in advance the sphere in which meeting takes place" (Fuchs 1964, 129).

We seem to have good reasons to read this question as genuine. I have argued throughout this chapter that Jesus seems to ask at least one genuine question of another character. Because Jesus typically interrogates or overwhelms others with questions, this one instance is exceptional. However, what the question means for individual readers or communities of interpretation is only resolvable on the level of determination of the plot—on the level of discourse. That is, whether Jesus poses a genuine question is relevant for a reader's understanding of the larger plot within which this fits as a "fact" within the world of the text. We will turn to address this in Chapter 9.

Part Three

The Existential Hermeneutic Circle: Questions Posed by the Deific Voice of the Text to Readers

Chapter 7: A Divine Voice Asks, "Where Do You Stand?"   137
Questions behind the Lines: The Torah as Unfurling Diasporic Dialogues   137
Questions beyond the Lines: An Authorial Voice Questions Readers' Ethical Embodiment   144
Culminating Reflection: A Divine Voice in Question   147

Chapter 8: A *Dharma* Heir Asks, "Why Conceive of Fulfillment as Outside Yourself?"   151
Questions behind the Lines: Crises and Reconstruction in Transmission Literature Production   151
Questions beyond the Lines: An Authorial Voice Questions Readers' Reflexive Awareness   155
Culminating Reflection: A Mastered Voice in Question   161

Chapter 9: An Evangelist Asks, "What Do You Have to Say for Yourself?"   165
Questions behind the Lines: A Canon Emerging in Colonization   165
Questions beyond the Lines: An Authorial Voice Questions Readers' Epistemic Accountability   168
Culminating Reflection: A Redemptive Voice in Question   172

In Part II, we examined the roles of questions in the direct discourse of deific figures represented in religious narratives. The following three chapters will be reflexive about the reading process, looking at the "deific voice" or subjectivity of the texts themselves in the dialogue between reader and text called interpretation. This deific voice can only be brought to the foreground by providing historical context as a constraint for interpretation. My primary goal is to apply what we developed in Part I about the nature of questioning and dialogue, the realization of dialogue between text and reader, and the unfurling of questions in the hermeneutic process. Recall that shared questions facilitate the transfer of complete thoughts from one person to another. We need to ask the question to which our conversation partners respond so that what they say will make sense to us. In this way, religious texts weave together communities in a broader social fabric of meaning and relevance. Also recall that there are four layers of questioning necessary for reading comprehension: on the lines, between the lines, behind the lines, and beyond the lines. Whereas we focused on what is "on" and "between" the lines in the preceding chapters, in the following chapters we will focus on questions about what is "behind" the lines and that go "beyond" the lines. That is, we are turning from the exegetical to the existential hermeneutic circle. As we pointed out, only the questions that go beyond the lines are properly hermeneutical: What does the text have to say to me, and what do I have to say to the text in response?

As I have suggested, it is plausible to think that genuine questions are among the elementary constituents of religious narratives, as actions performed by those deific figures endowed with ultimate authority. However, this is not the only way in which genuine questions operate in the reading of religious narratives. *Indeed, in the order of understanding meaning, genuine questions shared by the implied author and the reader are more fundamental in that without them we would not be able to render the elements of the story intelligible.* It is on this level, the "narrational level" as Barthes refers to it, that genuine questions play their most crucial role in a reader's engagement with religious narrative. The elements of point of view, modes of authorial intervention, and various systems of representation are all part of the narrational level. Barthes writes, "This ultimate, self-designating, form of narrative (i.e., the narrational level) transcends both its contents and its properly narrative forms (functions and actions)" (Barthes 1975, 264). On this level, the genuine question is the key operation "by which a work lifts itself above the opaque depths of living, acting, and suffering, to be given by an author [internal to the text] to readers who receive it and thereby change their acting" (Ricoeur 1984, 53). The claim of Part III is that sacred texts display listening in posing genuine questions to readers and in responding to readers. In this way, genuine questions are operative in religious narrative on a more fundamental level than indicated within Part II. The most significant hermeneutic priority of questioning is on this narrational level. The religious text, which itself plays an authoritative role in contemporary religious communities, confronts readers with genuine questions. It is this subjectivity of the texts themselves, this speaker, who engages readers in genuine questions and dialogue in the interpretive process.

In Chapters 7–9, I will move through one religious text at a time like before, with an aim at isolating a genuine question—perhaps *the* genuine question—posed by the text to the reader. Before proceeding, I need to point out that the following chapters are not an extensive study of the narrative voice and rhetoric in Genesis, Mazu's discourse records, or Mark's Gospel. I assume that readers are already somewhat familiar with the stories and books, especially in the cases of HaShem and Jesus. Perhaps many readers have not heard of Mazu specifically or have not read the *Mazu yulu*. However, many people in the United States have heard of Zen in some way or other, perhaps through the popular writings of D. T. Suzuki, Thich Nhat Hanh, or even the Beatnik poets of the 1960s. For each case study, I will begin with some questions that lean more toward what is behind the lines, to provide some parameters for possible interpretations.

The development here is a sketch of the constraints that bring events of genuine questioning into the foreground as these converge with explicit interrogative acts in the texts. One could perform, for example, a study focused solely on the genuine questions as they emerge for readers from interpreting non-interrogative acts, such as in some of Jesus' parables or in a Buddhist master's exploitation of the metaphor of water for the mind. In these noninterrogative instances, the reflexive reader might find oneself caught up in genuine questioning (though, for obvious reasons, neither Jesus nor the master in these cases would be themselves participating in dialogue). At issue is merely to lay out some of the ways in which the narrators of these texts appropriate genuine questions posed by characters as their own questions posed to the reader. A further notion gives shape to each chapter, that dialogue with the other of the text itself only occurs in light of the use of historical-critical methods (see Wallace 2000, 83). Only in this way can the reader become reflexive about one's own historical situatedness as well as the historical situatedness of the text. Without situating both self and other, a fusion of horizons between the reader and text is not possible. This should not distract us to the point where we bottom out in historical-critical study of what is *behind* the text, even if it is the appeal to an author's original intentions or an original audience's perceptions. The dialogue between reader and text happens *in front* of the text (see Wallace 2000, 83).

Allow me to begin with a few general remarks before turning to specific texts. First, in none of the religious narratives do the narrators appear as characters within the drama. Thus, there is no necessity to distinguish between the implied author and the narrator in the analysis of these texts. Second, all the narrators refer to a deific figure, or, as Ricoeur calls it with regard to Christian texts, a "God-referent" (Ricoeur 1974, 45). This referent is, according to Ricoeur, both the coordinator of the various genres of discourse and events of the narrative and "the index of their incompleteness, the point at which something escapes them" (Ricoeur 1974, 45). Thus, the dialogue that ensues between narrator and reader does so over a subject matter constrained by these deific figures, but which is at the same time opened up by virtue of the ultimate concern or unconditioned regulative ideal shared by narrator and reader. Third, and most important for our purposes, the narrators seem to depict these deific figures as posing genuine questions at crucial and transitional moments in the broader plot. This accomplishes a reflexive symbolic mediation in that the genuine questions posed by ultimate figures are placed before readers and posed to the readers themselves. In this way, these genuine questions donate and convey the power of being itself to the reader in the form of *being heard*. This point will guide some of my meditations in the Conclusion. In what follows here, we will examine the strategies and aims of the narrators, and isolate specific genuine questions that they seem to ask of their readers.

For a quick primer on narrational rhetoric, let us briefly examine narrative appeals set out in the story of the *Three Little Pigs*. In the very naming of the pigs and the description of them as little, and in juxtaposing them to the "big bad wolf," the narrator appeals to the audience to identify sympathetically with the pigs and to be distanced from the wolf (Boomershine 1980, 114). Moreover, the narrator describes the wolf's actions as assaults on two of the pigs' homes. In accord with norms of judgments, the narrator attempts to elicit moral outrage about the wolf's hostile actions. The narrator shifts points of view from the outside of the homes to the inside for the final episode, where the pig plots to lure the wolf down the chimney into a boiling pot. The pigs celebrate the realization of this climactic reversal with dancing and singing. In this, the narrator invites the reader to share the pigs' joy at the wolf's demise. However, when a reader responds in sympathy for the wolf, it is apparent that the narrator's appeals have failed. As the New Testament studies scholar Thomas Boomershine explains, "a narrator's rhetoric is in fact a series of appeals or invitations which can either be accepted or rejected by the audience" (Boomershine 1980, 114). In what follows, we will examine the invitations to readers made by the narrators surrounding the climactic moments at which open questions arise between characters in the story.

These invitations are themselves genuine questions posed to the readers, asking (generically), "Do you understand and agree with what I am saying?" The existential hermeneutic circle is defined precisely by such questions that go beyond the lines. Chapter 7 will focus on the Torah as itself a teacher or rabbi instructing a reader-pupil. Chapter 8 will focus on Mazu's discourse records as themselves a master provoking a reader-student. Chapter 9 will focus on Mark's Gospel as itself the Word engaging a reader-disciple.

A Divine Voice Asks,
"Where Do You Stand?"

In this chapter, I want to revisit the garden episode in Genesis, but this time on the level of narration rather than the level of story. I argue that through putting the text in historical context, we can foreground the voice of the text. And I argue that this deific voice appropriates the genuine question posed by HaShem and puts it to readers themselves. We will first look at questions about what is behind the lines, developing crucial historical dynamics from which our focal episode emerged. Then we will turn to isolate an authorial voice addressing readers, focusing in particular on the genuine question asked of readers. We will conclude this chapter by reflecting on the divine voice of the Torah.

Questions behind the Lines: The Torah as Unfurling
Diasporic Dialogues

What are some crucial features of historical context within which the selected excerpt (see Chapter 4) was produced? Decimated and displaced by the Babylonian Empire starting in 587 BCE, many former citizens of Judah sought to preserve their cultures and memorialize an ideal past era of political sovereignty. This past era was the Kingdom of Israel—a 400-year dynasty consolidated by David and his descendants, and a respectable feat for a nation occupying a small strip of land contested over by multiple empires. So began an effort to compile, standardize, and comment on inherited traditions, a polyphonic effort that continues to be a definitive aspect of all subsequent Jewish religious practice. In exile, a collective of rabbenu-redactors began artfully to weave these traditions together, transforming political and material loss of a kingdom into a transportable and hopeful social fabric of written text, the Torah—the first five and most authoritative books of the Hebrew Bible or Tanak.

The earliest evidence we have of a complete edition of the Torah is when the prophet Ezra brought one from Babylonia to Israel during the Second

Temple period near 445 BCE to propagate reforms of Judaism there, under the behest of Persian administrative efforts to categorize peoples into distinct groups (see Scheindlin 1998, 26–32; and Harris and Platzner 2003, 21–2). Yet the legendary, mythic, and diverse contents in the Torah are depicted as having occurred roughly 500–1000 years earlier, from the lives of Patriarchs like Abraham and Isaac to Moses leading Israelites liberated from Egyptian oppression to Mt. Sinai. Before standardization of materials during the exile, the religion of Israel is more appropriately conceived of as henotheistic Yahwism rather than what we have come to know as Jewish monotheism (see Gnuse 1999, 317–19). After the exile, Yahwism died out and from its ashes "arose a Judaism founded on the beliefs of the [HaShem]-alone movement" (Gnuse 1999, 319). Suggestions of polytheistic Yahwism are detectable in those few remnants mentioning HaShem outside of the Hebrew Bible. A Moabite inscription from the eighth century BCE commemorates the Moabite King Mesha's rebellion from Israel after Ahab's death, where Mesha claims to have destroyed Israelite cities and "seized sacred implements from a temple of [HaShem]" (Scheindlin 1998, 21). Large storage jars from Negev from the ninth century BCE have an inscription referring to "[HaShem] of Samaria" and "his Ashera" (Scheindlin 1998, 22; and Harris and Platzner 2003, 64). Ashera is a Goddess within Canaanite religions, raising a question about whether this inscription implies that Ashera is HaShem's wife.

Once they were exiled in Babylonia, previously disparate Israelite communities converged. These communities had relative autonomy from one another and preserved recognizably distinct traditions and primordial origin narratives. We can trace a similar recent development with diasporic Hindu communities in the United States over the last 100 years. Some Indian immigrants brought distinct religious traditions with them to the United States and found solidarity with other Indian Americans, leading to formulations of pan-Hindu ideas like "the Trinity" of Brahman, Vishnu, and Shiva, a notion absent from precedent traditions in India that came to be labeled "Hindu" by Muslim and British colonists before the 1800s (see Coogan 2003, 134–61; and Wuthnow 2005). That is, diasporic Jews in Babylonia were similarly perceived collectively as "the other," regardless of whether among themselves they recognized substantive differences in traditions and cultures. By means of the Torah, Persian authorities and their Judean emissaries regulated religious practice and citizen identity throughout the province. The Torah became the law of the land (see Davies 2003, 45).

Rigorous historical analysis of the Torah beginning roughly in the 1600s—such as with Spinoza (see Spinoza 2001, 107–15) and culminating with the work of biblical studies scholars Karl Heinrich Graf and Julius Wellhausen in the late 1800s (see Cohn-Sherbok 2003, 391–403)—has exposed four cultural pre-exilic and postexilic oral and written sources on which the Torah is probably based: J for the Yahwist sources, E for the Elohist sources, D for the Deuteronomist sources, and P for the Priestly sources. Before proceeding to elaborate on some of these, I want readers to note here that this framework analyzing the text into parts aims at an *explanation* of the Torah. Recall, however, that while explanation breaks something down into parts, an interpretation requires synthesizing these parts into a greater whole—a meaning to be understood, not just facts to be accepted (see Holstein 2002, 20). Yet, explaining something better allows us to interpret it even better. When trying to interpret this God's questions, we can already make our interpretation more rigorous by figuring out to which source the passages belong.

These sources are detectable by different key characteristics of social and political interests, regional settings, rhetorical styles, and character names—including those used for the God. And they can be located historically within distinct eras. For example, most of the J source material was probably produced around 950 BCE to consolidate David's and Solomon's power, and emphasizes the southern region of Judah by setting many travails of Abraham, Isaac, and Jacob there. The E source, alternatively, probably was produced around 750 BCE and emphasizes the northern region of Israel by setting many of the travails of the Patriarchs there. One major difference between the J and E sources, from which they receive their designations, is the words used to refer to the God. The J source predominantly uses the God's personal name, that which is replaced by HaShem, whereas the E source predominantly uses a more generic (plural) title "Elohim," like the English word "gods." Just as Zeus is the personal name of the highest God of Olympia in the Greek pantheon, HaShem is the personal name of the God of Judah. The J source has most devotees using HaShem from the beginning (see Gen. 4:26), but the E source depicts this God as keeping the name secret until revealing it to Moses (see Exod. 3:15). HaShem's name seems to be rooted in the ancient Hebrew verb "to be," and likely means "I am who I am" or "I will be who I will be."

A concern to be careful with this God's personal name grew in light of the prohibition not to take HaShem's name in vain (Exod. 20:7) (see Cohn-Sherbok and Cohn-Sherbok 2005, 5). By early 200 BCE, observants considered this name to be so sacred that a convention developed to avoid pronouncing it in ritual recitations and prayers, saying "Adonai" ("Lord" in English) in place of the written HaShem. Today, even Adonai is perceived as so sacred that many Jews use the word *HaShem* ("the Name" in English) instead. We can see this concern to respect the name intensify even into English usage, where a practice has developed among many observant

Jews to leave out some vowels in the names—to say and to unsay the words simultaneously—such as with G-d, L-rd, or even Alm-ghty. We can ask then, which name for the deity is used in our select passage? Does the passage belong to earlier or later material woven into the Torah's fabric? Before turning to this, I want to provide a little more historical context and development of rabbinic Judaisms so I can bring out more explicitly how this early polyphonic practice in Babylonia remains present throughout Jewish traditions of interpretation.

In addition to the Torah, the Tanak includes two further sets of content. The Neviim ("Prophets" in English) includes political history such as Kings I and II as well as narratives about major prophets like Isaiah and minor ones like Jonah. The Ketuvim ("Writings" in English) includes both pre-exilic poetry likely used in Judah's temple rituals such as the Psalms and postexilic narratives like Job and Esther, both of which seem to criticize institutionalized religion in the Second Temple period. Hence the acronym T(a)N(a)K is used for the Hebrew Bible in Jewish communities. There seems to be some consensus about the Prophets already between 200-100 BCE and discussion of other miscellaneous writings, but it appears that sages and scholars in the academy at Yavneh standardized the Tanak after Rome destroyed the temple in Jerusalem in 70 CE (see Harris and Platzner 2003, 22). That is, *the Tanak as we know it today only came together after the dissolution of temple Judaism and the emergence of varying Christian communities.* Like their rabbenu-redactor forbearers who produced the Torah, these scholar-sages at Yavneh weaved the Torah together with the Neviim and Ketuvim into the Tanak or Hebrew Bible, which is best conceived of as a library of books rather than one book. Just like the J source narrates episodes that purportedly happened 500 years earlier, postexilic books in the Neviim and Ketuvim narrate things purported to have occurred 500 years earlier.

Consider, for example, the postexilic writing of the Book of Jonah. It depicts events that occurred nearly 300 years before its composition. Likely composed after 500 BCE, the audience would remember that Nineveh destroyed the northern Kingdom near 800 BCE, where ten of the twelve tribes of Israel disappeared off the Earth. The audience would know this, and so would understand that Jonah is an argument about divine mercy represented by the divine figure versus rigorous application of justice represented by Jonah. Jonah puts his life on the line in objection to the God. The writer appears to be criticizing the deity, who, as Jonah points out, is too lenient, too lenient to a people the original audience knows are murderous genocidal imperialists who decimated the northern kingdom (see, for example, Crouch 1994). That is, by situating Jonah in its historical context of an original audience, we can see that Jonah's content is much more serious than children's cartoons make it out to be. Jonah would rather die, even die by suicide, than do what this God wants, and this God becomes so coercive as to take away from Jonah what often is seen as our last resort in utterly hopeless situations, suicide. Yet despite—or perhaps in spite of—its critical content, scholar-sages at Yavneh recognized its crucial role in ongoing conversations defining future Judaisms.

Moreover, early sages or Pharisees attempted to distill from these texts essential guidelines or *mitzvot* for Jewish practice in multiple Midrashim (commentary and interpretations) of specific books, such as investigating how to observe Shabbat properly—starting at dawn or at dusk? This ongoing conversation among Tannaim ("teachers" in English) such as Hillel and Akiba aimed at decisions about how best to observe *mitzvot* and culminated in Judah ha Nasi's redaction of the Mishnah near 200 CE (see Cohn-Sherbok 2003, 116). A particularly relevant feature of the Mishnah's genre for our purposes is that, in laying out the Tannaim's final decision, *it includes the minority's opinion and reasoning with the majority's opinion and reasoning.* That is, like the rabbenu-redactors of the Torah and Tanak, Judah ha Nasi produced a polyphonic text of inclusive and ongoing conversation. In fact, that conversation continued into the production of the Babylonian and Palestinian Talmuds circa 400–500 CE. The Talmud consists of the Mishnah and Gemara ("study" or "transmission of tradition" in English), which includes anecdotal digressions and dialogues with philosophical and ethical implications from the Amoraim ("speakers" in English), scholarly interpreters such as Abba Arika (or Rav) and Judah bar Ezekiel (or Rav Yehudah). I encourage readers to examine pages of the Talmud, where a visual representation of this spiraling conversation is represented textually—with a Mishnah passage in the center of the page, and commentary conversations circling around the centerpiece.

What I want us to glean from this is how inclusive dialogue and argument are definitive for Jewish engagement with the Torah. We cannot just pick up the "Old Testament" and read our primary passage, ignoring generations of interpretations. To become a respectable rabbi today includes demonstration of some mastery over what can seem like an unwieldly cacophony of interpretative traditions and involves being licensed by a genealogy or lineage traceable back to Moses himself. *The Torah's truths are not compromised through dispute and multiplicity but only emerge through this process* (see Kolbrener 2004, 283). In this way, rabbinic *midrash* or interpretive dialogue finds a middle way between the extremes of subjective relativism where everyone has their own truth and naïve fundamentalist absolutism where people claim direct access to objective and divine reality for themselves. Because human perspectives are limited, as we have pointed out above, we cannot claim some absolute correctness to our interpretations as if our perspectives do not affect our interpretations. In fact, the Talmud even rejects authoritarian (fascist?) divine intercession to settle questions (see Baba Mezia, 59a–b). No one who is genuinely engaged in the study of the Torah is excluded (Kolbrener 2004, 287). *By taking into consideration multiple voices and points of view, this dialogical tradition serves as an antidote to hegemonic and exclusive points of view, whether expressed as relativism or as absolutism.*

While we have outlined dialogues internal to the production of Jewish traditions and engagement with the Torah, we can also identify places in which the earliest rabbenu-redactors demonstrate engagement with broader culture. For example, the early Hebrew writers engaged Mesopotamian mythology, specifically the *Enuma Elish* with its creation narrative and the *Epic of Gilgamesh* with its flood narrative as well as the relationship between a leader protagonist and a hairy antagonist like Jacob and Esau. Genesis 1 has been identified as belonging to the P or Priestly source material, and either was written sometime before the final redaction of the Torah or was written for the sake of the final redaction sometime during the Babylonian exile or after 587 BCE. The rabbenu-redactors of the Torah likely belonged to this priestly community and tend to use Elohim rather than their God's personal name. They assembled originally separate codes and inserted them through the J and E epic narrative materials, emphasizing rituals, genealogies, and sacrifices, all of which consolidated and clarified the overarching jurisdiction of priests. They wove their version of the Flood into the J version and added both a primary creation account and an account of Moses's death—the latter two forming the opening and closing of the Torah to give it its final shape (see Harris and Platzner 2003, 89).

These priestly Judean exiles in Babylonia must have observed annual rituals that included recitation of the *Enuma Elish*, where the God named Marduk creates Earth and human beings from primordial undifferentiated waters in light of a cosmic conflict between generations of a multitude of Gods and Goddesses (see Cohn-Sherbok and Cohn-Sherbok 1999, 6; see also Eskenazi and Weiss 2008, ch. 1). That is, the priestly original audience knew this narrative well, so well that the priestly writers could assume knowledge of it in composing their alternative account, keeping allusions brief in order to get to their alternative point. The very process of creation in six steps parallels one another, both culminating in creation of human beings. A detectable allusion to the Mesopotamian pantheon occurs in Gen. 1:26, where Elohim appears to consult a council of deities, urging the creation of human beings in "our" image and "our" likeness. Later exclusive monotheisms try to explain this plurality away with appeal to alternative religious resources, such as in *midrashim* that the God only consults with angels there (see Gen. Rabbah 8.3-7; see also Feldman 1981; and Cohen 1990). These parallels are especially interesting where obvious scientific errors are made in the same places. For example, plants are created before the sun in both accounts. Of course, plants cannot survive without sunlight, and ancient Mesopotamians and Israelites knew this (see Greenstein 1990). To be charitable readers, we should resist the temptation to caricature ancient writers as ignorant. Instead, we should ask why they would choose to arrange their narrative sequence this way (see Kapelrud 1974)? On a careful literary reading, the organizing principle is increasing movement. Creation begins with the least moving—the unchanging horizon of sky and land (or ocean really) defining day and night. Each subsequent day or stage involves creation of things with slightly increased movements, such as plants and land. The celestial bodies can be seen to move much more than plants do, where they cross the entire sky and some of them, like planets, even do it unpredictably. That is, it is obvious that plants come before the sun because the sun moves a lot more than plants do, at least in terms of human perception (see Harris and Platzner 2003, 108–10). Then come the animals. And, finally, *the most moving thing of all: human beings.*

The priestly writers' dialogical argument with the Mesopotamian mythologists, agreeing with them in principle about the becoming and direction and movement of creation, is on the nature of human beings as the crucial focus of reader or audience attention. For Mesopotamians, human beings are *lullu*, or the Sumerian word for "highlander" or "criers." It is interesting to consider the ambiguity here in the name for human beings itself, as if the human choice is either a war cry of revolt against subjection to divine fate and subordination or a whimpering in acceptance of fate, as illustrated by the Gilgamesh narrative. The priestly writers, alternatively, name human beings "adamah," or earthling, of the dirt (see Alter 1981, 176–80). Thus, they frame human beings as full of fertile potential or uninhabitable land. It is the moving drama of human-to-human interaction, of human civilization, that is of focus for these rabbenu-redactors, as opposed to the cosmic conflicts among deities that Mesopotamians and even the Greeks make their focus. Humans are large and center stage in Genesis; humans are mere cast members for the others. Reading Genesis as if it were a literal description of some creation sequence makes us miss this literary argument, a conversation between cultures that sets precedents for the polyphonic conversation constituting Jewish traditions as a whole.

Questions beyond the Lines: An Authorial Voice Questions Readers' Ethical Embodiment

Before turning to the enigmatic Eden episode in Genesis, and the first acts of questioning in the Torah, it is helpful to examine a clear-cut case where authors confront readers with a question placed in the direct discourse of the God of the Tanak. The Book of Jonah is the single text that ends with a question posed by this God. There HaShem asks Jonah (Jon. 4:11), "And should I not be concerned about Nineveh, that great city, in which there are more than a hundred and twenty thousand people who do not know their right hand from their left, and also many animals?" The elliptical ending, where readers are not given any more details about what ensues upon the question, leaves the issue in suspense to be taken up by readers themselves. Does Jonah reply? Has Jonah died? What is this God's perspective on the relation between compassion and justice? What is my perspective, as a reader? This is the genuine question with which the narrator of Jonah confronts the reader. Similarly, a question placed in the direct discourse of HaShem is asked of the reader in the enigmatic Eden sequence.

Tradition attributes Genesis, or *Bereshit*, to Moses. Moses is the dominant prophet within the Hebrew Bible. As many in Jewish traditions construe it, HaShem gave Moses the Torah during the Mosaic revelation on Mount Sinai (Rosenberg 1984, 35; and Fishbane 1998, 18). Historically speaking, we can know that Moses did not write these texts. As Spinoza writes,

> It is clear beyond a shadow of a doubt that the Pentateuch was not written by Moses, but by someone who lived many generations after Moses... There are no grounds for holding Moses to be the author of the Pentateuch, and such an opinion is contrary to reason.
>
> (Spinoza 2001, 109–10)

Moses' death occurs in Deuteronomy, for example. However, materials and traditions traceable to Moses or Moses' time were incorporated into the Torah. Nevertheless, the voice of the text is referred to as Moses—keeping in mind that this is the narrator's voice or authorial voice, not the historical person with the appellation "Moses." Readers engage with this voice in dialogue in the interpretive process.

On a basic level, the plot of Genesis is twofold. First, the God creates human beings, but relationship with them seems strained by a series of failures and misunderstandings. Second, this God seems to try to overcome this alienation through the election and cultivation of a specific people, the people of Israel (Holstein 2002, 30–1). The biblical narrator employs a number of means to appeal to and invite the reader into the world of the text: an extreme economy of description, anticipatory information, redundancy, symmetry, ellipsis, hyperbole, omission, and more (Rosenberg 1984, 37–51). The authorial voice systematically develops the first creation story (Gen. 1–2:3), for example, by circumscribing creation from the macroscopic view of the entire phenomenological cosmos to the microscopic view of humanity and our affairs (see Dickman 2020b). Through this, the authorial voice focuses readers' attention on and gives center stage to human beings and their activities—especially their discourse (Holstein 2002, 81). HaShem's genuine question of "Where are you?" marks the critical moment of transition where the divine and human reach a new understanding about a radically different state of affairs inaugurated by consuming the "forbidden" fruit. In creation sequences from the first story of Genesis 1, human beings played a relatively passive or nominal part in the unfolding of events. After HaShem's question, however, everyone in the text—the God, human characters, narrator, readers—understands that humans now play an active role in the unfolding of events. They have become, in other words, *responsible* agents full of fertile potential.

Narrational reticence to flesh out both characters and context with descriptive language forces the reader's attention onto the discourse and dialogue of characters (Alter 1981). Adam, for example, in the second creation account (Gen. 2:3-4), is not described as tall or short, or slender or muscular. However, he hears the God speak as well as speaks himself inasmuch as he names all the other animals. This leaves unaddressed whether Adam's selection of names sparked dialogue or controversy between HaShem and himself. Readers are not told—though *midrashim* address issues along these lines. Authorial reticence is especially significant because, in the case of the God, the God appears within the narrative primarily as a divine voice with some slight anthropomorphic descriptions, such as the God's "walking" through the garden. Indeed, the very process of creation unfolds in correlation with this voice's divine utterances in the first creation narrative. However, in the second creation narrative, this voice or presence does not create but forms and shapes. Omission of descriptive reference for the God serves to bring the God's discourse further into the foreground. This God's voice, White writes, "does not speak from a recognizable position within the social structure or spatial/temporal register within which [typical] characters exist" (White 1991, 101). The narrative voice presents the pivotal initial figures and characters in *Bereshit* as speaking agents, as discursive beings. From the outset, divine discourse forms their personhood (see White 1991, 102).

Main characters stand out from the rest of the cast and the broader atmosphere of the world of the text once this God addresses them. That is, they emerge as figures with more important roles than merely fitting within a spatiotemporal localization in the world of the text (White 1991, 102). As examples, the narrator or authorial voice locates Adam and Abraham within specific spatiotemporal coordinates, but they become agents or actors once the divine voice addresses them as "you" (White 1991, 102). In Gen. 2:16-17, HaShem addresses Adam: "Of every tree of the garden you are free to eat; but as for the tree of knowledge of good and bad, you must not eat of it; for as soon as you eat of it, you shall die." In Gen. 12:1, the God addresses Abraham: "Go forth from your native land and from your father's house to the land that I will show you." It appears that being addressed in the second-person singular by the divine voice is crucial for the narrator's development of the story, whereby the narrator grants responsible freedom to the character in response to a specific type of word (see Buber 1970; and White 1991, 103). As Buber explains, encounters between an I and a you suffer from the glacial drift toward objectification. He writes, "Only when the primal encounters, the vital primal words I-acting-You and You-acting-I, have been split and the principle has been reified and hypostatized, does the I emerge with the force of an element" (Buber 1970, 73). Only through being constituted as a "you" does someone become present (see Buber 1970, 63).

A crucial dimension of the divine word or call is its perlocutionary aspect, the intent to affect someone with what is said—such as when someone says, "I want to inspire you" in an inspiring speech. The perlocutionary aspect of discourse establishes and constitutes intersubjective relationships. It is not merely about your own intentions, or the content of what you mean. It is about impacting one another. HaShem's genuine question fulfills this sort of establishment of intersubjectivity. Whereas for Buber the primal word pair "I-Thou" establishes relationship, *genuine questioning performs it*. It is one thing for someone to speak *at* you; it is another thing entirely for someone to speak *with* you through asking you a genuine question. On this interpretation, the narrator does not present Adam and Isha's responsibility as established by the God's prohibition against eating from the tree of knowledge of good and evil. Instead, the authorial voice uses this God's genuine questions to do so. It is not, as Kierkegaard believes, that Adam and Isha were anxiously free and therefore responsible *before* consuming the forbidden fruit. The prohibition did not induce anxiety about their new freedom (cf. Kierkegaard 1980). Consuming the fruit did not lead to the realization they had choices to make. Rather, the God's first question grants the primordial human beings a space in which they are able to respond, to respond in a way with integrity instead of merely reacting or merely obeying. The narrational voice gives these characters "character" once they respond, once they "talk back" to their God. In this way, the narrational voice gives privilege to moments in which this God asks questions rather than those moments in which the God utters prohibitions.

What, then, is the narrator's question to the reader? The narrational voice uses a number of strategies to appropriate HaShem's question to primordial human beings as one's own question posed to the reader. As Wolterstorff explains, it is possible to appropriate the discourse of others through simple acts like saying, "I agree" (Wolterstorff 1995). It is not simply that the God asks something of the primordial human beings. It is that the authorial voice also asks this same question of the reader. Every episode in which later figures take on responsibility seems to allude back to this episode in *Bereshit* where the ability to respond first occurs: in Adam and Isha's taking up responsibility with regard to HaShem's genuine question. Abraham responds to the God's call with "Here I am" (Gen. 22:1). Jacob responds with "Here I am" to the God's call (Gen. 31:11). Moses responds to the God's call with "Here I am" (Exod. 3:4). Samuel says, "I am here" to the God's call (1 Sam. 3:4). Isaiah says, "Here I am" to the God's call (Is. 6:8). These intertextual references and allusions always return to the God's original genuine question. By pointing back to this moment, the authorial voice of the text itself appropriates HaShem's genuine question and continuously asks the reader, "Where are you?"

Culminating Reflection: A Divine Voice in Question

Maimonides argues that God revealed the entirety of the Torah and its commentary in the Oral Torah to Moses on Sinai (Manekin 2018, 133). That is, Moses is technically not the authorial voice; HaShem is. Moses' role in receiving the Torah—like the Prophet Muhammad's role in receiving the Quran—is to deliver it to the people (see Sells 2007). For Maimonides, since there is nothing anthropomorphic about this God, what people call the "speech" or "call" of God can be meant only metaphorically. This divine discourse is understood only by Moses yet is expressed through Moses in a way that people can read and understand what it means—if readers put in the work to read and hear what the text says (see Manekin 2018, 150). The Jewish theologian Abraham Joshua Heschel, alternatively, urges that the Torah is spoken in an utterly human and accessible language—though, of course, later rabbis like Akiva are called to interpret and savor every detail of the language (Heschel 2006, 47). The point here is that the voice of the text is less that of Moses and closer to HaShem's voice speaking to readers.

Yet for our hermeneutic reduction this might be misleading because it suggests there is a metaphysically existent supernatural being behind the book, as if a reader's goal is to understand the intentions of this writer resting behind the book. We might be tempted to look for some divine origin of the Torah, just like many are tempted to look for some divine origin of universe as a whole (see Dickman 2020b). Is the proper English translation of "*Bereshit bara Elohim*" best construed in chronological terms, as "in the beginning God created..."? Whose interests are served by directing readers' attention to chronological origins and—perhaps inadvertently—diverting attention away from ontological hierarchical principles (see Nasr 2006)? Similarly, we divert our attention away from our hermeneutic reduction if we turn to ask about some God's intentions behind the book.

This is precisely the direction some Christian philosophical theologians go, where they try to discern what the God means through the Bible. Wolterstorff, for example, argues that contemporary Christian believers are rationally entitled to believe that "God speaks" to them through the Bible (Wolterstorff 1995). Quinn, however, argues that Wolterstorff's argument is unconvincing. Not only is it not clear that the God even *can* speak but it is also not clear that even if the God can speak, the God *does* speak (Quinn 2001). Both Quinn and Wolterstorff take it for granted that the question "Can God speak?" makes sense. Recall that the question we should have ready in our back pocket is, "Which 'god'?" Do they mean Vishnu? Zeus? HaShem? Unlike Wolterstorff and Quinn, who take the question to make sense, where the word "god" signifies some metaphysical entity behind the book, we are looking at the divine authorial voice speaking in front of the text. It is this "god" with whom readers engage in dialogue. The "god" behind the lines must die, so that the "god" beyond the lines might live and engage readers in transformative dialogue (Dickman 2014, 554). As the philosopher of medieval Jewish and Islamic theology Charles H. Manekin explains, Maimonides believes that if anyone thinks even one word of the Torah is from Moses himself, then they deny the divine Torah (Manekin 2018, 135). We agree. However, it is not the God behind the lines but the God before the lines who addresses readers.

Because HaShem is a character within the story, the authorial or narrative voice transcends identification with HaShem alone. The narrator maintains an anonymity, as the Hebrew Bible and Ancient Near Eastern studies scholar Edward L. Greenstein explains (Greenstein 1990, 151). The narrator submerges their identity and background, maintaining focus on the fate of HaShem's people, yet the narrator often tries to align with what seems to be HaShem's point of view. They are a hidden participant, as Rosenberg puts it (Rosenberg 1984, 70). In this way, they invite and anticipate a continuation of traditions and dialogues beyond the borders of the book. As Rosenberg writes, "Someone is teaching someone else about the repeated failure of society [and the individual] to govern itself. The text itself invites readership concerned with the problems of both personal and communal self-governance" (Rosenberg 1984, 70). In Jonah, for example, the narrative voice seems to criticize HaShem. Or, as postcolonial critics have pointed out, the authorial voice challenges the view of HaShem as a liberator. As the Hebrew Bible and contextual theology scholar Kari Latvus explains, HaShem blames the people and not the colonial powers for their exile into Babylon (see Latvus 2006, 188). The authorial voice seems at times to agree, struggling with internalizing this colonization.

While there is no specific identification of the authorial voice with the character HaShem in the story, it is still worthwhile to consider this voice as speaking "the word of God." In other words, it is still a divine voice. The narrative voice or voice of the text itself drastically shifts scope, from the personal, to the household, to the regional or national, to the global, and to the cosmic. The voice develops in unexpected ways that, as the Hebrew Scriptures scholar Carolyn J. Sharp explains, destabilizes loaded ideological ways of reading the Torah or the "Old Testament" (see Sharp 2009). Indeed, some have even seen in this expansiveness room for arguing that women wrote parts of the Hebrew Bible (see Milgram 2008). This ironic voice redirects attention from the story to what is unsaid, to address the reader with something more subtle, more complex and profound than the plot (Sharp 2009, 24). The voice seems to take delight in "circumventing the most revered of human conventions of power, status, and inheritance in order to highlight [HaShem's] disregard for the trappings of human vanity" (Rosenberg 1984, 68). The voice is both HaShem and not HaShem. The voice is both masculine and feminine. The voice is both focused on the past and focused on the future. In all these ways, the voice challenges convenient pigeonholing of the text into an easy singular answer, or what we can call the Magic 8-Ball method of reading the Bible—flipping through to find the magic or astrological sentence of what "god" is saying to you for the day.

For us, though, we are concerned less with what the text is saying and more with what the text is asking. Where do you stand? How does it go with you now? The deific voice asks the reader, calling on one's potential. We can frame this in terms of the argument the Hebrew writers have with the Mesopotamian writers over the nature of human beings. Are they made of earth, with the potential for growth? Or are they screamers, wailing and gnashing against their certain fate? Maimonides explains this in the difference between image (*tzelem*) and likeness (*demuth*) in Genesis 1 (see Maimonides 1995, 51). As Maimonides explains, tzelem is the essence and form of something. For human beings, Maimonides echoes Aristotle, our intellectual or discursive capacity really distinguishes us from all other things, and so makes us what we truly are. We share in conversation and thought with one another; we do not just graze alongside each other in the same pasture (see Aristotle 1999, 1170b11–14). Demuth, however, is more figurative. It is like calling someone a bear or lion to capture the power or courage they seem to exude. That is, demuth is solely on us, something that we must live up to with our potential. Are we capable of the risk necessary to make something of ourselves? Will we just accept the socially constructed roles already set out for us and internalize them? Here we ought to see a similarity to Sartre's famous definition of existentialism as "existence precedes essence" and Simone de Beauvoir's application of this to gender in her famous quip that "One is not born, but becomes a woman." That is, like existentialists, the divine question engages the reader in one's own existential comportment and responsibility. Where are you?

Who is asking whether HaShem asks a genuine question? Is this a concept I, as a reader, am merely imposing on the text? Is this a topic the writers had no interest in? That is, when we ask whether or not such and such a passage is historical (in the sense of our modern historiographic criteria), we need to realize that ancient authors were not interested in our modern distinction between fact and myth. *Did the ancient authors have no interest in sharing genuine questions? Might it be something they took for granted, such that it is obvious they are choosing to ask them throughout the text?* I have argued that through putting the text in historical context, we can foreground the voice of the text. And I argued that this deific voice appropriates the genuine question posed by HaShem and puts it to readers themselves. Again, though, it appears we are in abeyance rather than being able to determine with some certainty in this way or that whether there actually is a genuine question in the text itself being asked of readers. Perhaps it depends on where you are.

A *Dharma* Heir Asks, "Why Conceive of Fulfillment as Outside Yourself?"

In this chapter, I want to revisit the encounter dialogue episode where Mazu triggers Dahzu's enlightenment, but this time on the level of narration rather than the level of story. I argue that through putting the text in historical context, we can foreground the voice of the text. And I argue that this deific voice appropriates the genuine question posed by Mazu and puts it to readers themselves. We will first look at questions about what is behind the lines, developing critical historical dynamics from which our focal episode emerged. Then we will turn to isolate an authorial voice addressing readers, focusing in particular on the genuine question asked of readers. We will conclude this chapter by reflecting on the mastered voice of Mazu's *yulu*.

Questions behind the Lines: Crises and Reconstruction in Transmission Literature Production

What are some crucial features of historical context within which the selected excerpt (see Chapter 5) was produced? I want to look first at a particular moment in the lifetime of Mazu himself, 709–788 CE. The An Lushan rebellion from 755 to 763 CE decimated the populace of the Tang Dynasty by roughly two-thirds (Pulleyblank 1976). The rebellion destroyed state centralization and "ushered a period of regional autonomy during which separatist military governors maintained their independence from the crown" (de Bary and Bloom 1999, 574). The Tang attempted to maintain distinct, yet far-reaching, borders facilitating global commerce via the Silk Road. Numerous changes in Eurasian political organization, often fueled by the merchant class, created turmoil for Tang governmental maintenance (see Beckwith 2009). Uighur rulers overthrew Turkish ones on the Eurasian Steppe border to the northwest. Abbasids overthrew the Umayyad Caliphate on the Khurasan border to the southwest. All the while, the Tang was leading a campaign against the Tibetan Empire to the west. In the midst of all of this, the northern general An Lushan ran a campaign all the way into the Tang capital, Chang'an, dethroning the emperor.

The rebellion's aftermath included widespread migrations and disruptions to all economic systems and trade. Without centralized infrastructure, *millions* eventually starved to death. As Hershock writes,

> this left two out of every three people in the country either dead or missing, cutting the official population from 53 million to 17 million... It is impossible to overestimate the utterly devastating effect such a catastrophic loss of life must have had on the spiritual resources of the Chinese people.
>
> (Hershock 2009, 32–3)

The rebellion happens in the middle of Mazu's adult and professional life, and it is this context that Mazu's radical style of improvised immediacy seems to be attributed. Mazu, more than all other early Chan masters except maybe for Linji, established the irreverent tactics for which Zen masters are well known. Born in horror, the exigency of Mazu's teachings and methods has an urgency to it unlike others before (and after) him.

Literature about Mazu, however, was not finalized for centuries after his death. As discussed in Chapter 5, classical Chan is a genre constructed during the Song Dynasty, depicting the ideal past to which contemporary practitioners should strive. Between these moments—Mazu's life, on the one hand, and the compilations of lives of masters in the transmission literature, on the other hand—occurred a persecution of all forms of Buddhism by the Chinese State during the Huichang era, from 841 to 845 CE (Poceski 2007, 3). Unlike modern historiographic principles, anachronism was not considered a transgression of the process of "recording." We can claim with the celebrated Japanese scholar of Zen Yanagida Seizan, then, that Chan transmission literature presupposes an orientation to history significantly different from modern historians (see Yanagida 1983, and Wright 1992a). Given both the textuality and inaccuracy of the records, the image of Tang masters depicted in transmission literature is a construction of Chan imagination in the Song dynasty. This idyllic and uncorrupted past of Chan flourishing was used in the Song as a strategy to indicate present-day decadence that Chan had become more and more corrupt in the Song (see Faure 1986). It makes sense that later generations would look back to an era as the "golden age" before things were corrupted by persecution, before the Sangha had to rebuild itself on its ruins.

Again, the editorial criteria for compilation of material about masters like Mazu seem not so much to have been a matter of capturing the past as it actually occurred as much as a matter of how effective a story was for the purpose of transmitting the Dharma to future generations. Or, probably more importantly, the criteria for inclusion had to do with the intrapolitical vying for patronage among various Dharma transmission lineages. The imperial government patronized Buddhist monasteries, subsidizing translations and printing of imported Buddhist sutras (see Robson 2011, 325). It is difficult to tell whether there were many lay readers or how widespread literacy was at this time. Some scholars like Cole argue that everyone in the broader public wanted what the masters seemed to have—meaning that the majority of people could read these broadly circulating texts (see Cole 2009, 29). It is more likely these texts were merely circulating among the elite literate clerics and writers. It was not a wide readership but primarily only the educated literati. Yet these literate patrons often participated in intra-Buddhist debates and issues (see Halperin 2006). Monastic institutions produced literate monks serving in a vast variety of administrative roles (see Wright 2003, 263). Monks were among the few who could read and handle books. Due to worry about the growing power of Buddhist institutions in this light, the Imperial government started implementing compulsory reading or literacy exams. These were massive endeavors (see Wright 2003, 264). The point here is to provide context about whom the discourse records writings were for. Who was reading them?

There are three primary features of transmission literature as a religious genre: narrativity, genealogy, and the presentation of a master prototype. The narrative structure of the of the *Jingde chuandeng lu*, for example, is two tiered. First, the text tells a story of a tradition as a whole by sequentially chronicling different individuals' enlightenments in distinct episodes. Second, it provides biographical narratives of individual masters from birth to death. There is no theoretical reflection on meanings of the narratives. Yet it does provide significant detail on the level of individual biographies (Wright 1998, 106). Between the events of a Chan master's birth and death, biographic details consist of stories presenting specific moments that were— and are—*read as manifesting a power and depth of that master's awakened state*. However, these specific moments are not always isolated events; they sometimes occur against the backdrop of a life narrative as well as a narrative of accumulative collective enlightenment (Dharma transmission lineages) defining a tradition.

Episodes often display masters in search of an heir to carry on their Dharma transmission lineage. Thus, *the texts complement as well as legitimize transmission genealogies*—where transmission certificates to this day license Zen masters, abbots, and abbesses. As scholar of Zen Studies Bernard Faure writes, "[Chan texts] played a crucial role in a ritual of transmission by legitimizing the patriarchal lineage" (Faure 1993, 229). The *Jingde chuandeng lu*, then, can be considered a family history, especially given the employment of family lineage terms such as *xiongdi* ("brother"), *shu* ("uncle"), and *zu* ("grandfather") to symbolize and describe the relationships among the members of a lineage (see Wright 1998, 107). As Schlütter explains, "This principle of organization was recognized by the Song state and reflected in sources such as the *Tiaofa shilei*, in which regulations for monastics and monasteries were placed in the 'Household and Marriage' (*huhun*) category" (Schlütter 2008, 83–4). The term *zong* ("ancestor") in particular carried pre-Buddhist Confucian connotations, which indicates, as Wright states, "knowing what it meant to belong to the [Chan] institution entailed knowing from whom it had been inherited, a historical knowledge transmitted and inculcated by means of narratives like the *Jingde chuandeng lu*" (Wright 1998, 107). As with any genealogy, determining one's position in the lineage locates one with regard to the past, present, and future. Transmission literature situates a purportedly ahistorical concept of enlightenment within structures of a narrative history and a genealogy in such a way that, as seems reasonable to claim with Wright, belonging to the Chan family serves as a condition of the very possibility of enlightenment (see Wright 1992a, 41). What is more, it serves as a condition of the possibility for taking up administrative roles at powerful temples and civic centers.

Readers are forced to interpret whatever a master does or says as a presentation of awakened enlightenment by the genre's conventions (see Foulk 2000, 40). In classical Chan philosophy, this is fundamentally the realization of inherent enlightenment, or, as the Song Dynasty master Dahui (1089–1163) puts it, the "merging" of oneself with inherent enlightenment (see Schlütter 1999, 113). If the activity or discourse were not the presentation of an awakened mind, then the records would appear odd and arbitrary, like an action movie without action. The genre's conventions themselves call for interpretation of the masters' mundane actions and words as indirectly about ultimate truth—to such a degree that, as Chan Studies scholar T. Griffith Foulk indicates, *the more mundane the act or statement, the more profound its meaning* (Foulk 2000, 40). The genre's conventions manufacture an image of Chan masters with a particular style of behavior in which they are interpreted as manifesting the Dharma through gestures such as shocking shouts and blows, as well as by means of paradoxical statements and counter-questions that confound their students (see McRae 2003, 76). *Their virtuosity in ordinariness makes the masters extraordinary.* Is asking a genuine question an ordinary or extraordinary act?

Questions beyond the Lines: An Authorial Voice Questions Readers' Reflexive Awareness

In the preface to the *Mazu yulu*, it is said that the collection was edited by Huanglong Huian (1002–1069 CE), a notable member of the Linji lineage (Poceski 2004, 55). While it is likely that Mazu's students transcribed his sermons, we know that his biographical sketch is traceable to an inscription composed by Quan Deyu (759–818 CE). We do not know who wrote the encounter dialogues unless they were composed along with the redaction of the collection. Whatever the case may be with regard to the historical origins of the material, at issue here is the narrator who speaks with the reader in the text. The basic plot of the encounter in the fourth dialogue of the *Mazu yulu*, where Mazu seems to ask a genuine question, is that Dazhu, seeking enlightenment, comes to study with Mazu. Mazu seems to refuse by turning Dazhu's question back on himself. Thereupon Dazhu attains enlightenment and eventually composes an accessible treatise on Chan practice and metaphysics.

The transmissions depicted in this literature reflect social practices of the Song State (960–1279), which established the foundation for the development of Chan traditions. Official documentation for a master's recognition of a student's awakening developed only during this time. It came in the form of a transmission certificate, which the student only received once the student ascended to the abbacy of a public monastery (Schlütter 2008, 92). That is, *transmission certificates accompanied assumption of institutional roles, not sheer inner experiential moments or profound recognitions between individuals.* In the literature, however, the most important condition for Dharma transmission, the master's recognition, often takes form in an exchange of words. Who is this exchange of words for, since it is probably not a record of something that happened? In contrast to calling on historical exegetical practices oriented toward uncovering real past masters as they were recorded and preserved, this Song construction of eighth- and ninth-century masters is marked by a rhetorical practice oriented toward a future, particularly a future public sphere of readers and a future of subsequent generations of Chan traditions (Faure 1993, 147). The literature impacted both the development of Chan traditions later in the Song dynasty and contemporary literati readerships since Chan abbots sought patrons to support their monasteries.

Through their dissemination to reading publics and later generations of Dharma heirs by means of transmission transcription, specific rhetorical episodes supplied basic models for subsequent Chan discursive practice. Once excerpted from the broader narrative context and commented upon by a later master, specific episodes became *gongan* ("public cases" or "precedents"). The term *gongan*, its origins in medieval Chinese jurisprudence, literally refers to the table or bench (*an*) of a judge (*gong*) (Foulk 2000, 18). By the end of the thirteenth century, *gongan* were being compared to legal precedent cases, indicating their role as authoritative standards for determining and authenticating purported levels of Chan experience and spiritual attainment (Foulk 2000, 18). Just as with any community, the shared concerns of Chan monastics were constituted by and expressed through their shared discursive practices, practices informed by the standards of excellence represented by *gongan* (see Wright 1992b, 124). These role models serve as regulative ideals (MacIntyre 1984, 187; see also Anderson 2001).

In his attempt to purify Chan practice as well as solicit patronage from affluent literati during the Song Dynasty, Dahui developed a method for the realization of one's inherent enlightenment through meditation on the *huatou* ("crucial phrase") of individual *gongan* (Schlütter 1999, 115; see also Schlütter 2004, 180). Reflection on *huatou* was central to Dahui's method of instruction aimed at producing overwhelming doubt in students, or what he called "the great ball of doubt," frustrating their discursive and grasping intellect while simultaneously preserving their investigative attitude (Schlütter 1999, 124; see also Foulk 2000, 22). The students' acquisition of skill to comment on *huatou* spontaneously and insightfully measured the students' success in the practice (see Foulk 2000, 23). This is the origin of what is known today as *koan* meditation practice, predominant in Rinzai monasteries but now showing up in all sorts of popular contexts, such as Jon Stewart's "Moment of Zen" closing to *The Daily Show*.

The Song readers of transmission literature, and *gongan* transcriptions in particular, probably consisted mainly of elite monastics and literati. The texts circulated among readers with varying levels of interest in Chan: from Chan enthusiasts to those committed to the collection and reading of texts due to their sheer rarity. Although printed texts were available and became increasingly common, they were still rare enough and thus were items of consumption for the book culture of the Song. Besides the rarity of the texts, what applied to readers then also applies to readers now. The literature allows readers to enter what is depicted often as quite private situations, intimate conversations between masters and students. Moreover, *the genre placates readers' egos by placing them somewhere between masters and students*, where readers can identify students' delusions yet can never fully be certain of what the master means. While readers might feel superior to the students, we are also like students insofar as we are—presumably—unenlightened.

In the Song, the iconoclastic discursive practices of classical Chan masters were enshrined in textual form as icons, inaugurating a form of veneration of words and actions of "past Buddhas"—replacing rhetorical practice with hermeneutical practice (see Faure 1993, 148). By interpreting the literature, Chan modes of being-in-the-world became live possibilities and regulative ideals for the readers, specifically the Song literati but also today's readers. While Schlütter notes one function of the literature was to solicit patronage from the literati (see Schlütter 2008), it also seems probable that the literature also functioned as a recruitment tactic of monastics insofar as leadership of public monasteries required many of the skills of educated literati. Training in the monastic community thus has come to require submission to literary traditions and to self-transformations that occur within Chan or Zen discursive practices. Only advanced members of the monastic community participate in the unusual and exclusive language (Wright 1992b, 126). Fluency in the rhetoric purports to display one's depth of experience in Chan. Thus, a crucial difference between the enlightened and the unenlightened is a discursive difference—a distinction between vastly different ways of participating in language (Wright 1992b, 132). As Hershock explains, it is about performing discursive actions with interactive and improvisational virtuosity (Hershock 2009, 134).

The shift from transmission narratives to *gongan* and *huatou* meditation practices divulge an increased tendency of students to publish, and thus publicize, the words of masters despite masters' persistent warnings that the soteriological power of their words is limited to singular moments (Faure 1993, 231). Like with Jesus, there is an intimacy or even secrecy definitive for the master-disciple relationship—yet this secret intimacy necessarily needs publicization to reach broader communities or future generations. Inscribing the discourses as if one were recording them restructures them in accord with literacy by freeing the discourses from any specific context and thus replacing direct reference in face-to-face dialogue with indirection and intratextual self-referentiality or, what Ricoeur calls, "productive reference" (see Ricoeur 1976). Such semantic autonomy facilitates the interpretive production of a "surplus of meaning," and one significant function of narrative texts like transmission literature of the Song is their capacity to disclose a possible form of life or way of being in the world to readers (Ricoeur 1976, 94).

The depiction of *wenda* (again, "question-and-answer") between masters and students, so central to Chan transmission literature, indicates the importance of orality to the Song imagination, an importance, Faure emphasizes, that is only enhanced by the literature (Faure 1993, 228). This is legitimately inferable from their dialogical structure, which also implies a dialogical and performative conception of writing and reading where just as the master seeks out an interlocutor, so also does the text seek out a reader. However, as Faure points out, this engagement has been assumed to be about uncovering a reference to some kind of superior experience or about the study of Buddhist doctrine rather than about the ritual and performative features of the narratives (Faure 1993, 225). As Faure writes, "It is significant that what may (or may not) have been at first spontaneous encounters... eventually became a literary genre—that is, a highly ritualized form of discourse with a given sociocultural setting and specific role expectations" (Faure 1993, 215). The specific role expectations for masters and students were shaped by the rhetorical practices presented in transmission literature, and these roles are replicated in the event of reading where the "student-reader" submits to the judgment of the "master-text" rather than the other way around. Classical Chan challenges modernist subjective aesthetics where audiences use their faculty of taste to judge the work.

The life of literary texts, especially those bearing a dialogical structure, parallels the performative surrounding of musical scores, *a literary genre where subsequent readers interpret the texts by literally performing them*. Each performance tries to get the piece correct or right. As Gadamer writes,

> I am not convinced by the objection that the performance of a musical work of art is interpretation in a different sense from, say, reaching an understanding in reading a poem or looking at a painting. All performance is primarily interpretation and seeks, as such, to be correct. In this sense it, too, is "understanding."
>
> (Gadamer 2013, xxvii)

According to Gadamer, the interpreter's performance of reading or co-speaking always accompanies literary texts in their life in a community (Gadamer 1989, 46). Both reading silently and reading aloud involve the same structure insofar as they are dialogical. When one reads a text, whether aloud or silently *to* oneself, one reads it *for* someone, which means one engages in dialogue. Just as in live dialogue, the dialogue that occurs in reading bears many marks of orality in the moment of performance. Like a guardian sounding out voices of characters as they read a bedtime story to a child, readers only understand to the degree they bring the sound into harmony with the meaning as they read to themselves (see Gadamer 1989, 147). What musicality is needed in reading encounter dialogues? What tones are master and student questions put? Might we discover a voice of genuine questioning in the texts?

As Schlütter points out, works such as the *Mazu yulu* served religious and didactic purposes such that students presumed they could gain enlightenment by reading and listening to lectures on the activities of classical masters (Schlütter 2008, 9 and 16). Moreover, the elite literati—almost all of whom would have been acquainted with and interested in Buddhist literature— seemed to have been tantalized especially by the encounter dialogues of Chan masters (Schlütter 2008, 178). "Chan's rhetoric," writes Schlütter, "seems to have convinced many literati *that they had an understanding of Chan equal to, or even surpassing, that of much of the Chan monastic community*" (Schlütter 2008, 178; my emphasis). With the proliferation of "Zen" in American culture during the last century, something similar can be said of today. We can call it the propensity to the presumption of Buddhahood.

The narrator of the *Mazu yulu* employs a number of strategies in order to appeal to readers. The most obvious is the utter lack of context. By means of this strategy, the narrator appeals to readers to use their imagination in order to provide their own context. McRae points out that this is especially useful for teachers who lecture from the text (McRae 2003, 82). McRae employs media theorist Marshall McLuhan's terminology in order to elaborate this point: "this is a 'hot medium,' like radio, that makes readers or listeners actively imagine what is happening, rather than a 'cold medium,' like television, that gives viewers just enough sensory input to turn off their minds" (McRae 2003, 82). The narrator, then, gives the narratival argument an enthymematic structure, in which the audience supplies the "premises" and thereby supports the argument's development. Moreover, just as with the Torah narrator, the narrator in the *Mazu yulu* emphasizes the actions and discourse of the characters by omitting context and physical description. The narrator places the characters in motion, always in action or speaking. In this way, the authorial voice draws the reader's attention to what the characters say and how they say it.

The narrator also develops this dialogue in accord to conventions of the encounter dialogue genre. McRae describes this genre as corroborating the transmission lineage by establishing genealogical links between specific masters and students, who in their turn become masters of other students in later encounter dialogues (McRae 2000, 68–9). "The Chan genealogical model requires," writes McRae, "some form of mutual interaction, some confrontation, between teacher and student" (McRae 2003, 97). In such dialogues, the students implicitly represent an individualistic conception of the spiritual path to enlightenment, where the solitary individual gradually acquires and develops proficiency in different techniques to overcome one's ignorance. The master, alternatively, responds to the students in ways that reorient them toward an encounter conception of spiritual cultivation. "The teacher reacts to [student] assumptions," writes McRae, "by forcing the student into dialogue, into engaged interaction. Thus, the unipolar ... style of practice is changed into a bipolar encounter, in which a sudden insight can be achieved by a fundamental change in perspective" (McRae 2003, 97–8). The narrator clearly abides by this convention in the fourth dialogue of the *Mazu yulu*: Dazhu literally states that he, like a reader, is seeking enlightenment, and Mazu responds first with a testing question and then with—what is arguably—a genuine question.

The narrator appropriates the question as the narrator's own in such a way that the entirety of the *Mazu yulu* could be reduced to its essence in this question, "Why are you seeking outside?" The crucial move made by the narrator in order to accomplish this seems to be by means of allusion to Mazu's first sermon. In the sermon, Mazu expounds upon the Mahayana thesis of nonduality as it pertains to the individual striving for enlightenment. He teaches saying, "All of you should believe that your mind is Buddha, that this mind is identical with Buddha" (Cheng Chein 1992, 62). Further, he cites a passage from the Vimalakirti Sutra, one of the most influential sutras in Mahayana Buddhism, which says, "Those who seek the Dharma should not seek for anything" (Kumarajiva 1997, 74–5). The narrator has Mazu say all this within the first few sentences of his very first sermon. Moreover, the narrator has approximations of this question reverberate throughout the rest of Mazu's dialogues, at roughly the one-third mark of the way into the sequence of dialogues at dialogue eleven, and then at two-thirds of the way through them at dialogue twenty-one. The following is the latter: "Someone asked, 'What is the meaning of [Bodhidharma's] coming from the West?' 'What is the meaning of your asking at precisely this moment?' replied the Patriarch" (Wright 1998, 215). In these later cases, the narrator represents Mazu as addressing his interlocutor reflexively in order to stimulate their self-awareness or display the lack there of. As Wright writes,

> This was Ma-tsu's [Mazu's] favorite line and the text has him present it to all his students at precisely the right moment: the moment when, through prior cultivation, the "I" is prepared to emerge into self-awareness. This is about you, not "the self" in general, or some other self! Who are *you*, and *what are you doing*?
>
> (Wright 1998, 215; my emphasis)

By so reverberating the question through the rest of Mazu's encounter dialogues, as well as connecting the question and the sermons, the narrator brings the question into the foreground as a crucial question in Mazu's corpus and thereby engages the reader herself with it. The narrator, like Mazu, calls into question the seeking stature of the reader and listens to what the self-aware reader has to say in response.

Culminating Reflection: A Mastered Voice in Question

The *yulu* literature came to be treated with the same veneration as traditional Buddhist sutras imported from India. This literature frames masters like Mazu as full-fledged Buddhas themselves (see Bucklew 2019). It is not merely the masters depicted within the text, though. The voice of the text itself is a Buddha—the Buddha teaching the Dharma to the reader. In Chan traditions, the expectation ideal readers have for engaging with the *Mazu yulu* is to experience transformative power within the text (see Wallace 2000, 85). Moreover, this transformative experience happens not in solitary reading, the Buddhist studies scholar Vensa A. Wallace explains, but in a dialogue among a community of "real readers about and with the text" (Wallace 2000, 86). Such a dialogue challenges naïve or conventional distinctions between self and other (see Simmer-Brown 2000, 322). Via interdependence, Buddhahood is distributed among all who are openly engaged in the dialogue. Put differently, the interpretive dialogue helps make explicit the Buddhanature inherent in all things. The hermeneutic and phenomenological reduction necessary for engaging with texts in dialogue suspends our propensity to objectification within our natural and naïve attitude toward the world. This suspension opens readers to a new perception of the world. As the phenomenologist and Chan studies scholar Philip J. Bossert explains, it is not the world that substantively changes through a reader's grasp of the Buddha's Dharma. Instead, our expectations and attitudes change (Bossert 1976, 274).

In the realization that the voice of the text is the voice of Buddhanature or the Buddha's Dharma, we can specify how "mind to mind" transmission of the Dharma happens in Chan lineage (see Morrison 2010, 51–2). It is not some mystical and nonlinguistic telepathic event, despite the rhetoric of transmission "outside letters and books." When we see the Chan trope that "reading too much leads to indigestion," *the irony is that we are reading it in a text* (see Froese 2017). As the Zen studies specialist Steven Heine explains, there is an ironic overemphasis on this in such a way that it leads many to overlook all the sophisticated rhetoric in Chan texts (Heine 2015). With the destabilization of "self" and "other," there is an accompanying destabilization of "inside" and "outside" letters and books as well as destabilization of "master" and "student." As Heine writes, "Whoever is master and whoever is the disciple is relative and shifting" (Heine 2003, 538). Just as some students overturn the master within encounter dialogues, so do readers overturn the text in this second order dialogue between text and reader. Just as in encounter dialogues where masters and students cross lines for mutual development, so also do text and reader. We transcend the binary of either subordination or hierarchical authoritarianism, and we come to stand out in the realm of open and constructive exchange (see Heine 2003, 538).

The critique of language—and reading in particular—propounded in classical Chan must be specified against the default kinds of reading proliferating throughout society in the Tang and Song dynasties. We can recognize similar concerns about kinds of reading today as popular media articles go viral about how social media ruin our ability to maintain enough attention to read critically. This irony—that a critique of social media skimming goes viral on social media—should not be lost on us. It is the inverse of the substance of Chan irony about reading. How can we really allow the voice of the other to reach us, to transform us, if we are just skimming or imposing the need for only 240 characters (such as on Twitter)?

And this says little to nothing about contemporary readers' engagement with purportedly sacred texts. Consider the practice of what I call the Magic 8-Ball method of reading the Bible: Christians will flip pages at random to find a passage that they take to be a mystical coincidence of "What God is saying to me today." With regard to Buddhism, on any social media site, we can see viral memes of the Buddha's "deep thoughts" without any accompanying citation to a source. Such "reading" is a symptom of toxic positivity promulgated by feel-good quacks and capitalists like Eckhart Tolle. Chan masters appear to have been concerned with empty recitation of texts (see Wright 2003, 264–5). Just as many Vajrayana Buddhists use prayer flags with mantras or sutras where the wind blowing over them "recites" the passages and thus accrues karmic merit, many in Song China used mechanistically revolving bookshelves like prayer wheels that moved the books in such a way for similar merit procurement. This way of "reading" put texts to use for ritual, without regard to the meanings of the texts. Indeed, many monks made a living through public recitation of sutras. In none of these is literacy necessary. One can memorize sutras or glance at a sentence out of context. Moreover, even scholarly accumulation of books—whether just on the shelves or accumulating their contents as mere additional knowledge—is also a target of this critique of reading. That is, although a scholar is perceived often as an ideal reader, Chan ironic critique points out through metaphors of digestion and gluttony that these sorts of collectors do not really understand the meanings of the very texts they purport to know (see Wright 2003, 267). In all these cases, readers fetishize the book itself rather than engaging the text in dialogue. Thus, Chan masters (and their discourse records) do not really reject reading as such. Instead, as Wright points out, they "redefine" and rethink the practice. In Chan, reading provides spiritual sustenance.

Is Mazu's question addressed to us the readers? Why are we seeking outside? To accrue more information? For spiritual transformation? Unless that question becomes the text's question, and unless we ourselves share that question with the text itself, readers are in no position to understand what is being said. That is, readers are in no position to receive the Dharma taught by the Buddhas. Reflecting on this, Wright reflects,

> How is the text conceived? Is it a human spiritual product intended to assist in human self-cultivation, or one that in some way emerged from a divine source? Correspondingly, on which side of the reading equation does the power of religious transformation lie: in the sacred text itself or in the quality of the reader's practice?... To say that subjectivity is "empty," or that there is "no self," is to say, among several things, that the reader comes to be who he or she is dependent upon the qualities of language—the texts—that have been incorporated into oneself, and that the self is never the sole agent of that transformation.
>
> (Wright 2003, 269–70)

Buddhanature flows through all, extending back through the transmission lineage, but also extending into contemporary readers as well as future readers. Who is this "I" that in seeking awakening creates duality between the "I" and its aim? Why do we project this division between what is in us and what is outside us? Throughout this chapter, I have argued that we can isolate and foreground the voice of the text itself in part through putting the text in its historical context. This deific voice puts the genuine question posed by Mazu to readers themselves.

An Evangelist Asks, "What Do You Have to Say for Yourself?"

In this chapter, I want to revisit the Gospel episode where Jesus questions Peter, but this time on the level of narration rather than the level of story. I argue that through putting the text in historical context, we can foreground the voice of the text. And I argue that this deific voice appropriates the genuine question posed by Jesus and puts it to readers themselves. We will first look at questions about what is behind the lines, developing critical historical dynamics from which our focal episode emerged. Then we will turn to isolate an authorial voice addressing readers, focusing in particular on the genuine question asked of readers. We will conclude this chapter by reflecting on a redemptive voice in the Gospel attributed to Mark.

Questions behind the Lines: A Canon Emerging in Colonization

What are some crucial features of historical context within which the selected excerpt (see Chapter 6) was produced? Adapting to centuries of decimation by empires from the Babylonian and Persian to the Hellenistic and Roman, the people living on the small fertile land of Palestine could not successfully mount a military or political revolution for gaining permanent sovereignty. There were many attempts at revolution despite this. The most effective was the Maccabean revolt against the Syrian empire starting in 167 BCE, where they eventually established a small Jewish state. They appointed a member of the Hasmonean family as the ruler and high priest, breaking with the ancient tradition of appointing a priest from the line of Zadok (Ehrman 1999, 107). In 63 BCE, however, Pompey brought the Roman Empire to the gates of Jerusalem, and allowed the priest to maintain a liaison position with local Jewish leadership. Rome appointed a king to rule over Palestine in 40 BCE, Herod the Great. Through building projects and mass employment of labor, he brought the region of Judea into economic prominence over other regions such as Galilee. In light of his brutality in exercising control, though, he was perceived by many in the regions as opportunistic and as a collaborator who maintained Roman control (Ehrman 1999, 107). Given both the previous Hellenization of Palestine centuries earlier during Alexander the Great's reign and the additional imposition of Roman rule with Herod the Great, Jewish culture at the time was mixed with many elements of Greco-Roman culture (see Evans 2001, 12).

It is crucial to contextualize Jesus' life and teachings within this horizon of political subordination of Jewish desire for a sovereign state of Israel in first-century Palestine. In this context, the people could not hope to make a material dent in the Roman Empire, though. Thus, many in Jewish communities sublimated their religious longing for liberation from political ideals to spiritual ideals. Such overwhelming circumstances should be kept in mind when we hear apologists for Christianity say it is "superior" to Islam. They might say Jesus lived by nonviolence, whereas Muhammad purportedly used the sword to dominate others. Muhammad, though, could have hope of victory in militia skirmishes with the Quraysh, which was a mafia-like organization with economic control over the Kaba in Mecca (see Aslan 2011, 50–75).

Throughout Palestine was a general sense of tension between two things. On the one hand, strong observance of the Torah and faith to their God seemed to fulfill their side of the Abrahamic covenant. On the other hand, they still witnessed subjugation by a foreign ruler. Even more troubling was that the foreign ruler claimed to be the embodiment of the divine. Since Jews and Christians in the Roman Empire did not worship the emperor, they were all perceived as "atheists," that is, treasonous. The problem is how to reconcile belief in the God's promise of political sovereignty with direct evidence to the contrary. On this basis, the notion of the "messiah" transformed from primarily being conceived of as a political monarch to being conceived of as a priest and judge, connected to a belief that the God will correct this imbalance of power at a later time. That is, for many Jews apocalypticism formed a new mode of resistance as an alternative to the failures of direct armed resistance (see Ehrman 1999, 107). Galilee was a particularly fertile ground for both forms of resistance within a twenty-year span. John the Baptist and Jesus both led separate nonviolent marches on or rallies at the Temple. Shortly after that, a band of Galilean zealots and others attempted to restore the priesthood of Zadok's lineage through armed guerilla warfare at the Temple (Crossan 1995, 52–3; cf. Aslan 2013).

Jesus' date of birth can be traced roughly to between 6 and 4 BCE, near the time of Herod's death (Evans 2001, 13). He appears to have been a follower of John the Baptist's apocalyptic nonviolent movement. This movement emerged in response to Antipas' change of capital city of Perea—a neighboring region to Galilee—from Sepphoris to Tiberias. This put greater demands on the Jewish populace in the area, from labor to food to taxes (see Crossan 1995, 42). John the Baptist's mission was to offer a welcoming populist community and countercultural movement, set against both state-sanctioned exploitation and hierarchical centralization of religious devotion represented by the Temple. His message seemed especially emotionally rousing to the majority of listeners, though he encouraged waiting on the God's time for overthrowing government and religious institutions. That is, John's apocalyptic movement focused on a future age of his God's reign. State and religious officials seem to have been particularly concerned about the growing mass of followers, perceiving John's movement as a threat to their power. So, John was executed (Crossan 1995, 46).

As a witness to this result, Jesus seems to have revised John the Baptist's message from one of a delayed or later apocalypse to one of *imminent* apocalypse (Ehrman 2013, 304–6). For Jesus, time seems to be up. The kingdom of God is not a place people will go to when they die, but a place here on Earth where love and justice prevail over forces of injustice. Observance of the Torah is the way to prepare for and inaugurate the new kingdom, which the Turkish journalist and Islamic studies scholar Mustafa Akyol calls the faith *of* Jesus not the faith *about* Jesus (Akyol 2017, 35). Living ethically in light of the spirit of the Torah—rather than its exact letters—is what Jesus advocates (see Keen 2004, 25). Jesus' message, then, seems less Temple-centered than the Sadducees, less austere than the Pharisees, and less isolationist than the Essenes (Ehrman 2013, 310). Jesus, just like Hillel before him, taught loving one's neighbor is what matters most, as well as maintaining devotion to the God (Goldin 1946, 273). All the other laws should be interpreted and applied in light of this. Jesus did not abandon Judaism but challenged other interpretations of it—especially the institution of the family and the Temple cult (see Ehrman 2013, 319–22). If the world was ending soon—within one's lifetime—the family represents a future incompatible with that. He took this message to Jerusalem on Passover, enacting a symbolic destruction of the Temple, and was executed for this and treason against Rome in claiming to be a king (see Sanders 1985). He probably meant the claim to kingship apocalyptically.

We know that Jesus was likely a peasant or middle-class (see Evans 2001). A number of stories about him suggest he was at least moderately literate, but more importantly he was a genius storyteller (see Levine 2015). Even the synoptic Gospel writers themselves try to domesticate Jesus' teachings by priming readers to interpret some parables allegorically. For example, the writers of the Gospels of Luke and Matthew preface and interject throughout the parables about the mindless shepherd, the widow who loses count of her coins, and a father who neglects his eldest son with strict parallels to sinners being the lost sheep or missing coin or "prodigal" son (see Levine 2015, 34–5). This forces readers to interpret Jesus' parables as allegories, where the shepherd or father represents the God and those that are lost represent sinners. As if a sheep or coin could be grateful for being found! And, if the shepherd and father represent the God, then it would seem only fair that the woman represents the God in the one centered on the coin. The point is that the parables are not allegories even if the Gospel writers try to tame the parables into allegorical messages. What this helps us see, through the method of dissimilarity, is that Jesus likely taught these specific parables. Why would the writers feel a need to control the meaning of a parable if they could just invent any allegory they wanted? That is, the writers seem to be obligated to remain loyal to inherited traditions of Jesus' authentic sayings.

We need not be too preoccupied with the quest for the historical Jesus here, though. Our concern is with the construction of Jesus, particularly in the synoptic Gospels—those with a relatively "shared view" of Jesus: Mark, Matthew, and Luke. As Bultmann writes,

> The sources offer us… the message of the early Christian community, which for the most part the Church freely attributed to Jesus. This naturally gives us no proof that all the words which are put into his mouth were actually spoken by him. As can be easily proved, many sayings originated in the church itself, others were modified by the church.
>
> (Bultmann 1934, 12)

As we have noted multiple times, historical context provides constraints for interpretations, but we need to focus our attention to what is on and between the lines as much as if not more than what is behind the lines. A crucial historical analysis not only includes the quest for the historical Jesus but also examines the historical context of the differing Gospels themselves.

Questions beyond the Lines: An Authorial Voice Questions Readers' Epistemic Accountability

Very few Palestinians could read and write in Jesus' day, and all of the disciples were peasant class. Thus, Jesus' disciples were likely unable to read and write. Even if they could, it would be in Aramaic. The canonized Gospels, however, are composed in Greek. Whoever their writers were, they must have been fluent in a foreign language. Indeed, they must have been so fluent as to compose brilliant works of art like the Gospels (see Ehrman 2013, 47–8). While Christian traditions ascribe two of the canonized Gospels to disciples—Matthew and John—no one has ever taken the other two—Mark and Luke—to be eyewitness accounts of Jesus' life.

In terms of putting the canonized Gospels into historical order, Mark is probably the oldest one, likely composed near 70 CE. It is clear because both Matthew and Luke are based partially on Mark. Thus, both of these are composed later, probably near 80 CE. John, however, is quite different in composition, containing very few of the teachings in the other Gospels—particularly the parables—and adding unique philosophically or theologically oriented longer discourses not in the other Gospels (Barton 2001, 173–4). John was probably composed between 90 and 100 CE and shows extensive influence by Greek philosophy. In this light, the texts themselves are composed decades after Jesus was executed, nearly an entire generation later. Just as Judaism adapted to a portable textual tradition after the destruction of the second Temple, and just as later generations of Dharma heirs constructed images of classical Chan masters, so also did Jewish and Gentile Christians adapt through the composition and standardization of Gospel texts. It is likely that these writers had access to many earlier written accounts and sources, such as Luke's claim to know many earlier authors (Ehrman 2013, 79). It should seem like a striking decision to include only these four Gospels in the Christian canon (see Barton 2001, 170). It was not until 367 CE, in a letter by the early Church father Athanasius, that we see a list of twenty-seven books corresponding to those in the New Testament. Before this, many gospels were in circulation—from the Gospel of Thomas and the Gospel of Mary to the Gospel of Peter. The four canonized ones became the most common, likely due to the invention of the codex—a device that served as an alternative to scrolls where up to four separate books could be collected and bound together (see King 2003, 7–12; and Barton 2001, 180).

It is well known that although the Gospel writers, or evangelists, wrote narratives about the same subject matter, they did so with different interests and aims and by different means. It is plausible to claim, then, that they all felt invited—if not also compelled by their commitment (see Lk. 1:1-3)—*to share what they thought about this subject matter with regard to a specific genuine question*. In addition to the evidence that the Matthew and Luke Gospels draw on the material in Mark's text, New Testament scholars have also reached further consensus on the existence of a source text of Jesus' sayings, simply named Q, an abbreviation of the German word for source, *Quelle*. Q accounts for other parallels in the Gospels of Matthew and Luke. Each of these three writers—Mark, Matthew, and Luke—constructs a narrator with their own story to tell about a similar subject matter, and with their own collection of details to arrange in their own way. That is, we can consider the creation of and composition of Gospels in similar ways to the redaction of the Torah and the production of Chan transmission literature. Focusing specifically on Mark's Gospel, I want to sketch a way in which the narrator poses a genuine question to the reader with reference to Jesus' seemingly genuine question in Mk. 8:29.

The specific passage, Mk. 8:29, initiates the central and transitional argumentative and narratival sequence (roughly Mk. 8–10) of, as the New Testament scholar Ian H. Henderson writes, "the Gospel's message about discipleship in imitation of Jesus' anointed death" (Henderson 2000, 48). With this passage, Mark's narrator introduces the first of three predictions Jesus makes about his impending death (the other two in Mk. 9:31 and 10:33-34). As the New Testament and comparative sacred texts scholar Vernon K. Robbins shows, in each of these three episodes, the method in Mark is to unfold the actions of Jesus in sequences of three steps (Robbins 1981). According to Robbins, "the final step [of each episode] introduces the dramatic conclusion to Jesus' action in the form of emphatic speech *that summons and commands*" (Robbins 1981, 102; my emphasis). Questions, at least deficit-driven ones as we explained, embody this combination of summons and commands. All three episodes begin with the first step describing Jesus in motion, going from one place to another, accompanied by his disciples. The second step situates Jesus in a more intensive interaction with his disciples, such as mediating debates that have arisen between them. And in the third step, Jesus summons or calls all the disciples and teaches them about the implications of following him. "The three units," Robbins writes, "reach their highpoint in a final part that emphasizes the authoritative status of Jesus as a teacher" (Robbins 1981, 105).

The narrator's mention of motion symbolizes the crucial character of these transitional moments. And insofar as the latter episodes repeat this tripartite structure, they refer to the first episode in which Jesus poses the question, "Who do you say I am?" That is, the narrator uses repetition to point back to this question. Repetition stresses the importance of the events, and the question, if addressed, allows for the integration of those events into a coherent whole. Through this repetition, the narrator appropriates Jesus' question for themselves. Jesus' question becomes the narrator's question as well, in the sense that the narrator poses the question to the reader—*or, what amounts to the same thing, requires that the reader ask it of herself as the reader.* Booth describes this feature of narrative voice as the questions that are "insisted upon by the text" (Booth 1979, 238). According to Booth, texts demand that readers ask certain questions rather than others. Appealing to readers to ask a question need not take the form of a "demand." Indeed, if the reader understands the question which the narrator poses, then the reader asks it as well. There is no cleavage between understanding a question and asking it in need of mediation with the operation of a demand. Merely stating that a text asks a reader a question or set of questions is enough; we do not need, with Booth, to appeal as well to the supposed demands a text makes on the reader.

In order to understand what Mark's narrator is saying and asking, then, the reader needs to ask the question proffered by the story. The narrator appeals to readers to consider this question and ask it themselves. Furthermore, just as the discussion of movement connotes crucial changes in the narrative, so does the question connote a crucial change in the reader's involvement with the text. In being asked that question, and in coming to ask that question oneself, the reader transitions into Mark's ideal audience. If readers ask this question with the narrator, and even attempt to answer it for themselves, they will find the narrator's answer to the question as a live possibility. That is, inasmuch as Mark's portrait of Jesus is as a servant-martyr, this only makes sense to readers who actually ask the question, "Who do I say Jesus is?" Only in this way can a reader come to consider Mark's answer as a potential option for the reader to appropriate as their own answer. Matthew and Luke, too, as readers of Mark saw themselves as responsive contributors to this unfolding dialogue.

Repetition stresses the importance of the events; allusion integrates the events such that what happens in one is associated with the others. By means of these, the narrator attempts to raise and address the question by presenting Jesus as an authoritative teacher on the subject of discipleship, especially as this requires martyrdom. In this way, the narrator takes seriously what the reader thinks and listens to what the reader has to say as well as responds to it. By way of assimilating Jesus' question to the level of narration via poetic strategies like allusion and repetition, the implied author poses the question as a genuine one to the reader.

This is precisely the way in which a number of Jesus' questions have been read. As an example of this with regard to *all* of Jesus' questions is a devotional book titled *The Questions of Jesus* (see Dear 2004). These sorts of exercises, however, read against the narrative function of many of Jesus' questions, as we noted in Chapter 6. Ricoeur, echoing Frei, believes that Jesus' second question, where he asks, "Who do you say I am?," sufficiently summarizes the entirety of the Gospels if not the entire New Testament (Ricoeur 1995, 185). It is the main topic that coordinates and integrates all the other narrative elements into a whole. Who is this person? What is the meaning of his life, teachings, and death? What relevance does it have for one's own life? Ricoeur writes, "It is a fact that the identity of Jesus remains an acute question throughout the Gospels" (Ricoeur 1995, 185). I think that we can go even further and claim that this question, as a genuine question, grounds the proliferation of Christian traditions. Without this *question*— as the condition of the possibility of the various proposed answers or perspectives—the variety of Christian traditions would not be possible.

Culminating Reflection: A Redemptive Voice in Question

Overall, Mark's Gospel is a passion narrative, "with extended introduction" (Henderson 2000, 48). In many ways, the Gospel of Mark is a working set of notes with rough arrangement. It is open-ended enough for later authors to make use of it in producing their own tailored and modified compositions (see Larsen 2018). The textual "unfinishedness" of Mark invites dialogue between the text and readers. As the New Testament studies scholar Raj Nadella explains, though in his case with regard to the Gospel of Luke, readers are distanced from the subject matter and this distance allows for a more comprehensive perspective to bring it into dialogue with the text itself (Nadella 2011, 111). Just as Jesus' family and friends in Nazareth dismiss his message even though they are the first to hear it, *readers who are "too close" to the subject matter are likely to have auditory atrophy*. Not only is Mark unfinished then, *critically engaged readers are the precise kind of outsiders who can appropriate meaning from the text*. As the Christian origins scholar Michael J. Thate writes, "something startling happens for the Reader: they become the star of the Markan Script, and themselves become the missing ending/new beginning of" the Gospel (Thate 2013, 270). The reader and text reach what Gadamer calls, inspired by Kierkegaard, "contemporaneity," where they interact in dialogue across a vast distance of time (Gadamer 2013, 129). It is the "outsidedness" that makes dialogue unfold in multiple layers and from ever-diversifying perspectives given the unique life issues faced by different readers.

In this way, as the New Testament studies scholar Mitzi J. Smith explains African American biblical interpretation,

> all biblical interpretation… is political, seeking to expose oppressive ideologies in texts, contexts, and in ancient and contemporary readers and readings. This political agenda includes the debunking of respectability politics, which claims that people of color and poor people will always be treated with dignity, justice, and respect in a racialized, patriarchal, and class-conscious society *when they exhibit acceptable behaviors*. Unacceptable behaviors, according to a politics

of respectability, like responding to injustice or resisting and protesting systemic racism, sexism, and violence from authority figures, should result in negative, harmful outcomes, particularly when the actors are persons of color.

(Smith 2017, 65; my emphasis)

Respectability politics demands that all people submit to the norms of white patriarchal capitalism, and deviations from these norms will be reined in, punished brutally, or even eliminated. Specific intersecting interests, privileges, and marginalizations shape all readers. And these shape readers' perspectives and capacities and directions for dialogue with the text. The broader and ongoing dialogue must be inclusive of a multiplicity of perspectives, with particular attention paid to the voices of the oppressed— *even at the cost of what may seem to be crucial elements of the biblical text.* For example, Smith advocates overturning parables that emphasize the interests of enslavers and the purported foolishness of virgins (Smith 2017, 77–93). With regard to the Syrophoenician woman's "dialogue" with Jesus we discussed in Chapter 6, recall that she persists despite his dismissal of her. Smith underscores the importance and dangers of "sass" and backtalk, comparing the woman's successful persistence to Sandra Bland's death by hanging (ruled a "suicide"), where she questioned the police officers detaining her for "failure to signal change of lane" (see Byron and Lovelace 2016, 95–112). Many others have approached this episode between the woman and Jesus in terms of moral judgment, such as by determining who is the victim or the hero of the exchange. Women of color, however, often face such situations of being minimized or treated as "too aggressive" where tactical navigation is necessary *as matters of survival.* The woman does whatever it takes. As the womanist homiletics scholar and reverend Raquel A. St. Clair emphasizes, biblical interpretation must take into consideration unique issues faced by African American women in particular (St. Clair 2007, 59; and St. Clair 2008, 11). Through grounding the dialogue of interpretation in the concrete reality of Black women's lives, we can develop a hermeneutic of wholeness supporting the spirituality of all people.

Just as Smith promotes sass and backtalk as a tactic for challenging oppressive authoritarianism, readers should have this tactic ready for talking back to the text itself. This is so especially when one's reading might seem to go against the status quo, exposing the political and policed norms for what and who counts as "legitimate" readers of New Testament texts. Indeed, inasmuch as the text asks genuine questions of readers, the text itself invites readers' self-attestation. What is said in the text might be less significant than how it is said. Is the text itself asking readers questions in a tone of genuineness or in a tone of interrogation—where the latter assumes there is a correct answer? How do readers hear the voice (see Dawsey 1986, 24)? Is it actually a conversation? Who is excluded from answering? Who isn't asked the questions? The biblical studies scholar Mary Ann Tolbert explains that the Gospel of Mark was like a popular Greek novel of the era, written for a wide spectrum of society (Tolbert 1996, 71). Yet given the low literacy rates in first-century Palestine, this audience must have been among the educated elite—like in Song-era China (see Chapter 8). That is, as literacy rates have increased, the "wide spectrum of society" has also increased in diversity, turning interpretation into an ever-broadening cacophony of voices in dialogue.

This radical inclusiveness might seem to lead to more and more disagreements, where the differing voices may hold contradictory perspectives on many topics. The concern we might have is who has the authority to determine "the" answer definitively? Do some usurp this power? Some people have been marginalized systemically in their capacity to respond by those in power, excluded from being perceived as legitimate contributors to the dialogue by privileged white men. As biblical studies scholar and Pastor Larry L. Enis underscores, postcolonial hermeneutics expose how status quo interpretations preserve classist, racist, sexist, and ableist hierarchies, and offer methodologically diverse alternative *strategies and tactics of reading as resistance to complicity* (see Enis 2005). Because of all of our participation in these dialogues, we all have the chance to change our positions, to change our ways toward better material conditions for all. What do you have to say for yourself as a reader? I have argued that through putting the text in historical context, we can foreground the voice of the text. And I argued that this deific voice appropriates the genuine question posed by Jesus and puts it to readers themselves.

Conclusion: Human Responses to Questions Asked by Deific Figures

What does it mean that religious narratives display deific figures, such as Gods and Buddhas, as asking questions? What does it mean for readers to experience sacred texts as deific voices, voices that ask questions of them? What if some of their questions are genuine ones? The appearance of questions in deific voices stands in need of demythologizing or, what I call elsewhere, "anapotheotics" (Dickman 2022). For my conclusion, I want to explore ways anapotheotics works to help overcome what we can call a kind of spiritual alienation (see Feuerbach 1989). I also want to dwell with the hermeneutic difficulty of reading genuine questions within deific voices and emphasize what is at stake with questioning together. Sharing questions—the point of genuine questioning—is one among many tactics to challenge authoritarianism and fascism.

Anapotheotics: Bringing Divine Discourse Down to Earth

I am writing this in the middle of the worst mass casualty event in US history. The number of deaths in the United States alone from the coronavirus pandemic has exceeded 734,611 as of October 12, 2021. There have been 4,872,884 deaths globally. Even by October 3, 2020, there were 260,000 deaths caused by Covid-19, with findings by the CDC that there were likely greater than 300,000 "excess deaths," those preventable deaths likely related to—though not necessarily directly caused by—Covid-19 (Rossen et al. 2020). We also know that these deaths and the number of illnesses faced from contracting the virus reveal vastly disproportionate effects on systemically marginalized and oppressed communities. While there appears to be some hope in vaccines distributed throughout the world even against the Delta and Lambda variants, the polarized US population does not show many signs of increased community care and justice. We know from the study of political and social determinants of health that this pandemic, and the inordinate death and infection numbers as well as the inequitable death and infection rates affecting oppressed communities in the United States specifically, that much of this catastrophe is a result of failed leadership by the Trump administration (see Dawes 2020; and Dickman and Chicas 2021). All this has happened in addition to the Trump administration's attempt at a coup by suing for recounts in numerous states, where Donald Trump finally seemed to concede formally to a clearly determined vote outcome in Joe Biden's favor on January 8, 2021 (Sorkin 2020). On Wednesday, January 6, 2021, many privileged white Trump supporters, or petite bourgeoisie, barged into the halls of Congress and interrupted the Electoral Vote count. How could they take a weekday and afford to fly (without masks?) for this horrible attack? And this says nothing about the ongoing Black Lives Matters protests against police brutality erupting as the result of the murders of George Floyd, Breona Taylor, Ahmaud Arbery, and too many more. I highlight all of this because, perhaps, we are living in a time with partial similarities to that of the writers of the Hebrew Scriptures, the writers of the *Mazu yulu*, and the Gospel writers. That is, just as they all seem to have found spiritual inspiration despite or in spite of political catastrophes, we too may be living in a time of spiritual inspiration in the face of our current catastrophes. What we may be witnessing is a spiritual alienation, unique to our time, where social divide and upheaval simultaneously accompany a division within ourselves, where individuals are similarly disintegrating spiritually under these conditions of our existence (see Tillich 2000). How can we find the courage to be, to affirm ourselves as individuals and as members of a greater global community, in the face of all these threats of nonbeing? I want to turn to make one contribution, which is only among many more that are needed as we build coalitions with others where we mobilize together to bring about a more just and more beautiful pluralistic society.

Despite the end of religion, I do think religious resources can provide orientation for our human aspirations. Demythologization is the primary framework within which anapotheotics works, so allow me to explain it in brief. Demythologization is not, as the name might seem to suggest, the getting rid of *mere* myths. This distorts the deeper meaning of myth or the ancient Greek *mythos* as the kind of discourse that has the power of authoritarian tradition and narrative backing it—as it is distinct from *logos*, discourse backed up by reasons (see Plato 1991, 442–3; and Lincoln 1996). In colloquial talk, people often use myth as synonymous with "falsehood," as in popular shows focused on myth-busting. The notion of myth at stake here, though, is that kind of discourse that addresses things not susceptible to direct description, or what Ricoeur calls our possibilities for modes of being or forms of life (Ricoeur 1976, 94). The task is not to get rid of myth. That is not possible because what we access through myth is only available through myth. The task instead is to appropriate or understand the meanings made available through and in myth. For Bultmann, that involves the existentialist interpretation of myth (see Bultmann 1989; and Congdon 2015).

I use anapotheotics to emphasize the critical and reflexively thorough retrieval of meaning from its drift into some ethereal "divine" or metaphysically transcendent realm. The method is to expose not what a religion says about a God or a Buddha but *to redirect our attention to what religions are really about: us.* The modern philosophical anthropologist Ludwig Feuerbach gets at this through his method of transformational grammar, where we invert the relations between subjects and predicates in religious discourse. For example, the sentence "God is love" puts our love into an alien entity existing in some realm separate from us, one that transcends ours. Through this reification and objectification, we are alienated from ourselves. Feuerbach believes we can overcome this spiritual alienation through retrieving the meaning of the complete thought, which takes inverting it into "Our love is divine" (Feuerbach 1989, 53). That is, as we have emphasized throughout this book, religious symbols—such as the word "God" or "Buddha" or "Prophet" or "Christ"—are used properly as predicates and not as subjects of complete thoughts. The predicate brings out the significance and meaning of the subject. As Feuerbach writes, "The Word of God is really the divinity of the human word" (Feuerbach 1989, 79). Through imagination, Feuerbach explains, we reify our ideals into entities distinct from ourselves, as divine entities (Feuerbach 1989, 22-3). This reification alienates us from deific figures, where they are constructed as radically other than us. In this way, we escalate ordinary existential transcendence into a metaphysically transcendent entity. We misrecognize this through inverting grammatical subjects and predicates. Doing so alienates us from our power and courage.

Yet I want to take this even further, building upon both Bultmann and Feuerbach. This retrieval of meaning from its alienated reification is an immanent refiguration of our world here and now. I describe it as *the eminently immanent poetic redemption of the real.* I mean this in the best sense of poetry, appealing to the meaning of the Greek *poiesis*, or to make. Through religious poetic predicates, we can refigure our world, to make it intelligible. As the sociologist of religions Reza Aslan writes,

> The fact is no evangelist in any of the world's religions would have been at all concerned with recording his or her objective observations of historical events. They would not have been recording observations at all! Rather, they were interpreting those events in order to give structure and meaning to... their community, providing future generations with

> a common identity, a common aspiration, a common story. *After all,*
> *religion is… interpretation.*
>
> (Aslan 2011, xxiv; my emphasis)

Religious traditions orient individuals and communities toward ultimate fulfilment and provide a fundamental interpretation of experience or narrative in which events make sense. Anapotheotics has a negative moment relative to ways people often believe that their religious language works as representing metaphysically existent divine entities. On another level, though, this project is productive. By philosophizing about questions in religious narrative or fiction, we can show how people use religions *poetically to redeem the real*. It is not a denial of religion but a reorientation away from reified abstraction to existential appropriation and empowerment. Malcolm X elaborates on this problem with regard to his perception of African American Christians of his day. He states, "We were much better off than the [others] who would shout, as my father preached, for the pie-in-the-sky and their heaven in the hereafter while the white man had his here on earth" (X 1992, 8).

As Anderson emphasizes, accounts of what it is to be human require elaboration on our effort to be or human growth, including some notion of "projection" or "yearning" (Anderson 2001, 197; see also Dickman 2018c). Our effort is structured by "regulative ideals" (see Anderson 1998, 135–7). Regulative ideals are what we are left with to guide practical reason in the place of transcendent metaphysical entities (such as "god") after the destruction of traditional substance metaphysics. Discourse about metaphysical entities does not, as Anderson writes, "constitute knowledge. But [it] can direct human understanding toward a practical goal without forgetting the illusion of claiming to know what is beyond every given experience" (Anderson 2001, 137). Specific symbols and archetypes concretize our regulative ideals, which configure into narrative wholes or myths. They open up possibilities for our becoming. The symbols and myths are regulative ideals through which we project our yearning, and consequently *reappropriate ourselves through them for fuller self-realization*. As Ricoeur writes, "The religious has as its function the deliverance of the core of goodness from the bonds that hold it captive" (Ricoeur 2010, 30). This is the fundamental feature of culture, or the cultivation of fully realized human beings. For example, when one sits in meditation or performs *zazen*, one alienates one's self from oneself in striving to emulate a Buddha, and in so sitting, one returns to oneself having sat in emulation of such a Buddha (see Faure 2009, 28; and Dickman 2018c). This is one way in which symbols cultivate self-attestation.

The feminist philosopher Luce Irigaray argues that patriarchal societies limit the symbols for projections and reappropriations of feminine subjectivity (Irigaray 2007, 11). The quest for equality, in Irigaray's eyes, can serve to promote men as the symbolic ideal toward which women strive. Rather than a vague "equality," Irigaray urges respect for differences. Irigaray points out that "motherhood," if deployed as symbolic of a regulative ideal for cultivating feminine selfhood, can be made complicit with patriarchal social systems. She writes,

> So many young women and so many girls expect their cultural elders to give them a lead on the possibility of their becoming women without an exclusive subjection to motherhood, and without, for all that, being reduced to male identity. I think it shows that the goals of our liberation have remained tied to a culture that offers women no subjective opportunities, and that, for want of an identity of their own, many are, in a vague sort of way, trying to find a niche for themselves within a technological era that needs their energy to give itself the illusion of a future.
>
> (Irigaray 2007, 128)

Cultures function to cultivate human becomings through symbolic and mythic projections, and these are rooted in specific practices and rituals. Yet the lack of symbols, myths, and practices that could facilitate blossoming inhibits feminine subjectivities. While we can see how specific isolated symbols, such as Buddhahood, might work, as well as how their absence might inhibit a person's flourishing, we should also note ways in which narratives serve similar roles. For example, the Exodus narrative has served as a mythic embodiment and regulative ideal for liberation.

My concern is with what genuine questions mean under the anapotheotic method. What do genuine questions—in the mouths of deific figures or coming from the deific voice of the sacred text itself—tell us about human yearning? Why focus so much on questions posed by figures of ultimate authority? What does this symbolize? How ought we demythologize questions in their direct discourse, and questions posed by texts to readers themselves? As we have now seen, the narrators of Mark's Gospel, Genesis, and Mazu's *yulu* appropriate potential genuine questions posed by the deific figures within the narratives. In their turn, the texts themselves pose those genuine questions to readers to reach an understanding with them. Only by means of such genuine questions is the text itself able to respond to the reader and any subsequent reading she might undertake. The genuine questions asked of the reader become shared by the reader, too. In this way, readers are made responsibly self-aware so that what they say back to the text will have integrity. By means of these questions not only do the figures endowed with ultimate authority call their interlocutors to self-awareness, so also do the narrators call upon their readers to become the same. This will only work, however, if the narrators of religious texts hear what the readers then have to say. It is the irony that not only do "texts speak" but "texts listen" too (Dickman 2014). The texts do so in the very event of posing their open questions to the reader and engaging in the ensuing dialogue. Intersubjectivity grounds responsive integrity. The reader responds to an interlocutor who, in turn, responds to the reader. In this way, a dialogue ensues from the momentum initiated by genuine questions. It transforms the exegetical phenomenon of the genuine question into an existential phenomenon. Not only do readers speak with a text that speaks but readers are also heard by a text who listens, and in its listening, bears witness to an ultimate horizon of being heard in being itself. It symbolizes, in other words, our acceptance of being accepted (see Tillich 2000, 185).

I have addressed this elsewhere as the analysis of the transcendental enabler of responsibility (see Dickman 2018b). Is the fundamental enabler of our ability to respond a "call" or a "question"? Thinkers like Heidegger and Levinas converge in claiming it is a call—that the face of the Other (Levinas) or uncanny Dasein (Heidegger) calls one out into authentic or responsive existence. As we have seen, religious narratives interpreted with an aim at genuine questions open up an alternative clue to this transcendental enabler of responsivity: genuine and shared questions. In the preface to his philosophical reflection on the claim that "god speaks," Wolterstorff asks, "Might it be that God is a member of the community of speakers?" (Wolterstorff 1995, ix). My topic is of a more specific philosophical interest: Might it be that deific voices participate in dialogue? Do they ask genuine questions? It is not merely that HaShem, Mazu, and Jesus speak *at* their listeners but that—more importantly—they seem in some cases to speak *with* them. It is not merely that the sacred texts themselves speak at their audiences but with them. This depends on our hermeneutic, and the one we developed here opens up this possibility, yet it does not settle the matter definitively. I have tried to develop it as itself a genuine question—putting responsibility on readers to answer to this for themselves. Is it "there in the text"? If so, their dialogue partners are endowed with a deep and abiding form of responsibility grounded in being heard by the ultimate, as ones capable of response to an overwhelming authority. Their asking of questions in such a way as to enter into dialogue brings these figures "down to earth." This is the crucial moment that constitutes humans and deific voices as sharing a universe of discourse. In this sense, deific voices before the lines navigate between the overreaching "hypertheism" of fundamentalist groups clinging to some God behind the lines and the nihilistic "overhumanization" of militant atheists and reductive naturalists with an entirely absent god (see Klemm and Schweiker 2008, 14–15). Only between these extremes may we realize a genuine dialogue with deific voices by way of their "appropriated" texts.

Questioning Together Is Antifascist

We started this project by looking at contrasts between deific voices developed in sacred texts and institutional religious leaders. I want to end emphasizing how deific voices display virtues of hospitality, humility, and an embrace of uncertainty—*if they ask genuine questions*. Institutional religious leaders, such as preachers and monks, often fail at imitating these virtues; instead, they claim to have certainty, as if their religion is a transcendent key to existence providing them with answers to all the questions they and their followers might have. *Their goal seems to be to stop questioning rather than genuine shared questioning.* What we have developed through focus on shared genuine questions is a model of how religious existence can be marked by discursive hospitality with others, even others who belong to vastly different religious traditions or none at all.

These virtues are the same ones we would expect from a robust deliberative democracy, where people with radically different perspectives can still enter into civic conversations and make decisions about policies that shape society for all. Recognizing that questioning is a crucial element with religious meaning and understanding opens us to the recognition that people can embody this in their social and political life. That is, in seeking to emulate their God or their Buddha, religious participants do not need to be wishy-washy in their commitments to "tolerate" living in communal relations with others. Instead, political contributions can maintain a relation to one's religious inspiration because, through genuine shared questions, one also maintains an openness to other perspectives as well as a preservation of the importance of truth-seeking in pluralistic society.

Can we imagine fascist leaders sharing or even asking questions? In a sense, deficit-driven questions can easily become tools in their hands, as we noted in our discussion of interrogation in the Introduction. Again, we probably can imagine fascist interrogators and leaders asking questions in the service of discovery or creating culpability. For example, "Where were you last night?" Authoritarians might even say, "It is *we* who will ask the questions around here!" (see Žižek 1989, 182). The fascist politic traffics in imagery that creates divisions between "us" and "them," based on ethnic, religious, ableist, or national conflicts (see Stanley 2018). Like the petite bourgeoisie who attacked the US Congress, followers do not ask questions of their leaders. They demonstrate more loyalty to their leader than to truth, understanding, and—as we have seen with the Trump administration's response to the coronavirus—*science*. For example, Trump referred to Dr. Anthony Fauci, director of the U.S. National Institute of Allergy and Infectious Diseases, as a "disaster" and called other epidemiologists "idiots." How can leadership occur in the absence of questioning? Thus, it is crucial to emphasize the difference between deficit-driven questions and surplus-driven questions. Genuine questions—shared questions—cannot be put to the service of authoritarianism. The authority of genuine questioning comes from superior insight, not from coercive power over others. If deific voices do not and cannot ask genuine questions, if they do not and cannot share questions, then perhaps they are merely models for authoritarianism and fascism. Alternatively, if they do ask genuine questions—both on the level of story and on the level of narration—then they might serve as a source for an antidote to fascism. By questioning together in genuine questions, we overcome easy divisions and hierarchies between "us" and "them."

I want to close with a final comment and question. We can think about how close or far we are from overcoming fascist distinctions by considering some of the rights we are most vocal in defending. We spend great deal of effort advocating for and protesting infringements upon the freedom of speech. How many of us, though, have advocated for or protested infringements upon the freedom to listen, to understand with genuine shared questions? We hear a lot about the right to free speech. What about the right to freely listen, the right to freely understand?

Bibliography

Adler, Mortimer J., and Charles Van Doren. 1972. *How to Read a Book: The Classic Guide to Intelligent Reading*, completely revised and updated. New York: Touchstone.

Ahmed, Sara. 2005. *Queer Phenomenology: Orientations, Objects, Others*. Durham: Duke University.

Ahmed, Sara. 2006. *Queer Phenomenology: Orientations, Objects, Others*. Duke University.

Akyol, Mustafa. 2017. *The Islamic Jesus: How the King of the Jews Became a Prophet of the Muslims*. New York: St. Martin's Press.

Aland, Barbara, Kurt Aland, Johannes Karavidopouios, Carlo M. Martini, and Bruce M. Metzger (eds.). 1993. *Novum Testamentum Graece*. Stuttgart: Deutsche Bibelgesellschaft.

Alster-Elata, Gerda, and Rachel Salmon. 1993. "Biblical Covenants as Performative Language." In *Summoning: Ideas of the Covenant and Interpretive Theory*, ed. Ellen Spolsky. Albany: SUNY Press.

Altemeyer, Bob, and Bruce Hunsberger 1992. "Authoritarianism, Religious Fundamentalism, Quest, and Prejudice." *The International Journal for the Psychology of Religion* 2(2): 113–33.

Alter, Robert. 1981. *The Art of Biblical Narrative*. New York: Basic Books.

Alter, Robert. 2004. *The Five Books of Moses: A Translation with Commentary*. New York: W. W. Norton & Company.

Amoros, Celia, Ana Uriarte, and Lina Lopez McAlister. 1994. "Cartesianism and Feminism: What Reason Has Forgotten: Reasons for Forgetting." *Hypatia* 9(1): 147–63.

Anderson, Pamela Sue. 1998. *A Feminist Philosophy of Religion: Rationality and Myths of Religious Belief*. Oxford: Wiley Blackwell.

Anderson, Pamela Sue. 2001. "Gender and the Infinite: On the Aspiration to Be All There Is." *International Journal for Philosophy of Religion* 50: 191–212.

Aquinas, Thomas. 1993. *A Shorter Summa: The Essential Philosophical Passages*, ed. P. Kreeft. San Francisco: Ignatius Press.

Aquinas, Thomas. 2010. "Reasons for the Faith against Muslim Objections." *St. Francis Magazine* 6(4): 733–67.

Aristotle. 1999. *Nicomachean Ethics*, 2nd ed, trans. T. Irwin. Hackett.

Asad, Talal. 2007/2008. "On Suicide Bombing." *The Arab Studies Journal* 15(2)/16(1): 123–30.

Aslan, Reza. 2011. *No God but God: The Origins, Evolution, and Future of Islam*, Updated Edition. Random House Trade Paperbacks.

Aslan, Reza. 2013. *Zealot: The Life and Times of Jesus of Nazareth*. New York: Random House.

Averroes (Ibn Rushd). 2012. *On the Harmony of Religion and Philosophy*, trans. G. Hourani. Cambridge: Gibb Memorial Trust.

Barthes, Roland. 1975. "An Introduction to the Structural Analysis of Narrative." *New Literary History* 6:2 (Winter): 237–62.

Barthes, Roland. 1977. *Image Music Text*, trans. Steven Heath. New York: Hill and Wang.

Barton, Stephen. 2001. "Many Gospels, One Jesus?" In *The Cambridge Companion to Jesus*, edited by Markus Brockmuehl. Cambridge University Press.

Bayer, Oswald. 2003. "Hermeneutical Theology." *Scottish Journal of Theology* 56: 2.

Beatty, Joseph. 1999. "Good Listening." *Educational Theory* 49(3): 281–98.

Beckwith, Christopher I. 2009. *Empires of the Silk Road: A History of Central Eurasia from the Bronze Age to the Present*. Princeton: Princeton University Press.

Bell, Catherine. 2009. *Ritual Theory, Ritual Practice*. New York: Oxford University Press.

Bell, Martin. 1975. "Questioning." *The Philosophical Quarterly* 25(100): 193–212.

Berling, Judith A. 1987. "Bringing the Buddha Down to Earth: Notes on the Emergence of 'Yu-Lu' as a Buddhist Genre." *History of Religions* 27: 56–88.

Blofeld, John. 1962. Trans., *The Zen Teaching of Hui Hai on Sudden Illumination: Being the Teaching of the Zen Master Hui Hai, known as the Great Pearl*. London: Rider & Company.

Bloom, Edward, Wayne C. Booth, and Wolfgang Iser. 1977. "In Defense of Authors and Readers." *NOVEL: A Forum on Fiction* 11(1): 5–25

Boomershine, Thomas E. 1980. "The Structure of Narrative Rhetoric in Genesis 2–3." *Semia* 18.

Booth, Wayne C. 1979. *Critical Understanding: The Powers and Limits of Pluralism*. Chicago: The University of Chicago Press.

Bossert, Philip J. 1976. "Paradox and Enlightenment in Zen Dialogue and Phenomenological Description." *Journal of Chinese Philosophy* 3: 269–80.

Brownlie, Faye, Susan Close, and Linda Wingren. 1988. *Reaching for Higher Thought: Reading, Writing, Thinking Strategies*. Edmonton: Arnold Publishers.

Buber, Martin. 1970. *I and Thou*, trans. Walter Kaufmann. Touchstone.

Buber, Martin. 1996. *On Judaism*. New York: Penguin.

Bublitz, Wolfram. 1988. *Supportive Fellow-Speakers and Cooperative Conversation*. Philadelphia: John Benjamins.

Bucklew, Kevin. 2019. "Becoming Chinese Buddhas: Claims to Authority and the Making of Chan Buddhist Identity." *T'oung Pao* 105(3–4): 357–400.

Bultmann, Rudolf. 1934. *Jesus and the Word*, trans. Louise Pettibone Smith and Erminie Huntress. New York: Charles Scribner.

Bultmann, Rudolf. 1963. *The History of the Synoptic Tradition*, trans. John Marsh. Oxford: Basil Blackwell.

Bultmann, Rudolf. 1962. "On the Problem of Demythologizing." *Journal of Religion* 42(2): 96–102.

Bultmann, Rudolph. 1989. *New Testament & Mythology, and Other Basic Writings*, trans. Schubert M. Ogden. Philadelphia: Fortress Press.

Burridge, Richard A. 1992. *What Are the Gospels?* Cambridge: Cambridge University Press.

Byron, Gay L., and Vanessa Lovelace (eds.). 2016. *Womanist Interpretations of the Bible: Expanding the Discourse*. Atlanta: SBL Press.

Campbell, Joseph. 1991. *Joseph Campbell and the Power of Myth*, with Bill Moyers. New York: Anchor Books.

Capitanio, Joshua. 2015. "Portrayals of Chan Buddhism in the Literature of Internal Alchemy." *Journal of Chinese Religions* 43(2): 119–60.

Caputo, John D. 2006. *The Weakness of God: A Theology of the Event*. Bloomington: Indiana University Press.

Carlier, J. C. (Cedric Watts). 2000. "Roland Barthes' Resurrection of the Author and Redemption of Biography." *Cambridge Quarterly* 29(4): 386–93.

Chatman, Seymour Benjamin. 1978. *Story and Discourse: Narrative Structure in Fiction and Film*. Ithaca: Cornell University Press.

Cheng Chein (i.e. Mario Poceski). 1992. *Sun Face Buddha: The Teachings of Ma-tsu and the Hung-chou School of Ch'an*. Freemont: Jain Publishing.

Cherbonnier, E. LaB. 1962. "The Logic of Biblical Anthropomorphism." *The Harvard Theological Review* 55(3): 187–206.

Chisholm, Robert B. 1995. "Does God 'Change His Mind'?" *Bibliotheca Sacra* 152 (October–December): 387–99.

Cohen, Chaim. 1990. "Jewish Medieval Commentary on the Book of Genesis and Modern Biblical Philology. Part I: Gen 1-18." *The Jewish Quarterly Review* 81(1|2): 1–11.

Cohn-Sherbok, Dan. 2003. *Judaism: History, Belief and Practices*. London: Routledge.

Cohn-Sherbok, Lavina, and Dan Cohn-Sherbok. 1999. *Judaism: A Short History*. Oxford: Oneworld.

Cohn-Sherbok, Lavina, and Dan Cohn-Sherbok. 2005. *Judaism: A Short Introduction*. Oxford: Oneworld.

Cole, Alan. 2009. *Fathering Your Father: The Zen of Fabrication in Tang Buddhism*. Berkeley: University of California Press.

Cole, Alan. 2016. *Patriarchs on Paper: A Critical History of Medieval Chan Literature*. Berkeley: University of California Press.

Comay, Rebecca. 1991. "Questioning the Question: A Response to Charles Scott." *Research in Phenomenology* 21: 149–58.

Congdon, David W. 2015. *The Mission of Demythologizing: Rudolph Bultmann's Dialectical Theology*. Minneapolis: Fortress Press.

Coogan, Michael D. (ed.). 2003. *The Illustrated Guide to World Religions*. Oxford: Oxford University Press.

Corcione, Adryan. 2018. "For Those in Grief, Talking to a Dead Loved One Is Good for Mental Health." *Teen Vogue*. August 30.

Cox, Patricia. 1983. *Biography in Late Antiquity: A Quest for the Holy Man*. Berkeley: University of California Press.

Crites, Stephen. 1971. "The Narrative Quality of Experience." *Journal of the American Academy of Religion* 39(3): 291–311.

Crossan, John Dominic. 1995. *Who Killed Jesus? Exposing the Roots of Anti-Semitism in the Gospel Story of the Death of Jesus*. San Francisco: HarperSanFrancisco.

Crouch, Walter B. 1994. "To Question an End, to End a Question: Opening the Closure of the Book of Jonah." *Journal for the Study of the Old Testament* 62: 101–12.

Cummins, Sean, Melissa Streiff, and Maria Ceprano. 2012. "Understanding and Applying the QAR Strategy to Improve Test Scores." *Journal of Inquiry & Action in Education* 4(3): 18–26.

Daube, David. 1956. *The New Testament and Rabbinic Judaism*, Jordan Lectures in Comparative Religion, Vol. 2. London: Athlone Press.

Davidson, Kimberly. 2017. *Adapting the Question Answer Relationship Strategy for Middle School Students with Intellectual Disabilities*. Dissertation, Peabody College of Vanderbilt University.

Davies, Philip R. 2003. "Judaism and the Hebrew Scriptures." In *The Blackwell Companion to Judaism*, edited by Jacob Neusner and Alan J. Avery-Peck, 37–57. New York: Blackwell.

Dawes, Daniel E. 2020. *The Political Determinants of Health*. Baltimore: John Hopkins University Press.

Dawkins, Richard. 2008. *The God Delusion*, reprint ed. Boston: Mariner Books.

Dawsey, James M. 1986. *The Lukan Voice: Confusion and Irony in the Gospel of Luke*. Macon, GA: Mercer University Press.

De Bary, WM Theodore, and Irene Bloom. 1999. *Sources of Chinese Tradition: From Earliest Times to 1600*, 2nd ed. New York: Columbia University Press.

Dear, John. 2004. *The Questions of Jesus: Challenging Ourselves to Discover Life's Great Answers*. New York: Doubleday.

Dickman, Nathan Eric. 2009a. *Dialogue and Divinity: A Hermeneutics of the Interrogative Mood in Religious Language*. Dissertation. The University of Iowa.

Dickman, Nathan Eric. 2009b. "The Challenge of Asking Engaging Questions." *Currents in Teaching and Learning* 2(1): 3–16.

Dickman, Nathan Eric. 2014. "Between Gadamer and Ricoeur: Preserving Dialogue in the Hermeneutical Arc for the Sake of a God that Speaks and Listens." *Sophia* 53(4): 553–73.

Dickman, Nathan Eric. 2016. "The Questions of Jesus and Mazu: Human or beyond?" *Literature and Theology* 30(3): 343–58.

Dickman, Nathan Eric. 2017. What "Is the Difference between Religion and Philosophy"? In *Religion in five minutes*, edited by Aaron Hughes and Russell McCutcheon, 22–5. Sheffield: Equinox.

Dickman, Nathan Eric. 2018a. "Hermeneutic Priority and Phenomenological Indeterminacy of Questioning." In *The Significance of Indeterminacy: Perspectives from Asian and Continental Philosophy*, edited by Robert H. Scott and Gregory S. Moss. New York: Routledge.

Dickman, Nathan Eric. 2018b. "Call or Question: A Rehabilitation of Conscience as Dialogical." *Sophia* 57(2): 275–94.

Dickman, Nathan Eric. 2018c. "Feminisms and Challenges to Institutionalized Philosophy of Religion." *Religions* 9: 113.

Dickman, Nathan Eric. 2020a. "Master Questions, Student Questions, and Genuine Questions: A Performative Analysis of Questions in Chan Encounter Dialogues." *Religions* 11(72).

Dickman, Nathan Eric. 2020b. "Where, Not When, Did the Cosmos 'Begin'?" *Sophia*. Onlinefirst. https://doi.org/10.1007/s11841-019-00752-w

Dickman, Nathan Eric. 2020c. "Should Religion-Affiliated Institutions Be Accredited? Ricoeur and the Problem of Religious Inclusivity." In *Paul Ricoeur and the Hope of Higher Education: The Just University*, edited by Daniel Boscaljon and Jeffrey F. Keuss, 213–36. Lexington Books.

Dickman, Nathan Eric. 2021. *Using Questions to Think: How to Develop Skills in Critical Understanding and Reasoning*. New York: Bloomsbury.

Dickman, Nathan Eric. 2021b. "The Hermeneutic Priority of Which Question? A Speech Act Clarification of Interlocutionary Acts." *Informal Logic* 41(3): 485–508.

Dickman, Nathan Eric. 2022. "Anapotheotics: A Hermeneutic Approach to Religions as Symbolic Languages." In *What Paths—What Summits: A Multi-Entry Approach to Philosophy of Religion*, edited by Timothy D. Knepper and Gereon Kopf. Springer.

Dickman, Nathan Eric, and Roxana Chicas. 2021. "Nursing Is Never Neutral: Political Determinants of Health and Systemic Marginalization." *Nursing Inquiry*. Early View: e12408.

Dilthey, Wilhelm. 1972. "The Rise of Hermeneutics." *New Literary History* 3(2): 229–44.

Dilthey, Wilhelm. 1988. *Introduction to the Human Sciences: An Attempt to Lay a Foundation for the Study of Society and History*, trans. R. Betanzos. Detroit: Wayne State University Press.

Dupre, Louis. 1993. *Passage to Modernity: An Essay in the Hermeneutics of Nature and Culture*. New Haven: Yale University Press.

Ebeling, Gerhard. 1963. *Word and Faith*, trans. James W. Leitch. Philadelphia: Fortress Press.

Ehrman, Bart D. 1999. *Jesus: Apocalyptic Prophet of the New Millennium*. New York: Oxford University Press.

Ehrman, Bart D. 2000. *The New Testament: A Historical Introduction to the Early Christian Writings*, 2nd ed. New York: Oxford University Press.

Ehrman, Bart D. 2013. *Did Jesus Exist? The Historical Argument for Jesus of Nazareth*. New York: HarperOne.

Enis, Larry L. 2005. "Biblical Interpretation among African-American New Testament Scholars." *Currents in Biblical Research* 4(1): 57–82.

Eskenazi, Tamara Cohn, and Andrea L. Weiss. 2008. *The Torah: A Women's Commentary*. New York: CCAR Press.

Estes, Douglas Charles. 2012. *The Questions of Jesus in John: Logic, Rhetoric, and Persuasive Discourse*. Brill.

Evans, Craig A. 2001. "Context, Family and Formation." In *The Cambridge Companion to Jesus*, edited by Markus Bockmuehl. Cambridge: Cambridge University Press.

Fajans, Elizabeth, and Mary R. Falk. 1993. "Against the Tyranny of Paraphrase: Talking Back to Texts." *Cornell Law Review* 78: 163–205.

Faure, Bernard. 1986. "Bodhidharma as Textual and Religious Paradigm." *History of Religions* 25: 187–98.

Faure, Bernard. 1993. *Chan Insights and Oversights: An Epistemological Critique of the Chan Tradition*. Princeton: Princeton University Press.

Faure, Bernard. 2009. *Unmasking Buddhism*. Chichester: Wiley-Blackwell.

Fear-Segal, Jacqueline, and Rebecca Tillet. 2014. *Indigenous Bodies: Reviewing, Relocating, Reclaiming*. New York: SUNY Press.

Feinstein, Edward. 2005. *Tough Questions Jews Ask: A Young Adult's Guide to Building a Jewish Life*. Woodstock, VT: Jewish Lights Publishing.

Feldman, Louis H. 1981. "Josephus' Commentary on Genesis." *The Jewish Quarterly Review* 72(2): 121–31.

Feuerbach, Ludwig. 1989. *The Essence of Christianity*, trans. George Eliot. Amherst: Prometheus Books.

Fish, Stanley. 1976. "How to Do Things with Austin and Searle: Speech Act Theory and Literary Criticism." *Centennial Issue: Responsibilities of the Critic* (October): 1024–5

Fish, Stanley. 1980. *Is There a Text in This Class? The Authority of Interpretive Communities*. Cambridge: Harvard University Press.

Fishbane, Michael. 1998. *The Exegetical Imagination: On Jewish Thought and Theology*. Cambridge: Harvard University Press.

Forman, Charles C. "Koheleth's Use of Genesis." *Journal of Semitic Studies* 5(3): 256–63.

Foster, Nelson, and Jack Shoemaker (eds.). 1996. *The Roaring Stream: A New Zen Reader*. 1st ed. Hopewell, NJ: The Ecco Press.

Foucault, Michel. 1998. *Aesthetics, Method, and Epistemology*, Vol. II, trans. Robert Hurley. New York: The New Press.

Foulk, T. Griffith. 2000. "The Form and Function of *koan* Literature: A Historical Overview." In *Kōan:Texts and Contexts in Zen Buddhism*, edited by Steven Heine and Dale S. Wright, 15–45. New York: Oxford University Press.

Fox, Michael V. "Job 38 and God's Rhetoric." *Semeia* 19: 53–61.

Freiberger, Oliver. 2019. *Considering Comparison: A Method for Religious Studies.* Oxford University Press.

Froese, Katrin. 2017. "Laughing for Nothing in Chan Buddhism." In *Why Can't Philosophers Laugh?* Cham: Palgrave Macmillan.

Fuchs, Ernst. 1964. *Studies of the Historical Jesus,* trans. Andrew Scobie, Studies in Biblical Theology, no. 42. Naperville, IL: A.R. Allenson.

Funk, Robert W. 1966. "Saying and Seeing: Phenomenology of Language and the New Testament." *Journal of Bible and Religion* 34:3 (July, 1966): 197–213.

Gadamer, Hans-Georg. 1977. *Philosophical Hermeneutics,* trans. and ed. David E. Linge. Berkeley: University of California Press.

Gadamer, Hans-Georg. 1989. "Text and Interpretation." In *Dialogue and deconstruction: the Gadamer–Derrida encounter,* edited by D. Michelfelder and R. Palmer and translated by D. Schmidt and R. Palmer, 21–51. Albany: SUNY.

Gadamer, Hans-Georg. 2007. *The Gadamer Reader: A Bouquet of Later Writings,* trans. Richard E. Palmer. Evanston: Northwestern University Press.

Gadamer, Hans-Georg. 2013. *Truth and Method,* 2nd rev. ed., trans. Joel Weinsheimer and Donald G. Marshall. London: Bloomsbury Academic, Reprint Edition.

Gathercole, Simon. 2018. "The Alleged Anonymity of the Canonical Gospels." *The Journal of Theological Studies* 69(2): 447–76.

Geertz, Clifford. 1993. "Religion as a Cultural System." In *Interpretation of Cultures.* Fontana Press.

Gibney, Alex, Stacey Offman, Richard Perello, and Jeff Sharlet. 2019. *The Family.* Netflix studios. https://www.netflix.com/title/80063867

Gnuse, Robert. 1999. "The Emergence of Monotheism in Ancient Israel: A Survey of Recent Scholarship." *Religion* 29(4): 315–36.

Goldin, Judah. 1946. "Hillel the Elder." *The Journal of Religion* 26:4 (October 1946): 263–77

Greenstein, Edward L. 1990. "The Formation of the Biblical Narrative Corpus." *AJS* (Association for Jewish Studies) 15(2): 151–78.

Grosse, Philip Henry. 1857. *Omphalos: An Attempt to Untie the Geological Knot.* London: J. Van Voorst.

Gundry, Robert H. 1964. "The Narrative Framework of Matthew XVI 17–19: A Critique of Professor Cullmann's Hypothesis." *Novum Testamentum* 7:1(March).

Halperin, Mark. 2006. *Out of the Cloister: Literati Perspectives on Buddhism in Sung China, 960–1279.* Cambridge: Harvard University Asia Center Publications.

Hancher, Michael. 1988. "Performative Utterance, the Word of God, and the Death of the Author." *Semia* 41.

Harrah, David. 1982. "What Should We Teach about Questions?" *Synthese* 51: 21–38.

Harris, Stephen L., and Robert L. Platzner. 2003. *The Old Testament: An Introduction to the Hebrew Bible.* Boston: McGraw Hill.

Hartwig, Maria, Par Anders Granhag, and Aldert Vrij. 2005. "Police Interrogation from a Social Psychology Perspective." *Policing & Society* 15(4): 379–99.

Heidegger, Martin. 1971. *Poetry, Language, Thought*. Trans. Albert Hofstadter. New York: HarperCollins.

Heidegger, Martin. 2010. *Being and Time*, trans. Joan Stambaugh and Dennis J. Schmidt. New York: SUNY Press.

Heine, Steven. 2000. "Visions. Divisions. Revisions: The Encounter between Iconoclasm and Supernaturalism in Kōan Cases about Mount Wu-t'ai." In *The Kōan: Texts and Contexts in Chan Buddhism*, edited by Steven Heine and Dale S. Wright, 137–67. New York: Oxford University Press.

Heine, Steven. 2003. "Ch'an Buddhist Kung-ans as Models for Interpersonal Behavior." *Journal of Chinese Philosophy* 30(3&4): 525–40.

Heine, Steven. 2015. "Does Even a Rat Have a Buddha-Nature? Analyzing Key-Phrase (*Huatou*) Rhetoric for the Wu Gongan." *Journal of Chinese Philosophy* 41(3–4): 250–67.

Henderson, Ian H. 2000. "'Salted with Fire' (Mark 9: 42–50): Style, Oracles and (Socio)Rhetorical Gospel Criticism." *Journal for the Study of the New Testament* 23(80): 44–65.

Hershock, Peter. 2009. *Chan Buddhism*. New York: Oxford University Press.

Heschel, Abraham Joshua. 2006. *Heavenly Torah: As Refracted through the Generations*, trans. Gordon Tucker and Leonard Levin. New York: Continuum.

Hintikka, Jakko. 2000. *On Wittgenstein*. Belmont, CA: Wadsworth.

Hirsch, E. D. 1967. *Validity in Interpretation*. New Haven: Yale University Press.

Holstein, Jay. 1975. "Confronting the 'Old' in the Old Testament." *Religious Education* 70(1): 77–81.

Holstein, Jay. 2002. *The Jewish Experience*, 4th ed. Boston: Pearson Custom Publishing.

Houk, Cornelius B. 1998. "Linguistic Patterns in Jonah." *JSOT* 77: 81–102.

Hume, David. 1998. *Dialogues Concerning Natural Religion*, 2nd ed, edited by Richard H. Popkin. Indianapolis: Hackett Publishing.

Humphreys, W. Lee. 2001. *The Character of God in the Book of Genesis: A Narrative Appraisal*. Louisville: Westminster John Knox Press.

Hunsberger, Bruce, Michael Pratt, and S. Mark Pancer. 2002. "A Longitudinal Study of Religious Doubts in High School and beyond: Relationships, Stability, and Searching for Answers." *Journal of the Scientific Study of Religion* 41(2): 255–66.

Irigaray, Luce. 2007. *Je, Tu, Nous: Toward a Culture of Difference*, trans. Alison Martin. London: Routledge Classics.

Iser, Wolfgang. 1972. "The Reading Process: A Phenomenological Approach." *New Literary History* 3(2): 279–99.

Janicaud, Dominique (ed.). 2000. *Phenomenology and the "Theological Turn": The French Debate*. New York: Fordham University Press.

Jenkins, Stephen. 2002. "Black Ships, Blavatsky, and the Pizza Effect: Critical Self-Consciousness as a Thematic Foundation for Courses in Buddhist Studies." In *Teaching Buddhism in the West*, edited by Richard P. Hayes, Victor Sogen Hori, and James Mark Shields, 71–83. New York: Routledge.

Jia, Jinhua. 2006. *The Hongzhou School of Chan Buddhism in Eighth- through Tenth-Century China*. Albany: SUNY Press.

Junior, Nyasha. 2015. *An Introduction to Womanist Biblical Interpretation*. Louisville: Westminster John Knox Press.

Kafer, Allison. 2013. *Feminist, Queer, Crip*. Indiana University Press.

Kant, Immanuel. 2007. *Critique of Pure Reason*, trans. Marcus Weigelt. London: Penguin Classics.

Kapelrud, Arvid S. 1974. "The Mythological Features in Genesis Chapter 1 and the Author's Intentions." *Vetus Testaamentum* 24(2): 178–86.

Kassin, Saul M., Richard A. Leo, Christian A. Meissner, Kimberly D. Richman, Lori H. Colwell, Amy-May Leach, and Dana La Fon. 2007. "Police Interviewing and Interrogation: A Self-Report Survey of Police Practices and Beliefs." *Law and Human Behavior* 31(4): 381–400.

Keen, Ralph. 2004. *The Christian Tradition*. Upper Saddle River: Prentice Hall.

Kierkegaard, Søren. 1980. *The Concept of Anxiety*, trans. Reidar Thomte. Princeton: Princeton University Press.

Kierkegaard, Søren (as Johannes Climacus). 1985. *Philosophical Fragments, or a Fragment of Philosophy*, ed. and trans. Howard V. Hong and Edna H. Hong. Princeton: Princeton University Press.

Kierkegaard, Søren. 1990. *For Self-Examination and Judge for Yourself!*, trans. Howard Hong and Edna Hong. Princeton: Princeton University Press.

King, Karen L. 2003. *The Gospel of Mary of Magdala: Jesus and the First Woman Apostle*. Polebridge Press.

Klemm, David E. 2008. "Philosophy and Kerygma: Ricoeur as Reader of the Bible." In *Reading Ricoeur*, edited by D. Kaplan, 47–70. Albany: SUNY.

Klemm, David E., and William Schweiker. 2008. *Religion and the Human Future: An Essay on Theological Humanism*. Oxford: Blackwell.

Knight, Jennifer. 2017. "Guide Students to Answers According to Question Type: The Question-Answer Relationship." *Iowa Reading Research Center*. September 5. https://iowareadingresearch.org/blog/question-answer-relationship.

Kolbrener, William. 2004. "'Chiseled from All Sides': Hermeneutics and Dispute in the Rabbinic Tradition." *AJS Review* 28(2): 273–95.

Kotsko, Adam. 2018. *Neoliberalism's Demons: On the Political Theology of Late Capital*. Stanford: Stanford University Press.

Kumarajiva. 1997. *The Vimalakirti Sutra*, trans. Burton Watson. New York: Columbia University Press.

Larsen, Matthew D. C. 2018. *Gospels before the Book*. New York: Oxford University Press.

Latvus, Kari. 2006. "Decolonizing Yahweh: A Postcolonial Reading of 2 Kings 24–25." In *Voices from the Margin: Interpreting the Bible in the Third World*, edited by Rasiah S. Sugirtharajah, 3rd ed., 186–92. Maryknoll, NY: Orbis Books.

Levinas, Emmanuel. 1969. *Totality and Infinity: An Essay on Exteriority*, trans. A. Lingis. Pittsburgh: Duquesne University Press.

Levinas, Emmanuel. 1990. *Difficult Freedom: Essays in Judaism*. Baltimore: John Hopkins University Press.

Levinas, Emmanuel. 1998. "Dialogue: Self-consciousness and Proximity of the Neighbor." In *Of God Who Comes to Mind*, trans. Bettina Bergo. Stanford: Stanford University Press.

Levine, Amy-Jill. 2015. *Short Stories by Jesus: The Enigmatic Parables of a Controversial Rabbi*. New York: HarperOne.

Lincoln, Bruce. 1996. "Gendered Discourses: The Early History of 'Mythos' and 'Logos.'" *History of Religions* 36(1): 1–12.

Lopez, Jr., Donald S. 2016. *The Lotus Sutra: A Biography*. Princeton: Princeton University Press.

Macquarrie, John. 1977. *Principles of Christian Theology*. New York: Scribner.

Maimonides, Moses. 1995. *The Guide of the Perplexed*, abridged ed., trans. D. Frank, J. Guttman, and C. Rabin. Hackett Publishing.

Mair, Victor H. 1983. "The Narrative Revolution in Chinese Literature: Ontological Presuppositions." *Chinese Literature: Essays, Articles, Reviews (CLEAR)* 5: 1–27.

Manekin, Charles H. 2018. "Maimonides on the Divine Authorship of the Law." In *Interpreting Maimonides: Critical Essays*, edited by Charles H. Manekin and Daniel Davies, 133–51. Cambridge: Cambridge University Press.

Martin, Bill, Jr., and Eric Carle. 1967. *Brown Bear, Brown Bear, What Do You See?* New York: Harcourt Brace and Company.

Masuzawa, Tomoko. 2005. *The Invention of World Religions*. Chicago: University of Chicago.

MacIntyre, Alasdair. 1984. *After Virtue: A Study in Moral Theory*, 2nd ed. Notre Dame: University of Notre Dame Press.

McCutcheon, Russell T. 2003. *Manufacturing Religion: The Discourse on Sui Generis Religion and the Politics of Nostalgia*. Oxford: Oxford University Press.

McDonald, J. Ian H. 1998. "Questioning and Discernment in Gospel Discourse: Communicative Strategy in Matthew 11: 2-19." In *Authenticating the Words of Jesus*. edited by Bruce Chilton and Craig A. Evans, 333–62. Boston: Brill.

McKenzie, Steven L., and Stephen R. Haynes (eds.). 1999. *To Each Its Own Meaning: An Introduction to Biblical Criticism*. Louisville: Westminster John Knox Press.

McRae, John R. 1986. *The Northern School and the Formation of Early Ch'an Buddhism*. Honolulu: University of Hawaii Press.

McRae, John R. 2000. "Antecedents of Encounter Dialogue in Chinese Ch'an Buddhism." In *The Kōan: Texts and Contexts in Chan Buddhism*, edited by Steven Heine and Dale S. Wright, 46–74. New York: Oxford University Press.

McRae, John R. 2003. *Seeing Through Zen: Encounter, Transformation, and Genealogy in Chinese Chan Buddhism*. Berkeley: University of California Press.

Milgram, Hillel I. 2008. *Four Biblical Heroines and the Case for Female Authorship: A Critical Analysis of the Women of Ruth, Ester, and Genesis 38*. Jefferson, NC: McFarland & Co.

Miller, Robert J. 1997. "The Jesus of Orthodoxy and the Jesuses of the Gospels: A Critique of Luke Timothy Johnson's The Real Jesus." *Journal for the Study of the New Testament* 60: 101–20.

Moltmann, Jurgen. 1995. *Jesus Christ for Today's World*. Philadelphia: Fortress Press.

Morrison, Elizabeth. 2010. *The Power of Patriarchs: Qisong and Lineage in Chinese Buddhism*. Boston: Brill.

Müller, F. Max (trans.). 2013. *The Dhammapada*. New York: Routledge.

Nadella, Raj. 2011. *Dialogue Not Dogma: Many Voices in the Gospel of Luke*. New York: Continuum.

Nagarjuna. 1995. *The Fundamental Wisdom of the Middle Way*, trans. Jay Garfield. Oxford: Oxford University Press.

Nasr, Seyyed Hosein. 2006. "In the Beginning Was Consciousness." In *The Essential Sophia*, edited by Nasr and O'Brien, 199–206. Bloomington: World Wisdom.

Neusner, Jacob. 1988. *The Incarnation of God: The Character of Divinity in Formative Judaism*. Philadelphia: Fortress Press.

Neusner, Jacob. 1993. *The Way of Torah: An Introduction to Judaism*, 5th ed. Belmont: Wadsworth.

Nietzsche, Friedrich. 2008. *On the Genealogy of Morals*, trans. Douglas Smith. Oxford: Oxford University Press.

Nussbaum, Martha. 2010. *From Disgust to Humanity: Sexual Orientation and Constitutional Law*. New York: Oxford University Press.

Olson, Roger E. 2007. *Questions to All Your Answers*. Grand Rapids: Zondervan.

Owen-Ball, David T. 1993. "Rabbinic Rhetoric and the Tribute Passage (MT. 22: 15-22;MK. 12: 13-17;LK. 20: 20-26)." *Novum Testamentum* 35: 1.

Pagels, Elaine. 1989. *The Gnostic Gospels*. Vintage Books.

Pas, Julian F. (trans.). 1987. *The Recorded Sayings of Ma-tsu*. Lewiston, ME: Edwin Mellen.

Patel, Eboo. 2012. *Sacred Ground: Pluralism, Prejudice, and the Promise of America*. Boston: Beacon Press.

Pew Research Center. 2018. "When Americans Say They Believe in God, What Do They Mean?" April 25.

Pfau, Thomas. 1990. "Immediacy and the Text: Friedrich Schleiermacher's Theory of Style and Interpretation." *Journal of the History of Ideas* 51(1): 51–73.

Piazza, Roberta. 2002. "The Pragmatics of Conducive Questions in Academic Discourse." the *Journal of Pragmatics* 34: 509–27.

Pirsig, Robert M. 2000. *Zen and the Art of Motorcycle Maintenance*. New York: Perennial Classics.

Plato. 1991. *The Republic*, 2nd ed., trans. Alan Bloom. New York: Basic Books.

Plummer, Robert. 2010. *40 Questions About the Bible*. Grand Rapids: Kregel.

Poceski, Mario. 2004. "*Mazu Yulu* and the Creation of the Chan Records of Sayings." In *The Chan Cannon: Understanding the Classic Texts*, edited by Steven Heine and Dale S. Wright, 53–80. New York: Oxford University Press.

Poceski, Mario. 2007. *Ordinary Mind Is the Way: The Hongzhou School and the Growth of Chan Buddhism*. New York: Oxford University Press.

Poceski, Mario. 2016. *The Records of Mazu and the Making of Classical Chan Literature*. Oxford: Oxford University Press.

Poceski, Mario. 2020. "Disappearing Act: Calmness and Insight in Chinese Buddhism." *Journal of Chinese Religions* 48(1): 1–30.

Pojman, Louis P. 2003. *Philosophy of Religion: An Anthology*, 4th ed. London: Wadsworth.

Porter, Stanley, and Beth M. Stovell. 2012. *Biblical Hermeneutics: Five Views*. Downers Grove: Intervarsity Press.

Pulleyblank, E. G. 1976. "The An Lu-Shan Rebellion and the Origins of Chronic Militarism in Late T'ang China." In *Essays on T'ang Society*, Perry & Smith, 518–41. Leiden: E. J. Brill.

Quinn, Philip L. 2001. "Can God Speak? Does God Speak?" *Religious Studies* 37(3): 259–69.

Raphael, Taffy E. 1981. *The Effect of Metacognitive Strategy Awareness Training on Students' Question-answering Behavior*. Dissertation, University of Illinois at Urbana-Champaign.

Raphael, Taffy E. 1986. "Teaching Question Answer Relationships, Revisited." *The Reading Teacher* 39(6): 516–22.

Raphael, Taffy E., and Kathryn H. Au. 2005. "QAR: Enhancing Comprehension and Test Taking across Grades and Content Areas." *The Reading Teacher* 59(3): 206–21.

Raschke, Carl A. 1982. "Religious Pluralism and Truth: From Theology to a Hermeneutical Dialogy." *Journal of the American Academy of Religion* 50(1): 35–48.

Rashi. 2008. *The Complete Tanach with Rashi* (CD-ROM), trans. and ed. Rabbi A. J. Rosenberg. New York: Judaica Press. Chabad.org, 2001-2009. http://www.chabad.org/library/bible_cdo/aid/8167/showrashi/true

Ricoeur, Paul. 1969. *The Symbolism of Evil*, trans. Emerson Buchanan. Boston: Beacon Press.

Ricoeur, Paul. 1974. "Philosophy of Religious Language." *The Journal of Religion* 54(1): 71–85.

Ricoeur, Paul. 1975. "Phenomenology and Hermeneutics." *Nous* 9(1): 85–102.

Ricoeur, Paul. 1976. *Interpretation Theory: Discourse and the Surplus of Meaning*. Fort Worth: Texas Christian University Press.

Ricoeur, Paul. 1979a. "The Human Experience of Time and Narrative." *Research in Phenomenology* 9 (1979): 17–34.

Ricoeur, Paul. 1979b. "The Function of Fiction in Shaping Reality." *Man and World* 12(2): 123–41.

Ricoeur, Paul. 1980. "Narrative Time." *Critical Inquiry* 7:1.

Ricoeur, Paul. 1984. *Time and Narrative*. Vol. I, trans. Kathleen McLaughlin and David Pellauer. Chicago: University of Chicago Press.

Ricoeur, Paul. 1985a. *Time and Narrative*, Vol. II, trans. Kathleen McLaughlin and David Pellauer. Chicago: University of Chicago Press.

Ricoeur, Paul. 1985b. "Narrated Time." trans. Robert Sweeney. *Philosophy Today* (Winter).

Ricoeur, Paul. 1986. "Life: A Story in Search of a Narrator," In *Facts and Values: Philosophical Reflections from Western and Non-Western Perspectives*, edited by M.C. Doeser and J.N. Kraay, 121–32. Dordrecht: Martinus Nijhoff Publishers.

Ricoeur, Paul. 1988. *Time and Narrative*. Vol. III, trans. Kathleen Blamey and David Pellauer. Chicago: The University of Chicago Press.

Ricoeur, Paul. 1991. *From Text to Action: Essays in Hermeneutics*, Vol. II. trans. K. Blamey and J. Thompson. Evanston: Northwestern University Press.

Ricoeur, Paul. 1992. *Oneself as Another*, trans. Kathleen Blamey. Chicago: University of Chicago Press.

Ricoeur, Paul. 1995. *Figuring the Sacred: Religion, Narrative, and Imagination*, ed. Mark I. Wallace, trans. David Pellauer. Minneapolis: Fortress Press.

Ricoeur, Paul. 2000. "Experience and Language in Religious Discourse." In *Phenomenology and the "Theological Turn": The French Debate*, edited by Dominique Janicaud, 127–46. New York: Fordham University Press.

Ricoeur, Paul. 2010. "Religious Belief." In *A Passion for the Possible: Thinking with Paul Ricoeur*, edited by Brian Treanor and Henry Isaac Venema. New York: Fordham University Press.

Robbins, Vernon K. 1981. "Summons and Outline in Mark: The Three-Step Progression." *Novum Testamentum* 32(2): 97–114.

Robson, James. 2011. "Formation and Fabrication in the History and Historiography of Chan Buddhism." *Harvard Journal of Asiatic Studies* 71(2): 311–49.

Rorty, Richard. 1999. *Philosophy and Social Hope*. New York: Penguin Books.

Rosemont, Henry, Jr. 1970. "The Meaning is the Use: Kōan and Mondō as Linguistic Tools of the Zen Masters." *Philosophy East and West* 20(2): 109–19.

Rosenberg, Joel. 1984. "Bible: Biblical Narrative." In *Back to the Sources: Reading the Classic Jewish Texts*, edited by Barry W. Holtz, 31–82. New York: Touchstone.

Rossen, Lauren M., Amy M. Branum, Farida B. Ahmad, Paul Sutton, and Robert N. Anderson. 2020. "Excess Deaths Associated with COVID-19, by Age and Race and Ethnicity — United States, January 26–October 3, 2020." *Morbidity and Mortality Weekly Report* 69: 1522–7.

Rowe, William. 2006. "Friendly Atheism, Skeptical Theism, and the Problem of Evil." *International Journal for Philosophy of Religion* 59: 79–92.

Rubenstein, Richard. 1992. *After Auschwitz*, 2nd ed. Baltimore: John Hopkins University Press.

Said, Edward W. 1979. *Orientalism*. New York: Vintage Books.

Sanders, E. P. 1985. "Jesus and the Temple" in *Jesus and Judaism*. Philadelphia: Fortress Press.

Sandifer, D. Wayne. 1991. "The Humor of the Absurd in the Parables of Jesus." In *Society of Biblical Literature 1991 Seminar Papers*, Vol. 30, edited by Eugene H. Lovering, Jr., 287–97. Atlanta: Scholars Press.

Sasaki, Ruth Fuller. 2009. *The Record of Linji*, ed. Thomas Yuho Kircher. Honolulu: University of Hawai'i Press.

Scharlemann, Robert P. 1993. "The textuality of texts." In *Meanings in Texts and Actions: Questioning Ricoeur*, edited by D. Klemm and W. Schweiker. Charlottesville: University of Virginia Press.

Scheindlin, Raymond P. 1998. *A Short History of the Jewish People: From Legendary Times to Modern Statehood*. Oxford: Oxford University Press.

Schilbrack, Kevin. 2014. *Philosophy and the Study of Religions: A Manifesto*. Malden, MA: Wiley Blackwell.

Schleiermacher, Friedrich. 1977. *Hermeneutics: The Handwritten Manuscripts*, ed. Heinz Kimmerle, trans. James Duke and Jack Forstman. Missoula: Scholars Press.

Schleiermacher, Friedrich. 1978. "The Hermeneutics: Outline of the 1819 Lectures." *New Literary History* 10(1): 1–16.

Schlütter, Morten. 1999. "Silent Illumination, Kung-an Introspection, and the Competition for Lay Patronage in Sung-Dynasty Ch'an." In *Buddhism in the Sung*, edited by Peter N. Gregory and Daniel Getz, 109–47. Honolulu: Hawai'i University Press.

Schlütter, Morten. 2004. "The *Record of Hongzhi* and the Recorded Sayings Literature of Song-Dynasty Chan." In *The Chan Canon: Understanding the Classic Texts*, edited by Steven Heine and Dale S. Wright, 181–206. New York: Oxford University Press.

Schlütter, Morten. 2008. *How Zen Became Zen: The Dispute Over Enlightenment and the Formation of Chan Buddhism in Song Dynasty China*. Honolulu: University of Hawai'i Press.

Schlütter, Morten. Forthcoming. *The Evolution of the Platform Sūtra and the Changing Notions of What Zen Should Be*. University of Hawai'i Press.

Schmidt, Lawrence. 2006. *Understanding Hermeneutics*. Stocksfield: Acumen Publishing.

Schuhmann, Karl, and Barry Smith. 1987. "Questions: An Essay in Daubertian Phenomenology." *Philosophy and Phenomenological Research* 47(3): 353–84.

Schweitzer, Albert. 1978. *The Quest of the Historical Jesus: A Critical Study of Its Progress from Reimarus to Wrede*. New York: Macmillan.

Scott, J. Martin C. 1996. "Matthew 15: 21-28:A Test-Case for Jesus' Manners." *Journal for the Study of the New Testament* 63: 21–44.

Searle, John. 1969. *Speech Acts*. Cambridge: Cambridge University Press.

Searle, John. 1992. "Conversation." In *(On) Searle On Conversation*, edited by Herman Parret and Jef Verschueren, 7–30. Philadelphia: John Benjamins.

Sells, Michael. 2007. *Approaching the Qur'an: The Early Revelations*, 2nd ed. OR: White Cloud Press.

Shanmugasundaram, Swathi. 2018. "Anti-Sharia Law Bills in the United States." *Hatewatch*, with the Southern Poverty Law Center. February 5.

Sharf, Robert. 1995. "Buddhist Modernism and the Rhetoric of Meditative Experience." *Numen* 42: 228–83.

Sharlet, Jeff. 2008. *The Family: The Secret Fundamentalism at the Heart of American Power*. New York: HarperCollins.

Sharp, Carolyn J. 2009. *Irony and Meaning in the Hebrew Bible*. Bloomington: Indiana University Press.

Sheng-yen. 1988. "Zen Meditation." In *Zen: Tradition and Transmission*, edited by Kenneth Kraft, 30–43. New York: Grove Press.

Shuchat, Wilfred. 2006. *The Garden of Eden and the Struggle to be Human: According to the Midrash Rabbah*. Israel: Devora Publishing.

Simmer-Brown, Judith. 2000. "Pluralism and Dialogue: A Contemplation on the Dialogue Relationship." In *Buddhist Theology: Critical Reflections by Contemporary Buddhist Scholars*, edited by Roger R. Jackson and John J. Makransky, 312–30. Surrey: Curzon Press.

Simmons, J. Aaron, and Bruce Ellis Benson. 2013. *The New Phenomenology: A Philosophical Introduction*. New York: Bloomsbury.

Smith, Jonathan Z. 1993. *Map Is Not Territory: Studies in the History of Religions*. Chicago: University of Chicago Press.

Smith, Mitzi J. 2017. *Insights from African American Interpretation*. Minneapolis: Fortress Press.

Sorkin, Amy D. 2020. "Trump and a Lesson in How Coups Fail." *The New Yorker*. November 25.

Spinoza, Baruch. 2001. *Theological-Political Treatise*, 2nd ed., trans. Samuel Shirley. Indianapolis: Hackett Publishing Company.

St. Clair, Raquel A. 2007. "Womanist Biblical Interpretation." In *True to Our Native Land: An African American New Testament Commentary*, edited by Brian K. Blount et al., 54–62. Minneapolis: Fortress Press.

St. Clair, Raquel A. 2008. *Call and Consequences: A Womanist Reading of Mark*. Minneapolis: Fortress Press.

Stanley, Jason. 2018. *How Fascism Works: The Politics of Us and Them*. New York: Random House.

Sternberg, Meir. 1985. *The Poetics of Biblical Narrative*. Bloomington: University of Indiana Press.

Stout, Jeffrey. 1986. "The Relativity of Interpretation." *The Monist* 69(1): 103–18.

Stout, Jeffry. 2004. *Democracy and Tradition*. Princeton: Princeton University Press.

Strauss, Leo. 1988. *Persecution and the Art of Writing*. Chicago: The University of Chicago Press.

Suzuki, D. T. 1978. *Manual of Zen Buddhism*. New York: Grove Press.

Taves, Anne. 2011. "2010 Presidential Address: 'Religion' in the Humanities and the Humanities in the University." *Journal of the American Academy of Religion* 79(2): 287–314.

Taylor, Terri Graves. 1989. "*Review* of *Time and Narrative* by Paul Ricoeur." *The Journal of Aesthetics and Art Criticism* 47: 4.

Thate, Michael J. 2013. *Remembering Things Past?: Albert Schweitzer, the Anxiety of Influence, and the Untidy Jesus of Markan Memory*. Tübingen: Mohr Siebeck.

Thich Nhat Hanh. 2007. *Living Buddha, Living Christ*. New York: Riverhead Books.

Thich Nhat Hanh. 2011. *Peace is Every Breath: A Practice for Our Busy Lives*. New York: HarperCollins.

Thiselton, Anthony C. 1970. "The Parables as Language-Event: Some Comments on Fuchs's Hermeneutics in the Light of Linguistic Philosophy." *Scottish Journal of Theology* 23: 437–68.

Tillich, Paul. 1951. *Systematic Theology*, Vol. 1. Chicago: The University of Chicago Press.

Tillich, Paul. 1955. *Biblical Religion and the Search for Ultimate Reality*. Chicago: The University of Chicago Press.

Tillich, Paul. 1959. *Theology of Culture*. New York: Oxford University Press.

Tillich, Paul. 1975. *Systematic Theology*, Vol. 2. Chicago: The University of Chicago Press.

Tillich, Paul. 2000. *The Courage to Be*. New Haven: Yale University Press.

Tillich, Paul. 2001. *Dynamics of Faith*. New York: HarperCollins.

Todorov, Tzvetan. 1969. "Structural Analysis of Narrative." *NOVEL: A Forum on Fiction* 3: 1.

Todorov, Tzvetan. 1990. *Genres in Discourse*, trans. Cathrine Porter. New York: Cambridge University Press.

Tolbert, Mary Ann. 1996. *Sowing the Gospel: Mark's World in Literary-Historical Perspective*. Minneapolis: Fortress Press.

Vacca, Richard T., Jo Anne L. Vacca, and Maryann E. Mraz. 2017. *Content Area Reading: Literacy and Learning across the Curriculum*, 12th ed. Boston: Pearson Eduction.

Vawter, Bruce. 1977. *On Genesis: A New Reading*. Garden City: Doubleday.

Wallace, Vesna A. 2000. "The Methodological Relevance of Contemporary Biblical Scholarship to the Study of Buddhism." In *Buddhist Theology: Critical Reflections by Contemporary Buddhist Scholars*, edited by Roger R. Jackson and John J. Makransky, 78–94. Surrey: Curzon Press.

Wang, Jinjun. 2006. "Questions and the Exercise of Power." *Discourse & Society* 17: 529–48.

Wang Y. 2018. "Philosophical Interpretations of Hongzhou Chan Buddhist Thought." In *Dao Companion to Chinese Buddhist Philosophy*, Vol. 9, edited by Wang Y., Wawrytko S., 369–98. Dordrecht: Springer.

Warnke, Georgia. 1997. "Legitimate Prejudices." *Laval theologique et philosophique* 53(1): 89–102.

Warnke, Georgia. 2016. *Inheriting Gadamer: New Directions in Philosophical Hermeneutics*. Edinburgh: Edinburgh University Press.

Warnke, Georgia. 1993. "Feminism and Hermeneutics." *Hypatia* 8(1): 81–98.

Weberman, David. 2000. "A New Defense of Gadamer's Hermeneutics." *Philosophy and Phenomenological Research* 60(1): 45–65.

Welter, Albert. 2008. *The Linji Lu and the Creation of Chan Orthodoxy: The Development of Chan's Records of Sayings Literature*. Oxford: Oxford University Press.

Welton, Donn. 1999. *The Essential Husserl: Basic Writings in Transcendental Phenomenology*. Bloomington: Indiana University Press.

Westerhorff, Jan. 2009. *Nagarjuna's Madhyamaka: A Philosophical Introduction*. Oxford: Oxford University Press.

White, Hayden. 1982. "The Structure of Historical Narrative." *Clio* 1: 2.

White, Hugh C. 1991. *Narration and Discourse in the Book of Genesis*. New York: Cambridge University Press.

Wiggins, Grant, and Jay McTighe. 2001. *Understanding by Design*, special ed. Upper Saddle River: Prentice Hall.

Williams, Paul. 2009. *Mahayana Buddhism: The Doctrinal Foundations*, 2nd ed. New York: Routledge.

Wilson, Nance S., Dana L. Grisham, and Linda Smetana. 2009. "Investigating Content Area Teachers' Understanding of a Content Literacy Framework." *Journal of Adolescent and Adult Literacy* 52(8): 708–18.

Wolterstorff, Nicholas (1995). *Divine Discourse: Philosophical Reflections on the Claim that God Speaks*. New York: Cambridge University Press.

Wolterstorff, Nicholas (2006). "Resuscitating the Author." In *Hermeneutics at the Crossroads*, edited by K. Vanhoozer, J. Smith, and B. Benson, 35–50. Bloomington: Indiana University Press.

Wright, Dale S. 1992a. "Historical Understanding: The Ch'an Buddhist Transmission Narratives and Modern Historiography." *History and Theory* 31: 1.

Wright, Dale S. 1992. "Rethinking Transcendence: The Role of Language in Chan Experience." *Philosophy East & West* 42: 1.

Wright, Dale S. 1993. "Discourse of Awakening: Rhetorical Practice in Classical Ch'an Buddhism." *Journal of the American Academy of Religion* 61(1): 23–40.

Wright, Dale S. 1998. *Philosophical Meditations on Zen Buddhism*. Cambridge: Cambridge University Press.

Wuthnow, Robert. 2005. *America and the Challenges of Religious Diversity*.
    Princeton: Princeton University Press.
Wright, Dale S. 2003. "Empty Texts/Sacred Meaning: Reading as Spiritual
    Practice in Chinese Buddhism." *Dao: A Journal of Comparative Philosophy*
    11(2): 261–72.
X., Malcolm, and Alex Haley. 1992. *The Autobiography of Malcolm X*. New York:
    Ballantine Books.
Yanagida Seizan. 1983. "The Development of the 'Recorded Sayings' Texts of the
    Chinese Ch'an School." Translated by John R. McRae. In *Early Ch'an in China
    and Tibet*, edited by Lewis Lancaster and Whalen Lai. Berkeley: Lancaster-
    Miller Press. pp. 185–205.
Žižek, Slavoj. 1989. *The Sublime Object of Ideology*. New York: Verso.
Zornberg, Avivah. 2006. "Seduced into Eden: The Beginning of Desire."
    In *Longing: Psychoanalytic Musings on Desire*, edited by Jean Petrucelli,
    185–205. London: H. Karnac.

Author Bio

Nathan Eric Dickman (PhD, the University of Iowa) is an assistant professor of philosophy at the University of the Ozarks. His recent book, *Using Questions to Think* (Bloomsbury 2021), explores the hermeneutic priority of questions in relation to critical thinking, reasoning, and dialogue. He researches in hermeneutic phenomenology, philosophy of language, and comparative questions in philosophies of religions, with particular concerns about global social justice issues in ethics and religions. He has taught a breadth of courses, such as critical thinking, Islam, ethics, Zen, existentialism, and the historical Jesus.

Index

Abraham 91–3, 95, 99, 138–9, 146–7, 166
Adam 95–8, 145–7
Aesop's fable 63
Akiba, Abba 141
Alster-Elata, Gerda 92–3
Alter, Robert 37–9, 41–3, 52, 56–8, 66, 71, 91–2, 96, 143, 145
Amitabha Buddha 1
anapotheotics 175–8
Anderson, Pamela Sue 28, 53, 156, 178
Aristotle 5, 23, 88, 150
Asad, Talal 32
authoritarian leaders 11
authoritarian power 22
Avalokiteshvara 1

Babylonian Empire 137
Baizhang Huaihai 103–4, 115
Barthes, Roland 40, 43–7, 50, 68, 132
Bell, Martin 23, 36, 39
Bereshit 14, 39–40, 92, 96, 144–8
Bible 4, 38–9, 52, 148, 162
    God, depiction in 86
    Magic 8-Ball method of reading 5, 39, 149, 162
Bodhidharma 36–8, 48, 57, 105
Bodhisattvas 1, 103
Book of Job 6, 82
Book of Jonah 6, 95, 140, 144
Brahman (Advaita Vedanta) 2, 138
Buber, Martin 10, 146
Buddhist traditions
    answers to human suffering 4
    Chinese culture 107
    meditation rituals 78
    roles superior to Gods 1
    use of Siddhartha Gautama's title 87

Bultmann, Rudolph 14–15, 52, 77–9, 125, 127–8, 168, 177

Campbell, Joseph 52, 78–9
Caputo, John 87
Carle, Eric, *Brown Bear, Brown Bear, What Do You See?* 65
Chan Buddhism. *See* Zen Buddhism
Chatman, Seymour 40, 42–3
Cherbonnier, Edmond 89–90, 92
Chretien, Jean-Louis 9
Christianity. *See also* Gospel; Jesus, Christ
    answers to human suffering 4
    anti-Jewish preaching 71
    Christ in 2
    communion practices 78–9
    depiction of God 86
    evangelical movement 12
    first creation narrative 36
    literature 39
    "Peter's Confession" 127–9
    US culture 82
Cole, Alan 56, 153
copula 24
Covid-19, deaths in U.S. 175

Daoist traditions, Dao in 2
deficit-driven questions 5–6, 37, 76, 80, 85, 102, 118, 170, 181–2
    suspense aspects 26
deific figures 14, 33, 42–3, 81–3, 99, 132, 134
    human response to questions 175, 177, 179
deific voices 1–3, 5, 16
    authoritarianism model 11, 23
    demythologization 77–80
    genuine questions 8, 12–13, 21, 33, 47, 57, 175, 180

performance 47–8
perspectives 7
religious narratives 39, 48, 51, 64
story and discourse level 14, 18,
 40
Demuth 149–50
demythologization 77–80, 176
Dunhuang manuscripts (China) 55,
 83

Ezra, Prophet 137

Fish, Stanley 60, 67–8, 85, 102, 110,
 119, 144
Foulk, T. Griffith 111, 154, 156
Fox, Michael V. 93–4
Fuchs, Ernst 121, 129

Gadamer, Hans-Georg 20, 26–32,
 41, 44–7, 49, 54–5, 60, 72, 74,
 158, 172
Gautama Buddha 1
 Enlightenment 5
 expansion of horizons 6
 novice disciple 101–3
 past lives 103
 Truth body of 2
Genesis 14, 36, 39–40, 51, 66, 83,
 85, 92, 96–7, 133, 137, 142–5,
 149, 179
genuine questions
 deific voices 8, 12–13, 21, 33, 47,
 57, 175, 180
 as not interrogatives 21–4
 subjects and predicates 24–6
God. *See also* omniscience
 anthropomorphic notions 15,
 89–90
 authorial voice 144–7
 conception of the divine as
 omniscient 96–7
 death phenomenon 89
 monotheistic 88
 questions 1–15

Gospel 1, 6, 14–16, 40, 56, 67, 71, 83,
 117, 127, 129, 133, 135, 165,
 167–72, 174, 176, 179
 on Jesus' use of questions 121–5
Gosse, Philip Henry, *Ompholos: An
 Attempt to Untie the Geological
 Knot* 37
Graf, Karl Heinrich 138
Guanyin (China) 1

Hancher, Michael 92
Harry Potter series 51
HaSatan 6, 93
HaShem 1–2, 6–7
 Adam's response 97–8
 Ashera, wife of 138
 authorial or narrative voice 148–9
 creation story 95–6
 depiction of God 85–7, 90, 93–5
 genuine question 86, 93–5, 97, 99,
 137, 145–7, 150
 as God of Judah 139
 narratives about 89
 omnibeing philosophical
 theology 86–90
 personhood 91–2
 use of language 92
 Yahweh or YHWH 2, 138
Hebrew Bible 73, 83, 93–5, 98–9,
 137–8, 140, 144, 148–9
Heine, Steven 106, 161–2
hermeneutic priority 8, 12–13, 20,
 23–4, 32–4, 61–7, 69, 91, 133
hermeneutics. *See also* deific figures
 exegetical and existential circle 41
 level of narrative discourse 46
 phenomenology's influence 37–8
 priority of questions 19–21
 religious literature 32–4
 rigorous determination 8
higher- and lower-level thinking 62
Hillel 141, 167
Hinduism, the Trinity 138
Hintikka, Jakko 73

Hirsch, E. D. 60
historical-critical questions 61
historical criticism 8, 55, 73, 80
Hongzhou School 103
Huangbo Xiyun 103
Huian, Huanglong 155
Huichang era 152
Huineng, *Platform Sutra* 46
Hume, David 4, 89
Humphreys, W. Lee 42, 98
Husserl, Edmund 9, 37

Ibn Rushd 88
imams 1, 3
implied author 44, 69, 75, 132, 134, 171

Jataka tales 103
Jesus, Christ 1, 4, 6–7
    audience 120, 122–3
    authorial voice questions 168–72
    date of birth 166–7
    as a deific figure 119
    genuine question 119, 122, 124–6,
        129
    Gospel narratives 120–1, 123,
        126–7
    interrogatives 124, 126
    Jewish audience 71
    John the Baptist's message 167
    life and teachings 166–7
    questions 15
    questioning in redemptive voice
        172
    quotations from Mark, Matthew,
        and Luke 117–20
    resurrection 8, 36
    rhetorical questions 121–4
    understanding with others 124–9
    use of parables 118, 121–2, 124,
        129, 133, 167–9, 173
Jia, Jinhua 105
Judaism. *See also* HaShem; Torah
    creation story 142–3, 145
    diasporic dialogues 137–43

Gilgamesh narrative 142–3
God in 2
Oral Torah to Moses on Sinai
    147–50
Orthodox Judaism 36
perlocutionary aspect 146–7
political history 140
polyphonic practice 137, 139–41,
    143
postexilic writing 140
Reform Judaism 36
temple rituals 140, 167
tough questions 5
Yahwism 138

Kant, Immanuel 53
Kierkegaard, Søren 69–70, 96, 126,
    146, 172
    Either/Or 46
Klemm, David 16, 47, 181

Latvus, Kari 149
Levinas, Emmanuel 9, 26, 40, 78, 180
Levine, Amy-Jill 39, 71–3, 84, 120–2,
    167–8
Linji Yixuan 56, 103, 108–9, 152, 155
Lushan rebellion 151–2

Maccabean revolt 165
Madhyamaka philosophy 102
Mahayana Buddhism 2, 102–3
Maimonides, Moses 88, 147–50
Manekin, Charles H. 147–8
Marion, Jean-Luc 9
Martin, Bill, Jr., *Brown Bear, Brown
    Bear, What Do You See?* 65
Marx, Karl 4
Masuzawa, Tomoko 55, 70, 102
Mazu, Daoyi 1, 7, 14–15, 40, 56. *See
    also* Zen Buddhism
    biographical sketch 104
    Dahzu's enlightenment 151
    Dharma heirs 103–4, 113–14,
        155, 169

encounter dialogue 14–15, 40, 70, 104–11, 114–15, 125, 155, 158–61
final question 115
genuine question 101–2, 113–16, 155
historical image 105
life and teaching 101–2
Linji lineage 56, 103, 108–9, 152, 155
mastered voice in question 161–3
mind-to-mind transmission of the Dharma 102–3
narrative strategy 159–60
norm of hierarchy establishment 109–10
questions to readers 163
radical and iconoclastic image 105
Shitou's question 107–8, 110
Sijia yulu 103–4
student questions 111–13, 158
transmission of the Dharma 103, 105–8, 111, 114, 153–4
typical interrogative or sincere question 111–13, 114
understanding with others 113–16
"Why are you seeking outside?" 101–2, 114, 160
Ming dynasty 103
monks 3, 111, 153, 162, 181
Moses 88, 91, 95, 120, 138–9, 141–2, 144, 147–8
myth
existential interpretation 79
features 53

Nagarjuna 102
Nanquan Puyuan 111
Neusner, Jacob 91
Nietzsche, Friedrich 4, 39, 44, 55
nirvana 1, 10–11, 103, 107, 112
Nussbaum, Martha 71

omniscience 5, 43, 128
original audience 18, 46, 61, 71–3, 75, 122, 133, 140–2

Pagels, Elaine 8, 83
philosophy and religion 5, 9, 11, 15, 86–7, 90–1
Piazza, Roberta 11
Plato 26, 88, 176
  Lysis 76
  Republic 46
Poceski, Mario 103–4, 114–15, 152, 155
preachers 3, 181
priests 1, 3–4, 117–18, 142

Quan Deyu 155
"question answer relationships" (QAR) 61–4, 71, 74
questions. *See also* genuine questions; shared questions
  authorial discourse interpretation 68
  deific voices 77–80
  direct discourse 42–3
  four levels of reading 64
  hermeneutic priority 19–21, 65
  level of discourse 68–76
  level of story 65–8
  logical analysis 21–4
  in my head 63, 69
  passivity or nonintentional character 27–8
  proposed division 67
  QAR taxonomy 62–4, 68
  reductionist tendencies 22
  right there 63
Quranic recitation 39, 47

rabbis 1, 3, 96–7, 147
Raphael, Taffy, "Question Answer Relationships" (QAR) 61–2
reading, three-tiered framework 61
religious literalism

anti-religious atheism 36
devotional contexts 38
didactic purposes 38
face-to-face dialogue 45
imaginative dwelling 48–51
myth and history 51–8
nonreligious literature *versus* 38
physical and metaphysical
  realities 35
plot in 41–2, 48–50
positivistic assumption 36–7
semantic autonomy 47
story and discourse 40–8
story and discourse, level of 40–1
religious narratives
answers to questions 4
central characters 57
deific voices 1–2
descriptions 42
dialogical process 58
human figures in 3
nonnarrative discourse 40
questions 1–3
religious texts. *See* sacred texts
religious traditions
first and second order discourses
  9
global critical philosophy 11
interreligious dialogue 11
symbols and myths 9–10
Ricoeur, Paul 9, 19, 24–5, 32, 37–50,
  53–5, 60–1, 73–6, 99, 127–8,
  132, 134, 157, 171–2, 176, 178
Roman Empire 165–6
Rosemont, Henry 112–13
Rubenstein, Richard 89

sacred texts
character development 8–9
deific figures 82
deific voices 77
dialogical structure 158
hermeneutics 8
interrogatives and genuine
  questions 80

reader bias 72–3
semantic autonomy 60–1
"wax nose" problem 68
Salmon, Rachel 92–3
Sartre, Jean-Paul 9, 150
Satan 6, 117–18, 127
Schilbrack, Kevin 87
notion of "superempirical" beings
  2
Schleiermacher, Friedrich 41, 67–9
Schlütter, Morten 55, 83, 104–6,
  154–9
Shakyamuni 1
shared questions 26–32
four discrete layers 59–60
fusion of horizons 28–33, 41,
  50–1, 76
Shariah law 69
Sharp, Carolyn J. 149
Shigong Huicang 113
Socrates, *Crito* 76
Song dynasty 103, 152
iconoclastic discursive practices
  157
Star Wars (Lucas) 70, 78
surplus-driven questions 6–7, 182
suspense aspects 26
suspense, phenomenological
  perspective 25–6
symbols and myths 9, 79, 178

Ta-chu (Dazhu) 101, 114
Taliban 12
Tanak 14, 82, 89, 91–2, 94–5, 137,
  140–1, 144
Tang period 14, 69, 104–5, 151–2,
  162
Ta-yün (Dayun) Monastery 101
Temple period 138, 140, 166–7, 169
Theravadin Buddhism 103
Thich Nhat Hanh 3, 87, 133
Three Little Pigs 47, 63–4, 134
Tibetan Empire 151
Tillich, Paul 8–10, 16, 52–3, 79, 87,
  89–90, 176, 180

Torah 1, 14, 16, 39, 79, 91–3, 96
  authorial voice questions
    144–7
  diasporic dialogues 137–43
  divine voice questions 147–50
  historical analysis 138–9
  Jewish engagement 141–2
  rabbenu-redactors 141–3
  source material 139–42
Trump, Donald 11–12, 176, 182
Twain, Mark, *Adventures of*
  Huckleberry Finn 46

virtual dialogue 76

Warnke, Georgia 29, 75
Wellhausen, Julius 138
Welter, Albert 56
Western notions of Buddhism and
  Islam 70
White, Hayden 54

White, Hugh, C. 96–8, 145–6
Wittgenstein, Ludwig 35, 73
Wolterstorff, Nicholas 44, 56, 68,
  90–1, 147–8, 180
Wright, Dale S. 103, 105, 107–8,
  110–13, 115, 152–4, 156–7,
  160, 162–3

Yanagida, Seizan 152

Zen Buddhism 1–2, 5, 46, 70, 103
  being-in-the-world ideals 157
  default kinds of reading 162
  depiction of *wenda* 157–8
  Dharma heirs 155–6
  early and classical 105
  inherent enlightenment 154–6
  metaphysics and 155
  transmission lineage 8
Zizek, Slavoj 11, 22, 181
Zongmi, Guifeng 104